Lessons from Hosea

The Bridegroom's Call to Return

Lessons from Hosea

The Bridegroom's Call to Return

Vinu V Das

TP
Tabor Press

ISBN 978-1-997541-23-3

Table of Contents

Chapter 1. Redeeming Love— Understanding God's Covenant Heart

In the opening movement of Hosea's prophecy we encounter a narrative so disquieting—and yet so disarming—that it simultaneously shocks ancient sensibilities and stirs contemporary hearts. God commands Hosea to marry Gomer, a woman whose future unfaithfulness will embody Israel's own covenant breach (Hosea 1–3). At first glance the story appears tragic; yet, beneath every painful turn pulses a resolve of steadfast love that refuses to abandon its bride. This God who speaks through Hosea is not a distant legislator but a covenant-making Redeemer whose affection is both fierce and tender, judicial and restorative. By tracing the prophet's lived parable alongside the New-Testament revelation of Christ the Bridegroom (John 3:29; Ephesians 5:25-27), we discover that redeeming love is more than a doctrine to affirm—it is the atmosphere in which the believer is invited to breathe, live, and mature.

1.1. The Prophetic Marriage: Divine Love Embodied

1.1.1. Hosea's call and the eighth-century BC northern-kingdom context

Hosea son of Beeri first hears the voice of the LORD "in the days of Uzziah, Jotham, Ahaz, and Hezekiah" of Judah and "Jeroboam II" of Israel (Hosea 1:1), situating his ministry between roughly 755 and 715 BC when political turbulence and economic affluence co-existed uneasily. During Jeroboam II's reign, Israel's borders briefly returned to the glory days of the Omride dynasty (2 Kings 14:25-28), yet prosperity masked deep moral rot, as shrines at Dan, Bethel, Gilgal, and Beersheba flourished with syncretistic rites (Amos 4:4; Hosea 8:11). Assyria, though temporarily weakened, loomed in the northeast, extracting tribute and threatening invasion, creating a climate of anxious diplomatic maneuvering (2 Kings 15:19-20). Into this maelstrom God commissions Hosea not merely to speak but to live a prophetic drama, signalling that Yahweh's message cannot be quarantined to pulpit or scroll. The prophet thus serves at once as preacher, performance artist, and living text—his marriage, family life, and even his children's names (*Jezreel, Lo-Ruhamah, Lo-Ammi*) become interpretive keys to Israel's story (Hosea 1:4-9). This historical anchoring reminds modern readers that divine revelation intersects specific economic booms, military threats, and cultural moods, never hovering in abstract ether. Studying Assyrian inscriptions such as the annals of Tiglath-Pileser III helps us feel the geopolitical pressure Hosea's audience felt, adding urgency to his plea for covenant loyalty. Moreover, the contrast between external success and internal decay foreshadows Jesus' critique of whitewashed tombs (Matthew 23:27). When believers today inhabit consumer cultures that mirror Samaria's veneer of stability, Hosea's context calls them to prophetic sobriety. It also demonstrates that God chooses ordinary pastors from small villages—Hosea likely hailed from the rural north—to confront systemic apostasy. Finally, the chronology underscores divine patience: four Judean kings and multiple Israelite monarchs rise and fall before judgment falls in 722 BC, revealing a God who warns repeatedly before acting.

1.1.2. Gomer as living symbol of covenant infidelity

Gomer daughter of Diblaim enters the narrative not as a moral exemplar but as an embodied illustration of Israel's waywardness (Hosea 1:2). Scholars debate whether she was already promiscuous or became adulterous after marriage, yet the ambiguity itself heightens the shock that Yahweh commands His prophet to embrace scandal for redemptive ends. Her name, possibly meaning "completion," ironically underscores how fully Israel fills up the measure of betrayal (cf. Genesis 15:16). The marriage exposes the heartache God feels when His people chase fertility gods promising rain and crops, echoing Exodus 34:15–16 where intermarriage with idolaters leads to spiritual prostitution. Each betrayal by Gomer—hinted at in Hosea 2:5 where she says, "I will go after my lovers"—parallels Israel's treaties with Egypt and Assyria, choices rooted in fear rather than faith (Hosea 7:11). In the New Testament, James 4:4 crystalizes the typology: "You adulterous people, don't you know that friendship with the world means enmity against God?" Through Gomer, the invisible sin of idolatry acquires flesh and tears, forcing hearers to confront the relational cost of disloyal worship. Pastors may recoil at the vulnerability Hosea displays, yet the narrative reminds ministry leaders that shepherding sometimes involves bearing the reproach of the flock (Hebrews 13:13). Gomer also personifies the church before conversion—"while we were still sinners Christ died for us" (Romans 5:8)—thereby turning shame into an invitation to grace. Her children's symbolic names amplify the message: *Lo-Ruhamah* ("No Mercy") warns of the Assyrian sword, while *Lo-Ammi* ("Not My People") echoes Sinai covenant language reversed (Exodus 6:7). Yet later these names are dramatically reversed in Hosea 2:23, foreshadowing Romans 9:25-26 and demonstrating the gospel's power to reclaim tarnished identities. Ultimately, Gomer's portrayal asks contemporary disciples to examine the subtle romances of the heart—careerism, digital escapism, partisan tribalism—that threaten covenant fidelity to Christ.

1.1.3. Dramatic symbolism—prophecy performed, not merely spoken

Hosea belongs to the prophetic tradition of enacted signs (*'ôt*) where message and medium converge—Isaiah walks naked (Isaiah 20:2-4),

14

Ezekiel lies on his side (Ezekiel 4:4-8), and Hosea marries an unfaithful wife. Such action-parables grab attention more forcefully than abstract doctrine, confronting Israel with a visceral tableau that bypasses intellectual defenses. The narrative structure itself becomes sermonic architecture: marriage (Hosea 1), estrangement (Hosea 2), and costly redemption (Hosea 3) anticipate Israel's exile, wilderness, and restoration. By embedding theology in story, Yahweh acknowledges that people learn through imagination and empathy, a pedagogical insight Jesus will later employ with vineyard tenants and prodigal sons (Mark 12:1-12; Luke 15:11-32). Enacted prophecy bridges cognitive and affective domains, converting theological propositions into lived reality where pain and love intertwine. The dramatization also underscores that covenant violation wounds God personally, countering any deistic caricature of detached omnipotence. Modern homiletics can glean a theology of embodiment: sermons are heard most powerfully when preachers' lives resonate with their proclamations (1 Thessalonians 2:8). Moreover, the sign-act warns against divorcing public worship from private ethics; Israel cannot sing psalms in Bethel while sleeping with Baal (Hosea 8:11-13). In a media-saturated age, believers may need fresh, creative liturgical practices that re-enact gospel truths—such as foot-washing services or lament liturgies—to re-awaken holy affection. Hosea's performance art thus anticipates sacramental theology where bread and wine embody grace, inviting disciples into tangible participation rather than distant observation.

1.1.4. Parallels to Jesus' parabolic method (Luke 15; Matthew 21)

Jesus' teaching ministry frequently mirrors Hosea's strategy of storytelling to unveil divine logic to hearts dulled by routine religion. In Luke 15 the lost sheep, lost coin, and lost son crescend to depict a Father whose love defies social expectation, echoing Hosea's relentless pursuit of Gomer. The parable of the wicked tenants in Matthew 21:33-46 broadens Hosea's marriage metaphor to a vineyard, but the thematic core remains covenant breach met by patient, then judicial, love. Both Hosea and Jesus employ shocking reversals—prophet marries a prostitute; father welcomes a disgraced son—to dismantle conventional honor-shame frameworks and spotlight grace. Moreover, Hosea's children's names function as interpretive keys much like parable punchlines—"the last shall be first" (Matthew 20:16)—that reorient listeners' moral compasses.

15

Scholars note verbal echoes: Hosea 6:6 ("I desire mercy, not sacrifice") resurfaces in Matthew 9:13 and 12:7, showing Jesus self-consciously draws on Hosea to critique ritualism divorced from compassion. Both ministries provoke leaders; Hosea confronts priestly corruption (Hosea 4:4-9), while Jesus cleanses the temple (Mark 11:15-17). For disciples, recognizing these parallels deepens confidence in Scripture's inter-textual unity and invites them to read Hosea christologically. It also models communication—stories disarm defenses, invite imagination, and linger in memory longer than propositions alone. In personal evangelism, believers may find that sharing narratives of God's pursuit in their own lives echoes Hosea's and Jesus' approach, offering a bridge to post-modern hearers suspicious of declarative authority.

1.1.5. Pastoral lessons on incarnational ministry today

Hosea's willingness to inhabit divine pathos furnishes a template for shepherds called to embody gospel truths amid messy realities. First, the prophet's marriage illustrates costly identification; he does not preach from a sanitized pulpit but from the rawness of betrayal, encouraging pastors to lead with vulnerable authenticity (2 Corinthians 6:4-10). Second, Hosea's obedience prioritizes God's agenda over personal reputation, challenging ministers tempted by platform culture to guard image more than holiness. Third, the narrative trains leaders to read congregational dysfunction not merely as behavioral lapses but as relational breaches requiring covenantal restoration, echoing Galatians 6:1. Fourth, Hosea shows that prophetic confrontation and tender invitation must coexist; he alternates between severe oracles and wooing promises (Hosea 2:14-23), modelling balanced pastoral tone. Fifth, his story underscores patience—years elapse before any visible fruit, teaching ministers to trust God's slow redemptive processes. Sixth, Hosea's children signal that family life itself becomes a ministry arena; pastors must shepherd their households even when circumstances carry stigma. Seventh, Hosea invites churches to become communities of relentless welcome where prodigals find re-entry, reflecting Luke 15:20. Eighth, the prophet's example cautions leaders against burnout; only deep awareness of God's covenant heart sustains endurance amid repeated disappointment. Ninth, Hosea highlights the prophetic imagination's role in social critique; contemporary idols like consumerism require imaginative

16

counter-liturgies, not merely moralizing. Tenth, his ministry pattern encourages collaborative discernment—Hosea likely addressed Northern Israel amid a network of prophetic voices including Amos and Micah, reminding pastors to avoid lone-ranger mentalities.

1.2. Covenant Foundations: Marriage in Ancient Israel

1.2.1. Social-legal meaning of berît *and bridal contracts*

The Hebrew term *berît* signifies a binding agreement ratified by oath, sacrifice, or symbolic act, appearing over 280 times in Scripture and framing Yahweh's relationship with humanity from Noah (Genesis 9) to the New Covenant in Christ (Luke 22:20). In ancient Israel, marriage itself functioned as a covenant, often sealed with a written contract (*ketubah*) stipulating husbandly obligations—food, clothing, and conjugal rights (Exodus 21:10)—and penalties for neglect. The contractual aspect underscores that love, in biblical perspective, is not mere sentiment but legally accountable fidelity. Hosea leverages this worldview to portray Israel's worship of Baal as legal treachery, punishable under covenant law (Deuteronomy 17:2-7). Understanding *berît* reveals why prophetic oracles invoke courtroom imagery—"Hear, O mountains, the LORD's accusation" (Micah 6:2). For modern believers, recognizing marriage as covenant counters consumerist views that treat relationships as disposable when feelings fade; covenant insists on steadfast commitment mirroring God's own. Additionally, the contractual lens provides ethical ballast in a culture suspicious of vows; it motivates spouses to rehearse the gospel through fidelity, forgiveness, and mutual service (Ephesians 5:21-33). The study of ancient Near-Eastern treaties—Hittite vassal agreements or Mesopotamian law codes—further illuminates the structure: preamble, historical prologue, stipulations, witnesses, blessings, and curses. Such parallels enrich comprehension of Exodus 20 and Deuteronomy, which adopt treaty form to communicate Yahweh's kingship. By wedding Gomer, Hosea reenacts the Sinai marriage liturgy, highlighting that divine grace precedes law, for God first redeems Israel from Egypt before stipulating commands. Thus, covenant becomes the grammar of divine-human communication, and breaking it entails not only disobedience but marital infidelity.

1.2.2. Bride-price, betrothal, and the sealing of vows

Ancient Israelite weddings unfolded in two stages: *erusin* (betrothal) and *nissuin* (wedding). During betrothal the groom paid a *mōhar* or bride-price to the bride's family (Genesis 34:12; 1 Samuel 18:25), symbolizing economic security and earnest intent. Betrothal, though lacking cohabitation, was legally binding; so serious was this state that dissolving it required divorce (Matthew 1:19-20). Hosea 2:19-20 employs betrothal vocabulary—"I will betroth you to Me forever"—to depict God's promise of renewed intimacy, underlining His willingness to reinvest relational capital after betrayal. The groom additionally presented gifts to the bride, called *mattan*, paralleling Christ's distribution of spiritual gifts to His church (Ephesians 4:7-11). On the wedding day, the groom journeyed to the bride's house, accompanied by friends with lamps and shouts, an image Jesus evokes in the parable of the ten virgins (Matthew 25:1-13). Wine and covenant blessings sealed the union (John 2:1-11). Recognizing these customs enriches the resonance of Jesus' declaration, "I go to prepare a place for you" (John 14:2-3), echoing the groom's preparation of a bridal chamber. Furthermore, the bride-price typifies Christ's precious blood, "not with perishable things such as silver or gold, but with the precious blood of Christ" (1 Peter 1:18-19). In pastoral counseling, teaching believers the seriousness of betrothal encourages sexual integrity and relational patience. It also frames church life as a season of engagement: we await the consummation at the Marriage Supper of the Lamb (Revelation 19:7-9), called to fidelity as we anticipate His return.

1.2.3. Loyalty clauses in Near-Eastern suzerainty treaties

Suzerainty treaties bound vassal states to an imperial overlord, stipulating exclusive allegiance, annual tribute, and military cooperation. Violation invited curses listed in chilling detail, paralleling Deuteronomy 28's blessings and curses. Hosea references these clauses when he indicts Israel for "going to Assyria" (Hosea 7:11) or "making a treaty with Egypt" (Hosea 12:1), acts equivalent to a bride flirting with rival suitors. The first commandment—"You shall have no other gods before Me" (Exodus

20:3)—thus mirrors treaty exclusivity. The prophet's repeated designation of Yahweh as "King" (Hosea 13:10) underscores the political dimension of covenant faithfulness. Modern disciples glean that following Christ entails exclusive loyalty that shapes political, economic, and relational choices; syncretism can take the form of uncritical nationalism or consumer brand discipleship. Consciously reviewing baptismal vows can help believers re-affirm ultimate allegiance to the risen Lord. Studying treaties also sharpens hermeneutics: when Hosea describes Israel as "like a silly dove without sense" (Hosea 7:11), he draws on diplomatic imagery where doves symbolized fickle envoys. By connecting marital and treaty metaphors, Scripture presents a holistic vision where love and law intertwine—loyal affection energizes obedient action, and legal obligation protects covenant intimacy.

1.2.4. Blessings and curses (Deuteronomy 28) as marital stipulations

Deuteronomy 28 functions as the covenant's "terms and conditions," enumerating material prosperity, military success, and agricultural abundance for obedience alongside drought, disease, and exile for rebellion. Hosea's oracles of coming famine, miscarrying wombs, and exile (Hosea 9:11-17) directly echo these curses, affirming God's covenant consistency. Yet embedded within Hosea's warnings is the hope of reversal—planting vineyards and calling God "My Husband" (Hosea 2:15-16)—anticipating new-covenant blessings (Jeremiah 31:31-34). The marital analogy helps readers see curses not as vindictive but corrective, akin to a spouse's tough love aimed at restoration. New-covenant believers read Galatians 3:13—the Messiah became a curse for us—as the climactic fulfillment, absorbing covenant penalties to secure blessings for the nations (Genesis 12:3). This theological move compels gratitude and guards against presumption; grace is free but never cheap. Practical application includes cultivating thankfulness for daily bread as evidence of covenant faithfulness and interpreting hardships through the lens of paternal discipline (Hebrews 12:5-11). Church liturgies that alternate blessing and confession echo Deuteronomy 28 rhythmically, training hearts in covenant realism.

19

1.2.5. Ḥesed—*steadfast love anchoring the covenant*

The Hebrew term *ḥesed* resists single-word translation, blending loyalty, mercy, kindness, and covenant faithfulness, appearing 249 times in the Old Testament. Hosea 2:19 pledges betrothal "in *ḥesed,*" highlighting divine character rather than Israel's merit. Psalm 136 repeats "His *ḥesed* endures forever" 26 times, forming a liturgical refrain that shapes the worshiper's worldview. In the New Testament, *ḥesed* underlies the Greek *eleos* and *charis*, culminating in John 1:14, "full of grace and truth." Hosea's emphasis critiques religiosity devoid of *ḥesed*: "I desire *ḥesed*, not sacrifice" (Hosea 6:6). Daily discipleship thus centers on receiving and reflecting steadfast love—marriages practice *ḥesed* through forgiveness, businesses through just wages, and communities through hospitality to outsiders. Spiritual disciplines such as meditation on Psalm 103 and journaling instances of God's daily kindness strengthen *ḥesed* consciousness. Furthermore, *ḥesed* fuels social justice; Micah 6:8 pairs it with acting justly and walking humbly, reminding believers that charity divorced from covenant loyalty lacks staying power. Finally, *ḥesed* invites eschatological hope—Revelation 21:3–4 portrays a world where steadfast love eradicates tears, demonstrating that covenant commitment shapes eternity.

1.3. Love That Pays the Price: Hosea 3 as Gospel Prototype

1.3.1. *The auction-block scene and its shock value*

Hosea 3 opens with Yahweh instructing the prophet to "love a woman loved by another and an adulteress," thrusting Hosea into the public marketplace where slaves were sold naked to maximize buyer scrutiny. The image is deliberately humiliating, shattering any romantic gloss readers might overlay on prophetic marriage. Ancient audiences would have gasped at a prophet spending his own silver on a woman whose infidelity was notorious; such an act violated social norms of honor and purity. The scene prefigures Jesus dining with tax collectors (Luke 5:30) and touching lepers (Mark 1:41), demonstrating redemption's scandalous reach. Hosea's public purchase counters consumer logic: he values Gomer not for utility but for covenant promise. This reversal critiques cultures that commodify bodies—whether through pornography, human trafficking, or exploitative labor. Contemporary Christians are challenged to rescue the marginalized at personal cost, embodying Proverbs 31:8-9's call to defend the vulnerable. The auction also dramatizes substitutionary logic: Hosea stands in Gomer's place financially so she might stand beside him relationally, just as Christ stands in sinners' place judicially (2 Corinthians 5:21). Finally, the narrative anticipates Revelation 5:9 where worshipers sing, "You purchased people for God by Your blood," confirming Hosea 3's typological weight.

1.3.2. Fifteen shekels of silver + barley—economic nuances

The redemption price totals fifteen shekels of silver and one and a half homers of barley—roughly the value of a common slave (Exodus 21:32). Scholars debate whether Hosea lacked sufficient silver and supplemented with grain, underscoring his sacrificial investment. Barley, the grain of the poor, accentuates humility and pre-Passover timing (Leviticus 23:10-11), linking redemption to festival imagery. Silver in Scripture often symbolizes redemption—consider the half-shekel temple tax (Exodus 30:13) and Judas's thirty pieces (Matthew 26:15). The mixed payment signals that redemption draws upon every available resource; love spares no expense. For disciples, generosity becomes tangible evidence of gospel comprehension (2 Corinthians 8:9). The economic detail also critiques prosperity theology that evaluates worth by monetary abundance; Hosea's modest payment exceeds price tags by attaching covenant value. Moreover, the sum foreshadows Mary's offering of turtledoves as a poor woman (Luke 2:24), reminding readers that redemption's power is not limited by financial stature. Finally, chronicling such minutiae affirms historical reliability, inviting believers to trust Scripture's concrete particularity.

21

1.3.3. Kinsman-redeemer (gō'ēl) and Passover blood echoes

The concept of *gō'ēl* (kinsman-redeemer) appears in Leviticus 25:25-55 and culminates in Boaz's marriage to Ruth (Ruth 4:1-10), where family dignity is rescued through covenant loyalty. Hosea, while not explicitly called a *gō'ēl*, enacts the role by restoring Gomer to covenant status. The Passover backdrop looms large; just as Israel was purchased from Egypt by lamb's blood (Exodus 12:13), so Gomer is rescued from slavery to desire. This intertwining of familial and national redemption foreshadows the cross where Jesus, both our elder brother (Hebrews 2:11) and Passover Lamb (1 Corinthians 5:7), fulfills every redeeming institution. Theologically, *gō'ēl* emphasizes both kinship and cost—redemption is relational before transactional. Practical discipleship entails adopting a redemptive stance toward indebted relatives, incarcerated neighbors, or trafficking survivors, reflecting Isaiah 58:6's call to loose bonds of wickedness. Liturgically, Communion rehearses *gō'ēl* themes: shared cup signifies familial covenant and ransom price. Pastoral counseling can draw on *gō'ēl* imagery to assure believers battling shame that Christ claims them legally and affectionately, nullifying accusations (Romans 8:33-34).

1.3.4. Jesus' ransom language (Mark 10:45; 1 Peter 1:18-19)

Jesus declares the Son of Man came "to give His life as a ransom for many" (Mark 10:45), directly aligning Himself with Hosea's purchasing paradigm. The Greek term *lytron* denotes the price paid to free a slave, echoing Septuagint translations of redemption narratives. Peter extends the theme, reminding exiles they were ransomed not with "perishable things like silver or gold, but with the precious blood of Christ" (1 Peter 1:18-19), an explicit contrast to Hosea's mixed payment. The shift from metal to blood underscores qualitative superiority—divine life exchanged for human salvation. Such ransom language rebukes any notion that forgiveness is a mere divine wave-off; it required substitutionary sacrifice. For spiritual formation, meditating on ransom texts cultivates awe and fuels ethical transformation: "You were bought at a price; therefore honor God with your bodies" (1 Corinthians 6:20). It also empowers mission; awareness of costly grace propels believers to proclaim liberation to captives (Luke 4:18). The ransom motif critiques transactional religion; since the price is fully paid, disciples serve not to earn favor but from secure belonging.

1.3.5. Gratitude that births covenant obedience in believers

In Hosea 3:3 the prophet stipulates a period of abstinence—"You must dwell with me many days; you shall not play the whore"—signifying rehabilitative fidelity rather than punitive restriction. Likewise, gospel redemption aims not only to rescue from penalty but to reshape desire, producing the obedience of gratitude (Titus 2:11-14). Paul captures this dynamic: "The love of Christ controls us" (2 Corinthians 5:14), showing that internalized grace, not external compulsion, fuels holiness. Spiritual disciplines—Sabbath keeping, generous giving, fasting—become love responses rather than meritorious works. Corporate worship functions as covenant renewal ceremony where believers re-declare allegiance, mirroring Israel's periodic covenant readings (Joshua 24). Testimonies of transformed addicts, reconciled marriages, and vocational integrity serve as living proof that gratitude generates sustained obedience. Moreover, gratitude guards against legalism by rooting ethics in relational delight rather than rule performance. Neuroscience studies reveal thanksgiving rewires brain pathways, offering a physiological echo of spiritual renewal. Finally, eschatological hope energizes present gratitude; Hosea 3:5 foresees Israel returning and seeking "David their king" in the latter days, a messianic promise fulfilled in Jesus and consummated at His return. Anticipation of future communion cultivates present perseverance, ensuring redeemed hearts remain loyal to the Bridegroom until the wedding feast arrives (Revelation 19:7).

1.4. The Heartbeat of *Ḥesed*: God's Self-Revelation

1.4.1 ▪ *Word study—frequency and shades of meaning in Hosea*

The noun *ḥesed* appears six times in Hosea (e.g., 2:19; 4:1; 6:4; 6:6; 10:12; 12:6), and each occurrence adds a layer to the covenant portrait God is painting. In Hosea 2:19 it denotes the loyal affection that underwrites Yahweh's promise to "betroth" His people forever, anchoring restoration in His character, not theirs. Hosea 4:1 indicts

Israel for lacking *ḥesed*, highlighting that covenant love can be conspicuously absent from social behavior even while cultic activity hums. Hosea 6:4 shows *ḥesed* can be transient—"like the morning cloud"—indicating that divine love, though constant, may be mirrored by fickle human responses. Linguists trace the root ḥ-s-d to ideas of zeal and zeal-infused kindness, reminding readers that steadfast love is energetic rather than passive. The Septuagint renders *ḥesed* as *eleos* (mercy) or *charis* (grace), and the New Testament echoes both trajectories (Luke 1:54; John 1:14) to identify Jesus as the embodied fidelity of God. Scholars note that *ḥesed* often pairs with *'emet* (faithfulness) in the Psalms, forming an inseparable couplet that governs divine action (Psalm 85:10). Within Hosea this pair surfaces implicitly when God vows to "betroth in faithfulness" (Hos 2:20), indicating that *ḥesed* is covenant glue sustained by truthfulness. Theological dictionaries emphasize covenantal context: apart from a binding relationship, *ḥesed* collapses into vague benevolence and loses its covenant bite. By paying attention to Hosea's strategic distribution of the word, modern readers see a contrast between divine constancy and human volatility, sharpening awareness of grace. Practically, meditating on *ḥesed* refutes a transactional view of salvation; believers rest in God's settled affection even when feelings waver. Moreover, tracing *ḥesed* across Scripture reveals that God's self-description in Exodus 34:6 ("abounding in steadfast love") is not a slogan but the pulse that drives redemptive history. Hosea provides the laboratory where that pulse can be observed in a failing marriage, thereby demonstrating how theological vocabulary acquires emotional weight. Finally, the word study equips preachers and teachers to unfold Hosea's message without reducing it to sentimentalism, instead letting the robust covenant backdrop display the full color spectrum of divine love.

1.4.2 ▪ Mercy and justice held in creative tension

In Hosea mercy and justice are never rivals; they dance in synchrony to achieve covenant goals. Hosea 11:8–9 registers God's inner wrestle—He cannot surrender Israel to total ruin, yet He cannot

24

ignore blatant covenant treason—illustrating a holy dialectic where compassion tempers wrath. Hosea 6:5 shows prophets hewing God's people as with "hewn words," revealing that sharp rebuke is itself a form of merciful surgery meant to excise idolatry. The book's final plea (Hos 14:1–3) marries confession with assurance, demonstrating that justice provides the frame within which mercy can operate with integrity. Micah 6:8 reinforces the synthesis by calling Israel to "do justice" and "love *ḥesed*," showing ethical life flows from divine balance. The cross later embodies this tension: Romans 3:25–26 states God is both just and justifier, fulfilling covenant demands while pardoning covenant breakers. Hosea's agricultural imagery— sowing righteousness to reap *ḥesed* (10:12)—reminds disciples that moral actions sow seeds whose harvests reveal whether justice or mercy has been ignored. Pastoral care often requires similar balance: confronting destructive behavior while offering pathways to restoration echoes Hosea's method. Church discipline, when done biblically (Matt 18:15–17), makes tangible the dual commitments of holiness and healing. For social ethics, justice without mercy becomes retribution, while mercy without justice becomes enabling sentimentality; Hosea's dialectic corrects both extremes. Spiritual formation practices such as examen invite believers to hold their own hearts under the joint light of mercy and justice, confessing sin while receiving pardon (1 John 1:9). Studying Hosea equips believers to resist cultural binaries that separate accountability from compassion. Ultimately, the nexus of mercy and justice climaxes in the eschaton, where Revelation 21:4 foresees tears wiped away (mercy) after the final judgment seat (justice), a future that Hosea's poetry anticipates in miniature. Recognizing this creative tension energizes worship—songs like "Holy, Holy, Holy" and "Amazing Grace" belong together, not apart.

1.4.3 ▪ Refracted in Christ's table fellowship (Matthew 9:13)

Jesus quotes Hosea 6:6 twice (Matt 9:13; 12:7) while defending His choice to dine with tax collectors and sinners, thereby linking prophetic *ḥesed* directly to table ministry. In Matthew 9 the call of Levi culminates in a banquet where outsiders recline with the Messiah, turning Hosea's abstract indictment into a practical hospitality ethic. The Pharisees' protest parallels Israel's ritualism in

Hosea; both prioritize ceremonial purity over covenant love. By selecting a meal setting, Jesus showcases *ḥesed* as a social phenomenon, not merely an inner sentiment—covenant love rearranges seating charts. Luke 7:36–50 deepens the theme when a sinful woman anoints Jesus; her lavish gratitude mirrors the extravagant *ḥesed* she has received, echoing Hosea 3's redemption scene. Each meal becomes an enacted parable of Hosea's marriage: undeserving guests receive honor, prompting moral guardians to question the host's discernment. Table fellowship thus functions as a microcosm of the gospel, revealing that community formation is inseparable from covenant grace. Early church practice follows suit; Acts 2:46 depicts believers breaking bread daily, embodying Hosea's restored union in communal rhythms. When modern congregations celebrate Eucharist, they stand in the lineage of Hosea-inspired hospitality, where bread and cup proclaim God's steadfast love to the undeserving (1 Cor 11:26). Missional application emerges: inviting neighbors to share meals becomes a strategic avenue for demonstrating *ḥesed* in post-Christian contexts. The practice also challenges ethnocentric barriers, much like Jesus' meals crossed social boundaries, fulfilling Hosea's vision of a people once called "Not My People" now seated at the family table (Hos 1:10). Furthermore, table fellowship trains believers in gratitude, generosity, and listening—virtues necessary for covenant living. Theologically, Jesus' quote of Hosea in a dining context asserts interpretive authority: the prophet's message was not about abandoning sacrifices but about subordinating ritual to relational mercy. Finally, this refracted *ḥesed* suggests that evangelism is less a courtroom monologue and more a dinner invitation, inviting the world to taste covenant love.

1.4.4 ▪ Implications for relational ethics and church discipline

Because God's covenant heart throbs with *ḥesed*, Christian ethics cannot be reduced to rule enforcement; they must channel redemptive loyalty. Matthew 18:15–17 sketches a restorative process that mirrors Hosea's progression—private appeal, expanded witness, and covenant sanctions all aimed at winning the brother, not shaming him. 1 Corinthians 5 illustrates decisive action against unrepentant immorality, yet 2 Corinthians 2:6-8 urges forgiveness once repentance appears, balancing firmness with comfort in Hosea-like rhythm. Galatians 6:1 calls "spiritual" believers to restore trespassers "in a spirit of gentleness," a New-Covenant echo of Hosea's tender allure (Hos 2:14). Covenant ethics therefore prioritize relational repair over punitive closure, reflecting divine patience that barred judgment for decades before 722 BC. In marital counseling, Hosea's narrative legitimizes boundaries (faithful exclusivity) while holding out hope for reconciliation, offering a biblical framework for dealing with infidelity. Community life shaped by *ḥesed* fosters transparency; members confess sin trusting discipline will aim at healing, not ostracism (James 5:16). Financial ethics also flow from covenant love—debts are renegotiated or forgiven (Matt 18:27) rather than weaponized, mirroring Hosea's ransom purchase. Justice ministries inspired by *ḥesed* pursue systemic reform while proclaiming personal salvation, integrating deed and word. Church governance structures can bake in *ḥesed* by pairing accountability committees with care teams, ensuring discipline is couched in support. Preaching that highlights God's steadfast love helps prevent moral exhortations from slipping into legalism, embedding imperative within indicative. Personal discipleship plans should include periodic "covenant check-ups" where believers review relationships, finances, and habits through the lens of *ḥesed*, akin to Hosea's prophetic audits. Moreover, conflict resolution that employs active listening, sincere apology, and concrete restitution reenacts Hosea's restorative trajectory. By embodying these ethics, the church testifies to a skeptical world that steadfast love is not abstract but socially transformative, validating Hosea's theological vision.

1.5. Christ the Bridegroom: New-Testament Fulfilment

1.5.1 • Messianic resonance of Hosea's "Call Me My Husband" oracle

Hosea 2:16 foresees a day when Israel will shift from calling Yahweh "My Master" (*Ba'ali*) to "My Husband" (*'Ishi*), signaling relational warmth supplanting transactional religiosity. John 3:29

draws directly on bridal language when John the Baptist identifies himself as the "friend of the bridegroom," implicitly casting Jesus in the Hosea-promised role. This self-identification transforms Jesus' ministry from mere moral renewal to covenant courtship, reframing miracles and teachings as wooing gestures. Paul intensifies the image in 2 Corinthians 11:2, declaring he betrothed the church to one husband, echoing Hosea's betrothal vows. The shift in address from master to husband also counters pagan misunderstandings of deity, emphasizing intimacy over domination, thus critiquing authoritarian religious systems. Jesus' use of "Abba" for God (Mark 14:36) parallels the shift in Hosea, enabling believers to approach God with filial and spousal confidence. Early Christian writers like Ignatius of Antioch picked up the bridal motif, encouraging congregations to remain "undefiled" for Christ—a practical outworking of Hosea's prophecy. The bridal lens illuminates passages like Matthew 9:15, where Jesus calls Himself the bridegroom and fasting inappropriate during His earthly presence, connecting spiritual practices to relational dynamics. Hosea's oracle also signals exclusivity; a bride with one husband cannot share affections with Baal, foreshadowing 1 John 5:21's warning against idols. Liturgically, bridal imagery shapes Advent anticipation and Easter joy, structuring the church year around covenant milestones. Theologically, it preserves the transcendence-immanence balance: the groom is both sovereign and near, majestic and tender. Practical spirituality includes cultivating affectionate language in prayer—addressing Jesus as beloved mirrors Hosea's relational shift. Finally, the messianic resonance invites apologetic dialogue, demonstrating prophetic continuity that validates Jesus' identity for Jewish and Gentile seekers alike. Recognizing this resonance equips readers to see Hosea not as isolated morality tale but as foundational to New-Testament christology.

1.5.2 ▪ Jesus' wedding imagery (John 3:29; Matthew 25:1-13)

Throughout His teachings Jesus leverages wedding customs to explain the kingdom, embedding Hosea's covenant vision into parabolic form. In John 3:29 the joy of the friend hearing the bridegroom's voice underscores that Jesus' presence inaugurates messianic fulfillment, rendering old covenant waiting obsolete. The parable of the ten virgins (Matt 25:1-13) warns disciples to maintain readiness during the groom's delay, paralleling Israel's waiting

28

period in Hosea 3:4-5 before seeking Davidic leadership in "the latter days." Wedding imagery also surfaces at Cana (John 2:1-11), where Jesus' first sign of turning water into wine quietly signals new covenant abundance, echoing Hosea 2:22's promise of restored grain and wine. By casting the kingdom as a wedding feast (Matt 22:1-14), Jesus shifts perceptions of salvation from courtroom acquittal alone to celebratory union, resonating with Hosea's marital theme. The parables stress reciprocal responsibility: the groom prepares a place (John 14:2) while the bridal party keeps lamps trimmed, teaching modern believers to balance assurance with vigilance. They also critique complacency; bridesmaids without oil represent hearts inattentive to covenant maintenance, echoing Hosea's portrayal of fleeting *ḥesed*. When churches stage weddings, they unwittingly preach a sermon on eschatological hope, reminding attendees of the ultimate wedding to come. Spiritual disciplines— Scripture meditation, confession, communion—function like lamp oil, sustaining inner fire until the bridegroom arrives. Finally, Jesus' wedding stories offer a joyful corrective to grim depictions of holiness, ensuring Hosea's severe warnings are held within a larger narrative of godly celebration and delight.

1.5.3 ▪ Calvary as the ultimate dowry—blood sealing the New Covenant

In ancient culture the groom's payment secured the bride's future; at Calvary, Christ's blood secures an eternal covenant, surpassing Hosea's silver and barley. Hebrews 9:15 asserts that His death redeems transgressions committed under the first covenant, equating the cross with redemption price for historical and future infidelity. Ephesians 5:25-27 describes Christ loving the church and giving Himself up to sanctify her, directly mapping marital sacrifice onto atonement theology. The costly dowry underscores sin's gravity—if lesser currency sufficed, the divine Son's death would be disproportionate. 1 Peter 1:19 contrasts perishable silver and gold with imperishable blood, deliberately recalling Hosea 3 to highlight the superior ransom. By purchasing with blood, Jesus fulfills Passover symbolism (Exod 12:13) and kinsman-redeemer obligations (Lev 25:49), collapsing multiple redemptive strands into one act. Calvary also rewrites honor-shame calculus: the groom accepts public humiliation, much as Hosea faced scandal,

29

demonstrating love stronger than societal scorn (Heb 12:2). The dowry has ongoing implications: believers belong to Christ (1 Cor 6:19-20), making ethical choices an outgrowth of purchased identity. Communion commemorates the payment each time the cup is lifted, keeping covenant status before the community's eyes (Luke 22:20). In counseling guilt-ridden believers, pointing to the dowry equips them to anchor assurance in historical fact rather than emotional fluctuation. Moreover, the cross stands as the ultimate protest against utilitarian relationships, inviting married couples to model sacrificial love that seeks the other's flourishing. Missional giving likewise imitates the dowry, as churches allocate time and resources to rescue the exploited, aligning economics with Calvary's generosity. Finally, meditating on the dowry fuels worship, transforming songs about the blood from archaic to deeply relational when framed within Hosea's marriage motif.

1.5.4 • Spirit as arrabōn *(engagement pledge, Ephesians 1:14)*

Paul calls the Holy Spirit the *arrabōn*—a legal pledge or earnest—indicating that Pentecost is God's down payment guaranteeing the wedding to come. This legal metaphor mirrors ancient Jewish practice where the groom offered a token at betrothal, assuring the bride of his return, thereby aligning Hosea's betrothal language (2:19-20) with New-Testament pneumatology. 2 Corinthians 1:22 and 5:5 reiterate the pledge concept, emphasizing that the Spirit's indwelling presence is experiential evidence of covenant status. The Spirit trains believers in bridal virtues—love, joy, peace—preparing them for union much like Esther underwent months of preparation before meeting the king (Esther 2:12). He also seals identity, countering the shame of "Lo-Ammi" by witnessing that we are children of God (Rom 8:16). Spiritual gifts function as wedding presents for communal edification, ensuring the bride matures into full glory (1 Cor 12:7). The *arrabōn* metaphor elevates everyday guidance—promptings to forgive, serve, or evangelize—as engagement whispers from the groom, not generic moralism. Understanding the pledge guards against eschatological despair; delays resemble the groom's prolonged preparation rather than abandonment. It also fuels holiness, for grieving the Spirit (Eph 4:30) would be akin to rejecting the engagement ring. Charismatic experiences—prophecy, healing—serve as foretastes of the marriage supper, intensifying longing for consummation while

30

rooting hope in present reality. The pledge metaphor fosters ecological and social stewardship, as the Spirit empowers believers to demonstrate kingdom foretaste in creation care and justice pursuits (Rom 8:19-23). Finally, pneumatology anchored in Hosea's betrothal widens Christian imagination: the Spirit is not merely power for ministry but the relational bond drawing bride and groom toward imminent union.

1.5.5 ▪ *Marriage Supper of the Lamb—eschatological consummation*

Revelation 19:7–9 announces the marriage supper where the Bride, arrayed in righteous deeds, meets the Lamb, concluding the trajectory Hosea initiated. The imagery unites prophetic strands: Isaiah 25:6's feast on Zion, Hosea 2:21–22's agricultural abundance, and Jesus' kingdom banquet parables converge in the final celebration. The "fine linen" signifies deeds prepared in advance (Eph 2:10), showing sanctification is bridal attire woven by grace-empowered obedience. Hosea's reversal of children's names (2:23) finds ultimate fulfillment when Revelation 21:3 declares, "They shall be His peoples," ending the "Not My People" era forever. Eschatological vision nurtures perseverance; present suffering echoes Hosea's wilderness but points toward certain joy (Rom 8:18). The supper also resolves the mercy-justice tension— evil is judged (Rev 19:20) before the feast commences, ensuring celebration is untainted by unresolved sin. Worship liturgies that conclude with Communion anticipate the Lamb's table, training congregations in hopeful longing. Mission gains urgency from this teleology; invitations to the gospel effectively distribute wedding invitations (Luke 14:23). The supper underscores catholicity—saints from every tribe gather, vindicating Hosea's inclusive promise that Gentiles be grafted in (Rom 9:25-26). It also forecasts ecological renewal; feasting implies harvest, indicating creation itself participates in redemption, reversing Hosea's judgment of land barrenness (Hos 4:3). Bridal theology counters escapist eschatology by portraying the future as tangible celebration, not disembodied cloud-floating. Pastoral care employs this hope at funerals, reminding mourners that resurrection leads to a feast, not a void. Finally, the marriage supper invites ethical preparation; like brides ensuring readiness, believers cultivate purity (1 John 3:3) and lamp-lit watchfulness, harmonizing present life with future destiny.

1.6. Practicing Covenant Loyalty in Daily Discipleship

1.6.1 • Personal holiness framed as marital fidelity

Scripture consistently equates idolatry with adultery, so holiness becomes marital faithfulness rather than sterile legalism (Jas 4:4). Hosea's vivid portrayal of covenant breach makes purity an affair of the heart before it is a checklist of behaviors. 1 Thessalonians 4:3–8 links sanctification to sexual integrity, reminding believers that their bodies belong to the Bridegroom who purchased them. Paul's concern to present the church as a chaste virgin (2 Cor 11:2) heightens stakes of moral compromise, framing temptation as potential infidelity. Holiness therefore involves guarding eyes, thoughts, and affections, recognizing that spiritual adultery often precedes physical. Practices like fasting curb bodily appetites, training desire to seek satisfaction in covenant love rather than fleeting thrills (Matt 9:15). Accountability partnerships serve as modern eunuchs guarding bridal chambers, providing protection against unsolicited suitors—pornography, greed, resentment. Holiness also embraces positive virtue: cultivating compassion, patience, and humility adorns the bride in bridal jewels (1 Pet 3:3-4). Liturgical confession offers periodic bath, echoing Esther's beauty treatments, cleansing stains that inevitably accrue. Attending to language—truthful speech over gossip—honors the Bridegroom who is Faithful and True (Rev 19:11). Sabbath rest witnesses to marital security, refusing anxiety-driven productivity that courts idolatry. Finally, holiness fuels evangelism; a radiant bride attracts onlookers, validating gospel power (Phil 2:15).

1.6.2 • Spiritual disciplines that deepen intimacy (prayer, Word, Eucharist)

Intimacy thrives on communication, so prayer becomes more than request; it is covenant conversation where lovers exchange affection (Ps 27:8). Fixed-hour prayer rhythms—morning, midday, evening—mirror Jewish betrothal visits, keeping relational sparks alive. Lectio divina invites slow listening to Scripture, akin to reading love letters repeatedly, allowing the Spirit to personalize Hosea's wooing phrases. Memorizing passages like Hosea 2:14–20 instills covenant language into the heart, enabling spontaneous praise. The Eucharist functions as covenant meal, renewing vows each time bread is broken (1 Cor 11:25). Journaling responses to Scripture resembles Gomer learning to dialogue with Hosea rather than fleeing, building trust through transparency. Solitude retreats echo Hosea's wilderness allure, stripping distractions to heighten God-awareness (Mark 1:35). Corporate worship adds communal dimension; singing bridal songs such as "Draw Me Close" unites individual hearts in collective longing. Fasting amplifies spiritual sensitivity, turning hunger pangs into reminders of deeper desire for the Bridegroom (Matt 9:15). Service disciplines—hospitality, visiting prisoners—let love overflow horizontally, guarding against introspective pietism. Practicing daily examen reviews moments of consolation and desolation, tracking movements of affection toward or away from the beloved. Celebrating sacred anniversaries—baptism date, conversion milestone—reinforces covenant memory, much like Israel's festivals. Digital sabbaths reclaim attention, reallocating it from screens to Scripture, countering idolatrous distraction. Ultimately, disciplines are bridal training, nurturing anticipation and readiness.

1.6.3 ▪ Guarding the heart from modern idols—success, screen, self

Idolatry in the digital age often masquerades as productivity apps, social metrics, or self-optimization programs promising control— echoes of Baal's fertility guarantees. Proverbs 4:23 urges vigilance over the heart, recognizing that spiritual adultery germinates in unchecked desires. Social media's "likes" can become altars where identity is sacrificed, requiring disciplined detachment through periodic detox fasts. Career ambition can morph into Pharaoh-like taskmasters, demanding brick quotas at the expense of Sabbath rest, necessitating vocational discernment rooted in covenant priorities. Materialism tempts believers to measure worth by square footage rather than bridal price, compelling counter-formation via generosity. 1 John 5:21's admonition to guard from idols remains urgent when algorithms curate cravings at lightning speed. Cultivating wonder—walks in nature, art appreciation—redirects affection from consumer goods to Creator, strengthening covenant awe. Community accountability groups serve as watchmen, naming subtle idol drift before relationships fracture. Regular tithing dethrones Mammon, reminding hearts of ultimate ownership (Matt 6:21). Practicing Sabbath screens-off dinners restores face-to-face presence, mirroring Hosea's table fellowship aims. Confessing tech overuse in small groups breaks secrecy, initiating Gomer-like return journeys. Gratitude lists shift focus from accumulation to appreciation, subverting scarcity scripts that idols employ. Reading missionary biographies broadens horizons, diminishing self-absorption by showcasing sacrificial loyalty. Ultimately, hearts guarded from idols remain pliable to divine affection, securing marital fidelity.

1.6.4 • Forgiveness & reconciliation as covenant reflexes (Ephesians 4:32)

Covenant love predisposes believers to forgive as they have been forgiven, turning Hosea's redemption into communal practice. Ephesians 4:32 bases forgiveness on God's precedent in Christ, not on offender merit, mirroring Hosea paying for Gomer before behavioral change. Matthew 18:21-35 illustrates unforgiveness as spiritual amnesia regarding one's own debt, exposing hypocrisy that nullifies bridal witness. Reconciliation begins with truthful naming of offense, following God's candid diagnosis of Israel's adultery, avoiding superficial peace. Forgiveness is multidimensional—canceling debt, relinquishing vengeance, and pursuing relational restoration where safe and possible (Rom 12:19). Practically, believers can use "I feel…when…because…" statements to articulate wounds without accusation, fostering dialogue. Peacemaking often requires mediators—neutral elders or counselors—paralleling prophets bridging God and people. Communion provides tangible reminder; participants examine hearts, reconcile if needed, before partaking (1 Cor 11:28). When reconciliation is resisted, covenant community may employ structured intervention, echoing God's progressive steps in Hosea 2. Celebrating restored relationships publicly models redemption, encouraging others to pursue similar healing. Forgiveness does not erase consequences; Hosea lived through lingering stigma, teaching communities to balance grace with wisdom. Trauma-informed approaches recognize deep wounds may necessitate professional therapy alongside spiritual care. Cross-cultural forgiveness in diverse churches testifies to gospel power capable of bridging racial and social divides (Col 3:11-14). Ultimately, forgiveness frees both victim and offender to re-enter covenant joy, keeping the bride unburdened for the coming feast.

Since Hosea paid a price for Gomer, redeemed believers view resources as instruments for covenant blessing rather than personal hoarding. Acts 4:32-35 shows early Christians holding possessions loosely, reflecting redemption economics where no one among them lacked. Tithing embodies first-fruit devotion, signaling that the bridegroom, not Mammon, holds ultimate allegiance (Mal 3:10). Generosity subverts scarcity mentalities ingrained by market capitalism, mirroring Hosea's promise of abundant grain and wine post-repentance (Hos 2:22). Budgeting becomes spiritual formation when line items prioritize kingdom projects—missions, aid to poor—over status consumption. Hospitality costs money and time, but each shared meal reenacts covenant feasting, investing earthly resources in relational dividends (1 Pet 4:9). Environmental stewardship honors the Bridegroom's creation, refusing to treat the earth as disposable, aligning with Hosea's concern for land mourning under sin (Hos 4:3). Financial transparency within marriage reflects mutual trust, an earthly echo of God's open-handedness toward His bride. Debt reduction strategies function as exodus journeys from slavery to freedom, liberating disciples for generosity. Marketplace ethics—fair wages, honest scales—manifest covenant integrity, countering Hosea's indictment of commercial exploitation (Hos 12:7). Philanthropic giving is calibrated by gratitude, not guilt, ensuring cheerful hearts (2 Cor 9:7). Estate planning can include kingdom bequests, viewing death as final stewardship act before the marriage supper. Testimonies of divine provision fuel faith, reminding communities that generosity triggers surprising harvests, much like Israel's restored vineyards. Ultimately, possessions become love letters written in tangible form, translating covenant affection into backpacks for students, wells in villages, and meals for strangers, thereby extending Hosea's redemption arc into contemporary economics.

1.7. Missional Implications of Redeeming Love

1.7.1 • Evangelism re-imagined as inviting the world to a wedding

Evangelism shaped by Hosea's storyline begins with celebration rather than argument, positioning the gospel not merely as escape from wrath but as entry into a covenant banquet envisioned in Revelation 19:7-9. When believers share Christ, they are effectively handing out wedding invitations, echoing the parable of the great feast in Luke 14:16-24 where servants compel guests to come. This reframing shifts tone from combative persuasion to hospitable welcome, lowering defenses in a post-Christian culture distrustful of institutional religion. The invitation model emphasizes relationship, affirming that the Bridegroom wants hearts, not just converts tallied on charts. It also clarifies the urgency: a banquet has a start time, paralleling the eschatological closing of the door in Matthew 25:10-13. In practical terms, gospel presentations highlight God's pursuit, mirroring Hosea's relentless search for Gomer, thereby resonating with those who feel unworthy or overlooked (Hosea 3:1-3). Storytelling becomes a primary method—believers share personal redemption narratives as mini-parables of divine courtship. Apologetic conversations shift from abstract proofs to showcasing communal joy, inviting skeptics to "taste and see" by joining Christian community gatherings (Psalm 34:8). Baptism is explained as a public betrothal ceremony patterned on Hosea 2:19-20, giving ritual depth to conversion. Evangelists practice patient listening, recognizing that the Spirit often woos gradually; Hosea's multiyear ministry warns against pressure tactics. Follow-up discipleship emphasizes intimacy with Christ more than rule acquisition, reinforcing that new believers have entered a marriage, not merely signed a contract. Hospitality events—block-party barbecues, Alpha dinners—serve as fore-tastes of the marriage supper, embodying Hosea's festive restoration promises (Hosea 2:21-22). Churches train members to view workplaces and neighborhoods as fields where invitations are extended through kindness and credibility (Colossians 4:5-6). Evangelism teams pray Hosea 10:12, asking the Spirit to "break up fallow ground" so invitations find receptive soil. Finally, leaders guard against manipulative urgency; like Hosea, they trust covenant love, not coercion, to win hearts.

1.7.2 ▪ Social justice rooted in redemption economics (Hosea 12:6)

Hosea condemns Israel's dishonest scales (Hosea 12:7), linking economic exploitation to spiritual adultery, thus making justice a gospel issue, not a political add-on. Redeeming love therefore fuels advocacy for fair wages, debt relief, and housing equity, mirroring the prophet's concern that covenant faithfulness manifests in the

36

marketplace. The Jubilee legislation of Leviticus 25—land returns and slave liberation—provides historical precedent for structural mercy, and Hosea's purchase of Gomer dramatizes economic rescue in miniature. Modern disciples translate these principles into responsible consumer habits, supporting companies with ethical supply chains and challenging those profiting from exploitation (Proverbs 31:8-9). Churches create benevolence funds reflecting Hosea's ransom, offering micro-loans or grants that restore dignity without predatory interest. Mission partnerships focus on vocational training in underserved communities, embodying Isaiah 61:1's liberation agenda fulfilled in Christ. Advocacy work is framed liturgically: congregations lament systemic sin in prayer services patterned after Hosea's oracles (Hosea 4:1-3). Sermons connect sacrificial giving to the redemption price Christ paid, inspiring generosity beyond mere obligation (2 Corinthians 8:9). Justice ministries cultivate long-term relationships rather than paternalistic handouts, imitating Hosea's covenant endurance. Members study local budgets and zoning laws, discerning how policies impact the poor, then engage city councils as covenant ambassadors. The sacrament of Communion galvanizes justice commitment, reminding worshipers that broken bread obligates them to broken neighborhoods (1 Corinthians 11:29). Cross-cultural partnerships dismantle privilege and extend Hosea's promise to "Not My People" (Hosea 1:10) by including marginalized voices in leadership. Metrics of success shift from attendance numbers to stories of restored families and flourishing communities. Prayer teams intercede using Amos 5:24, asking that justice roll like a river, while acknowledging that only redeemed hearts sustain equitable systems. Ultimately, Hosea grounds social justice in the character of God, ensuring activism flows from worship rather than anger alone.

1.7.3 ▪ The local church as living parable of steadfast loyalty

A congregation shaped by Hosea becomes a public drama where covenant fidelity is visible to observers, much like the prophet's marriage. Members commit to one another through church covenants, mirroring God's *berît* with Israel and countering consumerist attendance patterns (Acts 2:42). Regular reaffirmation of vows—membership renewals, child dedications—cultivates the muscle memory of loyalty. Pastoral care teams pursue straying

37

members, applying Hosea 11:8's compassionate pursuit rather than silent deletion from rolls. Conflict resolution processes are transparent and restorative, demonstrating Hosea's blend of truth-telling and tenderness (Matthew 18:15-17). Multigenerational worship underscores covenant continuity, echoing Hosea's concern for future children's names and identities (Hosea 1:4-9). Financial stewardship reports are shared openly, reflecting the honesty Hosea demanded of Israel's merchants. Leaders model marital faithfulness, offering premarital classes and counseling to fortify households against cultural pressures. Mission committees support long-term global partners, resisting trend-driven project hopping, thus embodying persevering love. Corporate fasting during crises rehearses Hosea's wilderness discipline that leads to deeper intimacy (Hosea 2:14). Testimonies of restored prodigals are celebrated, reinforcing that no one is beyond redemption, thereby making the church a safe harbor for Gomers of every era (Luke 15:20). Architectural spaces—baptismal fonts near entrances—visually remind visitors of covenant entry points. Small groups function as covenant micro-families, meeting needs and holding members accountable in loving truth. Elder qualifications emphasize hospitality and blameless character (1 Timothy 3:2), upholding the integrity Hosea demanded of priests (Hosea 4:4-9). In all, the church becomes an enacted sermon of steadfast *ḥesed*, persuading doubters through consistency more than rhetoric.

1.7.4 ▪ *Hospitality & table fellowship as covenant signposts*

In both Testaments meals seal relationships—Abraham's feast with angels (Genesis 18) and Jesus' post-resurrection breakfasts (John 21:12)—so believers extend Hosea's covenant love by opening their tables. Weekly potlucks emulate Acts 2:46 and offer embodied inclusion for singles, refugees, and the elderly, subverting loneliness epidemics. Hosts pray Hosea 2:19 over guests, asking God to betroth them in *ḥesed* through shared bread. Dining spaces are curated for dignity: real plates instead of disposables signal worth, echoing the costly silver Hosea paid. Conversation guidelines promote listening, ensuring marginalized voices are heard, reflecting James 1:19's quick-to-listen ethic. Cultural foods are celebrated, anticipating the multinational feast of Revelation 7:9 and demonstrating that Hosea's restored people include Gentiles. Communion services bleed into potlucks, collapsing liturgical and ordinary tables into one covenant continuum (1 Corinthians 10:17). Families invite neighbors for holiday meals, turning secular celebrations into missional touchpoints. Hospitality budgets appear in church finances, sanctifying groceries as kingdom investment. Training workshops teach food safety and cross-cultural sensitivity, because love attends to details. Testimonies of salvation at kitchen tables encourage members that evangelism can simmer on a stove, not just behind a pulpit. Fasting rhythms punctuate feasting, reminding hearts that ultimate satisfaction is in the Bridegroom, aligning with Matthew 9:15. Digital invitations and carpool coordination ensure accessibility, paralleling the servant's compulsion in Luke 14:23. Finally, hospitality theology equips believers to see every meal as an altar where covenant grace is enacted, turning ordinary evenings into Hosea-style redemption stories.

1.7.5 ▪ Cultural apologetics—answering a cynical age with relentless love

Modern skepticism often stems from perceived hypocrisy, so Hosea's narrative offers apologetic leverage by spotlighting God's integrity despite human failure. Christian advocates emphasize that the same Bible naming sin also narrates divine pursuit, presenting a morally serious yet compassionate worldview. Storytelling is central: testimonies of addicts freed or marriages healed illustrate tangible *ḥesed*. Artistic expressions—film, poetry, visual art— translate Hosea's imagery for imagination-driven audiences, aligning with Paul's Mars Hill engagement in Acts 17:22-28. Philosophical arguments for morality or design are complemented by relational experiences of community, showing the gospel's coherence and beauty. Apologists highlight Hosea's prophetic accuracy—Assyrian exile and later restoration—to bolster Scripture's credibility without engaging in triumphalism. Dialogue forums address cultural idols—autonomy, identity politics— through Hosea's lens of misplaced loves, inviting hearers to consider the covenant alternative (Jeremiah 2:13). Online presence mirrors Hosea's honesty; bloggers admit church failings and repent publicly, disarming cynicism. Acts of costly service—disaster relief, pro bono counseling—precede verbal witness, echoing Hosea's purchase of Gomer with tangible currency. Intellectual humility is practiced,

39

acknowledging unanswered questions yet pointing to the Bridegroom's reliability (1 Corinthians 13:12). Scripture engagement is invitational: skeptics encouraged to read Hosea for themselves, trusting the Spirit to illuminate. Cross-disciplinary panels—psychology, economics, theology—demonstrate Christianity's integrated vision, reflecting Hosea's holistic concern. Persistent kindness, not click-bait outrage, marks social media responses, embodying Romans 12:21's admonition to overcome evil with good. Ultimately, apologetics aims to woo rather than win debates, paralleling Hosea's allure language (Hosea 2:14) and trusting love's persuasive power.

1.8. Formation & Reflection Tools

1.8.1 ▪ Lectio divina *on Hosea 1–3 with guided pauses*

Lectio divina begins with *lectio*, a slow reading where participants note recurring words—names of Hosea's children, covenant verbs—allowing the text's rhythm to settle into memory. During *meditatio*, readers imagine standing in the slave market of Hosea 3, engaging senses to feel the scandal and cost. In *oratio*, worshipers respond, thanking God for pursuing love despite personal wanderings, referencing Romans 5:8. *Contemplatio* invites silent resting, trusting that, like Gomer, they are now safe under the Redeemer's gaze. Facilitators suggest breathing the name "Yah-weh" to embody covenant exhale-inhale. A fifth step, *incarnatio*, propels action: participants write one way they will live loyal love in the coming week. Sessions encourage journaling insights, creating a personal commentary on Hosea over time. Group sharing respects vulnerability, reminding members that communal reflection mirrors Israel's corporate covenant identity. Visual aids—art depicting Hosea and Gomer—assist right-brain engagement. Time markers, such as bell chimes, pace the practice, preventing rush. Leaders emphasize that understanding grows with repetition; subsequent weeks revisit the passage in different translations to expose nuanced phrasing. Workshops train participants to inductively trace *ḥesed* across Scripture, reinforcing theological connectivity. Retreat settings—gardens, chapels—echo Hosea's wilderness motif for distraction-free listening (Hosea 2:14). Digital versions use audio recordings, aiding auditory learners. By intertwining text and silence, *lectio divina* transforms Hosea from ancient narrative into lived experience.

1.8.2 • *Prayer of surrender patterned on Hosea 2:19-20*

This guided prayer opens by acknowledging God's initiating betrothal—He "will" act—shifting focus from human effort to divine promise. Participants confess areas of resistance, naming specific idols—control, comfort, acclaim—mirroring Hosea's exposure of Baalism. They then articulate trust, echoing Mary's "let it be" posture (Luke 1:38), pledging loyalty like a bride accepting a ring. Leaders incorporate breath prayers: inhale "You betroth me," exhale "I am yours," syncing body with covenant reality. Scriptural promises—Jeremiah 31:3, John 15:9—are interspersed, grounding surrender in revelation, not emotion. A segment for lament welcomes grief over betrayal, resonating with Hosea 6:1's call to return. Intercession follows, asking that unbelieving friends experience the same wooing love, aligning prayer with missional impulse. The prayer closes with a symbolic gesture—opening hands—signifying relinquishment of self-ownership (1 Corinthians 6:20). Participants may sign a dated card summarizing commitment, providing a tangible memorial like the standing stones of Joshua 4. Follow-up encouragements include daily recitation of Hosea 2:20 to reinforce identity. Musical accompaniment—soft strings—creates atmosphere without distraction. Small groups debrief experiences, fostering communal accountability for surrendered living. Testimonies of answered prayers are shared monthly, nurturing expectancy. By rehearsing surrender, believers internalize Hosea's covenant vows, turning theology into daily posture.

1.8.3 • *Journal prompts for diagnosing divided affections*

Prompts begin with inventory: "List today's top three anxieties; what gods promise to fix them?" referencing Psalm 139:23-24's search request. Another prompt asks: "When did success last feel like salvation?" correlating to Hosea 10:13's trust in own way. Writers examine media habits: "Which notifications capture attention more quickly than Scripture?" echoing Matthew 6:21. A gratitude exercise records moments of undeserved kindness, combating entitlement that fuels idolatry (James 1:17). Reflection on spending: "Highlight purchases made for image-management

41

rather than stewardship," paralleling Isaiah 55:2's call against money for non-bread. Prompts include drawing two circles—one labeled Bridegroom Joy, the other False Lovers—and mapping weekly energy expenditure. Monthly review compares entries, tracking spiritual drift or growth, resembling Hosea's cyclical pattern of sin and rescue. Writers compose a letter from God's perspective, using Hosea 11:1-4 as template, to feel divine tenderness. Another exercise scripts a courtroom scene where conscience cross-examines motives, mirroring Hosea 4:1's lawsuit format. Seasonal prompts tie to liturgical calendar—Advent longing, Lent repentance—integrating personal story with church rhythms. Prompts are framed positively: identifying holy desires beneath sinful pursuits, fostering redemption rather than shame. Inclusion of artistic mediums—poetry, sketching—engages diverse learners. Journals remain private yet can be shared selectively in mentoring relationships for accountability. This disciplined introspection cultivates self-awareness, turning divided hearts toward singular devotion.

1.8.4 ▪ Small-group discussion guide & accountability questions

Groups open by reading Hosea 1–3 aloud, distributing parts to embody drama, enhancing engagement. Ice-breakers invite members to share a time they felt pursued by grace, relating personal stories to Hosea's narrative. Questions probe text: "What emotions surface imagining Hosea at the slave market?" encouraging empathy. Application moves to heart level: "Where might we be bargaining with modern Baals for security?" referencing Hosea 7:11. Accountability queries follow SMART pattern—specific, measurable—such as "Did you practice a media fast one evening this week to seek deeper intimacy with Christ?" Scripture memory challenges—Hosea 2:23—are reviewed together, reinforcing retention. Role-play scenarios rehearse confronting a wandering friend, practicing Hosea-style truth in love (Galatians 6:1). Groups schedule service projects—food-bank volunteering—to act out redeeming love. Prayer triads form, assigning partners to check-in mid-week via text. Facilitators teach conflict-resolution steps aligned with Matthew 18, ensuring group health mirrors covenant fidelity. Periodic testimonies celebrate growth, while failures receive grace and strategic adjustment. Curriculum cycles every six weeks, preventing stagnation. Yearly retreats explore themes in depth, using creative arts and silence for holistic formation. Evaluations solicit feedback, embodying teachability. This guide transforms small groups into laboratories where Hosea's lessons become communal lifestyle.

1.8.5 ▪ Suggested worship songs/hymns celebrating divine pursuit

Song selections interlace classic and contemporary pieces to root worship in historical breadth. "Come Thou Fount" resonates with prone-to-wander honesty mirrored in Gomer's story. "How He Loves" spotlights relentless affection, echoing Hosea 11:8's compassionate controversy. "Reckless Love" captures scandalous pursuit, offering modern language for redemption cost. "O the Deep, Deep Love of Jesus" provides maritime imagery paralleling Hosea's immeasurable *ḥesed.* "Living Hope" celebrates resurrection, tying to Hosea 13:14's promise of death's defeat. "Jesus, Lover of My Soul" frames Christ as Bridegroom refuge, suitable for reflective moments. "Your Grace Finds Me" juxtaposes everyday settings with grace, reinforcing covenant daily-ness. "The Church's One Foundation" anchors corporate identity in marital union imagery (Ephesians 5:25-27). "Great Is Thy Faithfulness" underlines steadfastness contrasting Israel's fickle love (Lamentations 3:22-23). "Run to the Father" shapes response posture akin to Hosea 6:1's return call. Leaders arrange set lists to narrate gospel arc— confession, assurance, commitment—mirroring Hosea's flow. Instrumentation varies: strings during lament, drums during celebratory reversal (Hosea 2:15). Visual slides feature artwork of Hosea's redemption scene, fostering imagination. Choir anthems on *ḥesed* Hebrew refrain teach theology through repetition. Teams introduce songs with brief Scripture references, educating congregants. Seasonal planning integrates wedding-themed songs at Easter, signifying covenant climax. By curating pursuit-focused worship, congregations internalize Hosea's message emotionally and theologically, fueling lives of loyal love.

Conclusion Having walked through Hosea's dramatic testimony of pursuit and purchase, we stand confronted with a love that not only pays the highest price but also reshapes the redeemed into loyal partners. The prophet's marriage points beyond itself to Calvary, where Christ secures the new covenant with His own blood (Mark

43

10:45; 1 Peter 1:18–19). Such a gift calls for more than admiration; it summons a life imbued with grateful fidelity—guarding affections, cultivating intimacy, extending mercy, and embodying justice in the everyday. As you step into the remaining chapters, let the vision of a God who turns auction blocks into altars ignite hope for personal restoration and energize missional compassion for a wandering world. Redeeming love is not merely Hosea's theme; it is the believer's daily reality and eternal song.

Chapter 2. The Pain of Betrayal— Recognizing Spiritual Adultery

The harshest ache in Hosea is not economic collapse or military defeat but the shattering of a covenant heart spurned by its beloved. When the prophet exposes Israel's dalliance with Baal, he is not delivering a dry indictment of improper rituals; he is diagnosing a broken marriage in which every sacrifice at a rival altar is an act of infidelity. By placing betrayal in relational—not merely legal—categories, Hosea helps believers recognize how easily the worship of Christ can be displaced by subtler lovers: security, acclaim, convenience, spectacle. This chapter invites readers to stand in the emotional whirlwind of divine pathos, to feel the grief behind the oracles, and to allow that grief to illuminate the many altars that line our own cultural landscape. Only in the light of Yahweh's wounded love does spiritual adultery become visible for what it is: a rejection of intimacy that drains joy, disorients identity, and fractures community. Acknowledging God's pain is the necessary first step toward healing ours, for only a lover who has been wronged can teach us the gravity—and the remedy—of unfaithful hearts (Hosea 11:1-9; James 4:4).

2.1. Idolatry Then and Now

2.1.1. Baal Worship in Hosea's Day—Fertility Rites & Political Flirtations

Baalism framed every aspect of Israel's agrarian economy, promising rain, crops, and wombs that produced heirs, so the temptation to participate was not merely theological but deeply pragmatic (Hosea 2:5). Cultic calendars synchronized ploughing and harvesting with seasonal festivals in which sexualized rituals were believed to stimulate divine procreation, turning religion into an agricultural technology. Temple prostitutes—both female and male—served as intermediaries, and Hosea's graphic language of "whoredom" borrows imagery the populace would have recognized from those rites (Hosea 4:13–14). Worshipers mixed Yahweh's covenant feasts with Baal's orgiastic ceremonies, attempting to hedge spiritual bets while keeping fields green, a syncretism that violated the first commandment (Exodus 20:3). Politically, Baal devotion functioned like an international brand: regional alliances with Tyre and Sidon often included sharing liturgies, so kings viewed Baal patronage as diplomatic currency (2 Kings 16:10–16). Archaeological evidence from Ugarit tablets reveals that Baal was lauded as "Cloud-Rider," the storm-bringing deity, making Hosea's later portrayal of Yahweh as the one who "responds to the skies" a deliberate polemic (Hosea 2:21). Sacrificial systems also diverged: while Torah sacrifices emphasized sin-atonement, Baal offerings sought manipulation—feed the god to get rain—revealing fundamentally different relational logics. Hosea exposes the irony that Israel credits Baal for blessings Yahweh actually supplies (Hosea 2:8). The prophet's marriage metaphor therefore functions culturally; Gomer's adultery mirrors a nation visiting Baal shrines under the pretense of securing livelihood. Farmers who once recited Deuteronomy's blessing-and-curse liturgy now invoked Baal hymns over seed sacks, illustrating spiritual amnesia (Deuteronomy 11:13-17). Hosea's denunciation underscores covenant exclusivity: to flirt with Baal is to breach marriage vows, not merely adopt novel farming techniques. The political dimension heightens culpability because kings institutionalized idolatry for strategic gain, trading covenant loyalty for perceived military advantage (Hosea 5:13). Modern readers must see that Baal worship was not quaint paganism but a sophisticated, empire-linked economic system; betrayal wore the mask of prosperity. Understanding these dynamics equips believers to discern contemporary idolatries that intertwine economics, sexuality, and geopolitics, reminding them that God's jealousy is the protective passion of a covenant spouse (Exodus 34:14).

2.1.2. Syncretism in the High Places—Bethel, Dan, Gilgal, and Beersheba

After the divided monarchy, Jeroboam I established calf shrines at Bethel and Dan to prevent pilgrimages to Jerusalem (1 Kings 12:26-30). What began as political expediency hardened into multigenerational tradition; Hosea calls Bethel "Beth-Aven" (house of wickedness), highlighting spiritual decay (Hosea 10:5). Gilgal, once memorializing covenant entry under Joshua, became a center of empty ritualism where sacrifices multiplied without heartfelt devotion (Hosea 9:15). Beersheba in Judah joined the circuit, demonstrating that geography offered no safeguard against syncretism (Amos 8:14). High places featured innovative liturgies—hybrid songs, mixed priesthoods, parallel feasts—so the people could claim Yahweh while soothing Baal anxieties, an early form of religious pluralism. Hosea laments that Israel "mixes herself with the peoples" (Hosea 7:8), an indictment using culinary metaphor: dough leavened with pagan yeast. The prophet's lawsuit language (*rib*) pictures Yahweh convening a courtroom where locations themselves testify to covenant breach (Hosea 4:1). The high-place phenomenon shows how idolatry becomes embedded in architecture and pilgrimage habits; stones preach as loudly as priests. Hosea's critique resonates today when believers compartmentalize Sunday worship from Monday marketplaces, essentially building modern Bethels in boardrooms or entertainment venues. Archaeological surveys of Tel Dan reveal monumental gates and cult pedestals, affirming biblical descriptions and underscoring the physical entrenchment of compromise. By contrasting these sites with Torah's command to seek "the place the LORD will choose" (Deuteronomy 12:5), Hosea reminds readers that convenience-driven worship inevitably distorts covenant truth. The prophet therefore calls for dismantling—both literal altars and internal loyalties—illustrated by his vision of thorn and thistle overgrowing abandoned high places (Hosea 10:8). Syncretism's danger lies not

47

only in wrong doctrine but in dulled discernment, as familiarity breeds acceptance. Contemporary parallels include church consumerism that blends gospel language with self-help mantras, diluting holiness. Hosea's geography becomes a map of the heart: where have we erected private high places and renamed them "Bethel," convincing ourselves God endorses them?

2.1.3. Contemporary Idols of Success, Self, and Spectacle

Twenty-first-century idols rarely sit on stone pedestals; they flash on LED screens, dominate algorithms, and shape vocational aspirations. Success idolizes achievement metrics—titles, growth graphs, social-media follower counts—and subtly redefines identity around productivity rather than adoption in Christ (Galatians 4:7). The self idol turns inward, baptizing preferences as immutable rights and elevating personal authenticity above covenant obedience (Judges 21:25). Spectacle worship thrives on constant stimulation, valuing experiences that generate dopamine spikes over disciplines that cultivate enduring character (2 Timothy 4:3–4). These idols promise agency, validation, and excitement, echoing Baal's allure of control over fertility and weather. They demand offerings: overtime hours that eclipse Sabbath, curated personas that mask weakness, disposable income spent on novelty rather than generosity. Hosea's indictment that Israel "feeds on the wind" (Hosea 12:1) applies when believers chase brand partnerships or viral posts that vanish like morning mist. The prophets' economic critique also fits; success idolatry often exploits labor, mirroring merchants with deceitful scales (Hosea 12:7). Self-idol tragically hollows community, for covenant identity gives way to individualized spirituality resistant to accountability (Hebrews 13:17). Spectacle distracts from contemplation, making Scripture reading feel tedious, thereby suffocating intimacy with God. Pastors must therefore name these forces explicitly, as Hosea named Baal, to free congregations from invisible chains. Spiritual formation counters these idols by re-anchoring worth in Christ's finished work (Philippians 3:7–8) and celebrating hidden faithfulness over public acclaim. Diagnosing modern idols through Hosea's lens reveals that betrayal persists, simply cloaked in technological glitz and psychological jargon.

2.1.4. Subtle Cultural Liturgies—Advertising, Algorithms, and Affection-Shaping

James K. A. Smith describes secular practices as liturgies that calibrate love; advertising is one such liturgy, preaching a gospel of deficiency and retail salvation. Hosea would recognize its cadence: declare lack, promise abundance, require offering. Algorithms intensify this catechesis by curating content that reinforces desires, much like Baal priests choreographed rituals to stoke appetite for rain. Social-media "feeds" mimic sacrificial tables, continually inviting users to consume images and identities, forming devotion through repetition (Romans 12:2). Push notifications act as modern bells calling worshipers to miniature altars dozens of times a day. Over time these micro-rituals reorder imagination: vacation envy replaces gratitude, doom-scrolling supplants lament, and influencer admiration edges out emulation of saints (Hebrews 12:1). Cultural calendars further disciple hearts—Black Friday, Super Bowl Sunday, award shows—becoming quasi-religious festivals complete with vestments and liturgies. Christian participation without critical reflection mirrors Israel's unexamined attendance at high-place feasts. Hosea's hedge of thorns (Hosea 2:6) suggests intentional friction: turning off autoplay, instituting screen-Sabbaths, or using grayscale mode to dull attraction. Church gatherings must craft counter-liturgies—call to worship, confession, Eucharist—re-inscribing covenant narrative onto neural pathways. Parents teach children to analyze commercials like modern prophets, exposing false eschatologies of endless upgrade. Communities practice corporate disciplines such as common purse initiatives or technology fasts, breaking enchantments. Recognizing subtle liturgies is crucial because visible idols are easier to flee; unseen scripts shape desire beneath conscious radar. Ultimately, Hosea urges believers to curate habits that prime affection toward the Bridegroom, not toward algorithms that monetize attention.

2.2. Diagnosing Divided Affections

2.2.1. Early Warning Signs of a Wandering Heart (Hosea 7:8–10)

Hosea compares Israel to a half-baked loaf—"a cake not turned"— illustrating inconsistency: warm on one side, raw on the other

(Hosea 7:8). Early indicators of spiritual drift resemble that uneven dough. Prayer becomes perfunctory, guided more by routine than relational hunger (Matthew 15:8). Scripture reading shifts from delight to duty checklist, signaling cooling affection (Psalm 119:97). Gratitude wanes; blessings are assumed rather than acknowledged, echoing Israel's forgetfulness (Hosea 2:8). Ethical shortcuts appear—minor expense reports padded, harmless gossip shared—betraying subtle erosion of holiness. Worship gatherings lose their magnetic pull; comfort or brunch feels preferable to fellowship, foreshadowing absenteeism that preceded exile (Hebrews 10:25). Private sin tolerance grows: the website visited "just this once," bitterness nursed quietly, mirroring Israel consorting with Assyria yet denying guilt (Hosea 7:11). Peer accountability feels intrusive rather than life-giving, showing autonomy trumping covenant mutuality. Emotional responses betray shifted trust: anxiety spikes when investments dip, revealing security in savings, not Savior (Philippians 4:6-7). Complaints multiply as entitlement displaces wonder, similar to Israel's vineyard boasting (Hosea 10:1). Prayer petitions center on comfort acquisition rather than kingdom advance, indicating self enthroned. An unteachable spirit emerges, resisting prophetic correction just as Israel rejected Hosea's words (Hosea 9:7). When confronted, defensiveness surfaces, masking shame; truth feels like threat, not liberation (John 3:20). Recognizing these subtleties allows course correction before hardened idolatry sets in, making repentance a daily micro-turn instead of crisis overhaul.

2.2.2. Emotional, Intellectual, and Volitional Drift—Three Levels of Betrayal

Spiritual adultery rarely erupts overnight; it seeps through concentric circles of the soul. Emotionally, affection transfers first—excitement once reserved for God now attaches to career milestones or romantic pursuits (Revelation 2:4). Intellectual drift follows as cognitive assent to biblical authority softens; inconvenient doctrines are reinterpreted or sidelined (2 Timothy 4:3). Finally, volitional betrayal manifests in actions: skipping church, ethical compromises, secret addictions (James 1:14–15). Hosea traces this progression in Israel: their heart is "false" (emotion), they "do not consider" God's ways (intellect), and they "deal faithlessly" (will) (Hosea 4:11–12). Emotional drift may disguise itself as burnout, yet beneath exhaustion lies misaligned love; Augustine called it *ordered*

50

affections. Intellectual wanderings often borrow cultural plausibility structures—scientism, expressive individualism—to justify distance. Volitional rebellion then solidifies drift into lifestyle grooves; practices reinforce beliefs, completing the loop. Addressing only behavioral symptoms without heart and mind renewal yields short-lived change. Hence discipleship must engage worship (emotion), catechesis (intellect), and obedience training (will), re-aligning the whole person (Colossians 1:28). Communities nurture emotional connection through testimony and lament, intellectual fidelity through teaching, and volitional strength through service projects. Leaders evaluate preaching for all three domains: does the sermon ignite love, clarify truth, and call to concrete action? Hosea's holistic diagnosis guards against reductionism that labels sin as mere ignorance or mere disobedience; it is both, born from misplaced love.

2.2.3. Practicing Daily Self-Examination—Psalm 139:23–24 as Diagnostic Prayer

David's prayer "search me, O God" provides a template for daily heart audit that prevents gradual drift (Psalm 139:23–24). Begin by inviting the Holy Spirit to spotlight hidden motives, trusting conviction as covenant kindness (John 16:8). Review the day hour by hour—*examen*—noting moments of consolation (movement toward God) and desolation (movement away). Ask: "Where did I sense God's presence? Where did I feel pull toward lesser loves?" Journal patterns; repeated desolations flag emerging idols. Incorporate bodily awareness: tension during status updates may reveal success worship; racing pulse when phone pings indicates digital dependence. Scripture reading becomes mirror; verses that sting often reveal pressure points, similar to Hosea's oracles piercing Israel (Hebrews 4:12). Confession follows discovery, naming sins specifically, refusing vague generalities that mask seriousness (1 John 1:9). Receive assurance of pardon, anchoring identity in redeemed status, not failure. Set small repentance steps: apologize to colleague, delete tempting app, schedule Sabbath walk. End with gratitude, reaffirming God's *ḥesed* that empowers change (Lamentations 3:22–23). Weekly, share insights with a mentor, embracing James 5:16's healing dynamic. Over time, self-examination cultivates discernment, enabling believers to detect

51

drift at the desire level before it matures into action. Hosea's call to "know the LORD" (Hosea 6:3) becomes lived reality through this daily diagnostic liturgy.

2.2.4. Case Studies: Saul's Half-Obedience, Solomon's Late-Life Compromise

King Saul epitomizes incremental betrayal: commanded to annihilate Amalek, he spares the best livestock "to sacrifice to the LORD," masking disobedience with pious veneer (1 Samuel 15:15). Samuel's rebuke—"to obey is better than sacrifice"—echoes Hosea 6:6, showing religious activity cannot compensate for partial loyalty. Saul's insecurity craves public approval; people-pleasing becomes his Baal, eventually spiraling into paranoid violence. Solomon illustrates another arc: early devotion marked by lavish temple worship shifts when foreign wives turn his heart to other gods (1 Kings 11:4). Intellectual tolerance—building shrines "for the sake of his wives"—precedes full-blown idolatry, proving affection alliances can override wisdom (Nehemiah 13:26). Both narratives demonstrate that giftedness or initial favor does not immunize against spiritual adultery; vigilance is lifelong. Saul's half-obedience warns modern leaders who adjust biblical commands to fit market research. Solomon's compromise cautions scholars who prize cultural engagement over covenant boundaries. Hosea would diagnose both as covenant breakers deserving exile—Saul loses kingdom, Solomon begets division. Yet their failures instruct disciples: repentance window closes when rationalization hardens. The church can redeem these stories by developing succession plans that prioritize character over charisma, preventing Sauline insecurity. Marital counseling addresses "unequally yoked" concerns, invoking Solomon's downfall as sober precedent (2 Corinthians 6:14). Ultimately, these case studies validate Hosea's thesis: betrayal devastates individuals and nations, underscoring need for steadfast love.

2.3. Guarding Relational Intimacy with Christ

2.3.1. Spiritual Disciplines That Cultivate Loyalty—Prayer, Word, Eucharist

Prayer nurtures conversational intimacy; Jesus withdrew often to solitary places, modeling dependence (Mark 1:35). Variety sustains engagement—adoration, confession, lament, intercession—each facet addressing different heart needs. Scripture intake feeds covenant imagination; lectio, memorization, and study anchor the mind in truth that counters cultural lies (Psalm 1:2). Regular Eucharist rehearses redemption narrative, re-enacting Hosea's purchase in tangible elements (Luke 22:19–20). Disciplines must be grace-based, not performance metrics; they are wedding tunes, not wage earning. Habit stacking—pairing prayer with morning coffee—builds consistency. Utilizing written liturgies can rescue dry seasons, lending borrowed language to tired souls. Corporate disciplines complement private ones; singing psalms together amplifies affection (Colossians 3:16). Silence and solitude function as detox from noise, allowing subtle Spirit nudges to surface. Fasting sharpens appetite for God, reminding believers that true sustenance flows from covenant table (Matthew 4:4). Service disciplines (foot-washing, hospitality) embody love, preventing introspective piety. Journaling captures insights, creating a testimony archive to recall in drought seasons, much like Israel's stone memorials. Disciplines should flex with life stages; new parents may convert diaper changes into breath prayers. Spiritual mentors provide guidance, ensuring practices remain relational, not ritualistic. Sustained over time, these rhythms cultivate loyal hearts resistant to seduction.

2.3.2. Building Rhythms of Remembrance—Fasts, Feasts, and Testimony Nights

Israel's calendar embedded memory: Passover, Weeks, Booths commemorated salvation history (Leviticus 23). Hosea laments that these feasts were co-opted by Baal worship, losing covenant meaning (Hosea 2:11). The church inherits and reinterprets such rhythms: Advent anticipates, Lent repents, Easter celebrates, Pentecost empowers. Regular fasting, personal or corporate, interrupts consumption cycles, echoing Hosea's wilderness season meant to reawaken dependence (Hosea 2:14). Celebration feasts—Resurrection brunches, harvest dinners—counter scarcity narratives, proclaiming God's provision. Testimony nights allow members to share deliverance stories, modern *Ebenezers* that fortify communal memory (1 Samuel 7:12). Practicing *Shema* moments at family tables—retelling redemption each night—teaches children covenant loyalty (Deuteronomy 6:7). Liturgical symbols—candles, banners—engage senses, rooting memory in embodied experience. Digital photo albums of mission trips become modern scrolls, reminding hearts of God's faithfulness. Churches might mark baptism anniversaries with letters, reinforcing identity yearly. Rhythms must balance lament and joy; annual grief rituals for miscarriage or injustice acknowledge wounds while awaiting restoration. Hospitality rotations ensure every member both hosts and is hosted monthly, mirroring reciprocal covenant love. Crafting communal liturgies around local histories—city revival anniversaries—makes remembrance contextual. Without such rhythms, forgetfulness breeds idolatry; with them, gratitude flourishes, resisting the pull of rival stories.

2.3.3. Accountability within Covenant Community—James 5:16 & Hebrews 10:24–25

God intends sanctification to occur in family, not isolation (Ephesians 2:19). Confession to trustworthy believers disarms shame and invites intercessory healing (James 5:16). Accountability relationships clarify specific goals—screen limits, financial generosity, reconciliation steps—and review progress regularly. Meeting frequency matters; fortnightly check-ins create momentum before relapse patterns harden. Hebrews 10:24–25 urges mutual provocation to love and good works, especially as the Day approaches; accountability embodies that command. Tools like covenant cards or shared habit-tracking apps add tangible structure. Groups agree on confidentiality, fostering safety for vulnerable disclosure. Scripture anchors conversations; members remind one another of promises and warnings, functioning as living epistles. Celebrating victories prevents legalistic vibe, highlighting grace's power. When failure occurs, restoration pathways emulate Galatians 6:1—gentleness, not condemnation. Diversity within groups—age, ethnicity—broadens perspective, mitigating blind spots. Leaders receive supervision to avoid lording authority, reflecting servant leadership (1 Peter 5:3). Churches provide training so accountability avoids therapy pitfalls and focuses on discipleship. Ultimately, communal vigilance erects spiritual guardrails, echoing Hosea's plea for corporate response, not individualistic reform.

2.3.4. Digital and Financial Boundaries—Modern Hedge of Thorns (Hosea 2:6)

God promised to block Israel's path with thorns so she could not overtake her lovers (Hosea 2:6). Digital and financial boundaries serve similar protective roles today. Setting device curfews—no screens after 9 p.m.—creates space for prayer and marital conversation. Installing accountability software like Covenant Eyes alerts partners when questionable sites are visited, deterring secrecy. Curating app folders or grayscale mode reduces dopamine loops, weakening spectacle idolatry. Smartphones stay outside bedrooms, turning sacred space into hedge. Budgeting frameworks—10-10-80 or zero-based—allocate generosity and savings before discretionary spending, limiting materialist drift (Proverbs 3:9). Automatic transfers to charity function as monthly tithe hedge, turning firstfruits into infrastructure, not impulse. Sabbath economics—abstaining from buying one day a week—breaks consumer liturgy. Couples discuss purchases above a set limit, fostering transparency. Debt-avoidance strategies protect from enslaving lenders, acknowledging "borrower is slave to lender" (Proverbs 22:7). Notifications are pruned; only relationally essential apps retain badges, reducing attention fragmentation. Social-media fasts each quarter recalibrate identity away from comparison traps. Investment ethics filter portfolios for companies aligned with biblical justice, refusing profit at the expense of laborers (James 5:4). Community challenges—30-day contentment challenges—build corporate momentum. By erecting such hedges, disciples redirect desire back to the Bridegroom, experiencing the freedom Hosea envisioned when allurements lose access to the heart.

2.4. The Anatomy of Spiritual Adultery

2.4.1. From Complacency to Infidelity—A Four-Stage Descent (Hosea 4–8)

Complacency begins when the memory of past deliverance fades and routine replaces wonder; Israel's confidence that "everything is fine" after Jeroboam II's expansion bred spiritual dullness (Hosea 4:7). Comfort then turns into entitlement, so blessings are treated as guaranteed entitlements rather than covenant gifts, and gratitude withers. The second stage is curiosity: exposure to pagan festivals and political entanglements awakens fascination with alternative sources of security; Assyrian alliances sparkle with promises that seem safer than trusting Yahweh (Hosea 7:11). Curiosity ripens into experimentation—attendance at a high-place gathering "just this once," or a small tribute gift to a neighboring deity "for rain insurance," actions that feel harmless but breach exclusivity clauses of the covenant (Exodus 34:14). Experimentation reshapes habits; new rituals embed themselves into calendars and the old rhythms of Torah feasts are crowded out, ensuring the heart drifts without immediate alarm. Stage four is full infidelity: political treaties formalize Baal patronage, priests legitimize hybrid liturgies, and conscience dulls so thoroughly that the people insist they still "know God" while ignoring prophetic warnings (Hosea 8:2). Throughout this slide, prophetic voices are first ridiculed, then silenced, and finally persecuted, illustrating the self-protective instinct of idolatry (Hosea 9:7). Each downward step is incremental, proving that large-scale betrayal usually hides in small daily compromises. The pattern repeats across history—Samson flirts before he falls, David strolls before he sins—showing the universal danger of spiritual drift (Judges 16; 2 Samuel 11). Disciples today must diagnose early complacency, not merely obvious rebellion, if they are to avoid repeating Israel's trajectory. Regular covenant renewal—through Communion, confession, and corporate worship—interrupts the slide by reawakening awe. Spiritual mentors act as early-warning systems, naming drift while it is still reversible. Vigilance also includes attentiveness to feelings of boredom with faith practices; boredom often signals the first move toward alluring alternatives. Leaders who model humility and repentance demonstrate how to pivot when complacency is exposed, preventing communal descent.

Hosea's four-stage descent therefore functions as a spiritual seismograph, sensitive to the first tremors that precede relational collapse.

2.4.2. Cognitive Dissonance—Confessing Yahweh, Serving Baal (Hosea 8:2-4)

Cognitive dissonance allows believers to recite orthodox creeds while engaging in practices that contradict them; Israel claimed covenant identity—"My God, we know you"—even as they kissed the golden calves (Hosea 8:2). The human mind resolves this tension by compartmentalizing: religious language remains in the sanctuary, while economic and political behaviors follow pragmatic pagan scripts outside. Over time, compartmentalization breeds self-deception, so critique feels like persecution rather than correction; prophets are labeled unpatriotic when exposing idolatry (Hosea 9:7-8). Selective memory aids the dissonance: Israel recalls Davidic victories but forgets wilderness discipline, celebrating triumph narratives that validate triumphalist politics. Misapplied theology strengthens the split—claiming divine favor as proof that current policies are blessed, just as calf worshipers argued that economic growth justified their religion (Hosea 10:1). Ritual multiplication masks guilt; more sacrifices are offered to silence conscience without altering behavior (Hosea 8:11-13). Cognitive dissonance thrives in echo chambers where only affirming voices are heard; royal priests in Samaria ensured dissenting Levites were marginalized. Modern parallels include business leaders invoking biblical values while exploiting labor, or churches championing family values while ignoring systemic injustice. Technology amplifies the dissonance by enabling curated identities; social feeds highlight devotional quotes alongside consumerist obsessions. Breaking dissonance requires truth-telling communities that refuse to flatter; Nathan's confrontation of David illustrates prophetic courage piercing royal denial (2 Samuel 12:7-9). Scripture meditation that emphasizes difficult passages—prophets, lament psalms—shreds selective reading habits. Eucharist confronts duplicity by forcing participants to reconcile broken relationships before taking the cup (1 Corinthians 11:27-29). Public confession disciplines the tongue to align speech and life; testimonies of failure and restoration normalize repentance. Without these correctives, cognitive dissonance ossifies into hypocrisy, provoking divine

57

judgment and public scandal. Hosea's critique warns that theological slogans cannot camouflage contradictory loyalties indefinitely; eventually fruits reveal the tree's true root.

2.4.3. Affection Hijack—How Desires Become Demands (James 1:14-15)

James describes desire conceiving sin and birthing death, a biological metaphor capturing how affection morphs into addiction (James 1:14-15). Hosea portrays Israel's affection for grain, wine, and oil mutating into dependence on the fertility god who supposedly guarantees them (Hosea 2:5, 8). Desire is God-given—hunger for security, beauty, relationship—but hijack occurs when legitimate longing detaches from covenant boundaries and seeks fulfillment apart from God. Marketing leverages this process, inflaming wants into perceived needs; Baal priests did similarly, staging sensual rituals to magnify agricultural anxiety. Emotional triggers like fear, loneliness, or envy accelerate hijack; Israel's fear of drought propelled them to Baal altars just as modern anxieties drive 24-hour news consumption. Once desire solidifies into demand, negotiation ceases; the heart insists, "I cannot be content unless..." thereby dethroning the Bridegroom. Ritual payments—ancient offerings or modern subscriptions—feed the habit, reinforcing neural and cultural ruts. The Holy Spirit convicting conscience becomes an irritant, prompting either repentance or deeper entrenchment. Hosea's hedge imagery suggests divine intervention limits the idol's supply line, exposing its inability to satisfy (Hosea 2:6-7). Practically, disciples combat hijack by tracing triggers through journaling—what emotion preceded the online splurge or illicit fantasy? Counter-liturgies of gratitude recalibrate desire, celebrating gifts as tokens of God's love rather than proofs of autonomy. Fasting weakens demand circuitry by denying immediate gratification, retraining desire to rest in divine timing. Community intercession provides external strength when internal resolve falters; shared struggle dismantles shame that fuels secrecy. Ultimately, affection hijack is reversed when the heart encounters superior delight in Christ, echoing Hosea's promise of singing in the restored vineyard (Hosea 2:15). Spiritual adultery thus yields to joyful fidelity as desires are re-ordered around covenant beauty.

2.4.4. Relational Consequences—Distorted Worship, Broken Community, Barren Land (Hosea 4:1-3)

When vertical loyalty fractures, worship distorts first: hymns turn into performance or manipulation, sacrifices into superstition, and liturgy into spectacle, mirroring Israel's empty festivals (Hosea 6:6; 9:1). Distorted worship erodes identity—priests forget Torah, teaching myths that validate excess (Hosea 4:6). The breach then ripples horizontally; deceit multiplies, oaths are broken, and interpersonal trust collapses, spawning a culture of suspicion (Hosea 4:2). Marriages mirror the divine-human fracture, experiencing infidelity and divorce as covenant concepts lose societal value. Economic relationships suffer; merchants adopt dishonest scales, seeing customers as targets rather than neighbors (Hosea 12:7). Leadership failure compounds the decay; kings enthrone themselves without seeking God, cycling through assassinations and coups (Hosea 8:4). Social safety nets unravel because generosity dries up when worship centers on self. Violence escalates; Hosea links idolatry to bloodshed, showing moral vacuum invites predatory behavior (Hosea 6:8-9). Even creation groans: drought, crop blight, and animal die-offs testify in court as witnesses against covenant breach (Hosea 4:3), illustrating ecological solidarity with divine order (Romans 8:22). Barren land further destabilizes economy, intensifying fear and accelerating idol pursuit, a vicious spiral. Communities once marked by hospitality become tribal and inhospitable to immigrants, mirroring Israel's refusal to welcome returning exiles. Prophetic voices lament in poetry because mere prose cannot capture the multi-layered ruin. Modern equivalents include relational fragmentation in urban loneliness, environmental degradation tied to consumer idolatry, and political polarization born of truth decay. Hosea thus presents broken community and barren land not as isolated crises but as relational symptoms of spiritual adultery. Healing, therefore, begins not with social engineering but with renewed covenant fidelity that re-enchants worship, justice, and ecology.

2.5. The Cost of Covenant Breach

2.5.1. Personal Fallout—Shame, Restlessness, Fear (Hosea 10:1-2)

Inner collapse precedes outer judgment; Israel's heart becomes "false," birthing shame that erodes confidence (Hosea 10:2). Shame triggers hiding behaviors—Adam and Eve behind fig leaves—now reenacted in secret alliances and covert idol rituals. Restlessness surfaces because idols cannot satisfy; Jeremiah calls it a cracked cistern that leaks, leaving perpetual thirst (Jeremiah 2:13). Emotional turbulence breeds haste; Israel "multiplies altars" seeking quick relief, a frenetic spirituality mirrored in modern church-hopping (Hosea 8:11). Fear shadows the adulterous heart; without covenant security, threats loom large—economic downturn, geopolitical shifts, personal illness. Insomnia becomes a metaphor—nights spent strategizing like King Ahaz counting Assyrian chariots (2 Kings 16:7-8). Guilt warps self-perception, fueling either self-loathing or defensive pride; both hinder authentic community. Cognitive dissonance drains mental energy; maintaining dual allegiances requires constant rationalization. Spiritual discernment dulls, making divine guidance feel silent—"They cry to me…He does not answer" (Hosea 5:6). Addictive cycles intensify as coping mechanisms—alcohol, pornography, shopping—falsely promise ease. Physical health can degrade; stress and secrecy manifest somatically, aligning with Proverbs' observation that crushed spirits dry bones (Proverbs 17:22). Depression and anxiety often accompany prolonged hypocrisy, confirming that body, soul, and spirit integrate. Personal fallout thus illustrates sin's boomerang effect: what promised pleasure delivers torment. Hosea exposes these inner costs so readers will flee idolatry before external calamity strikes. True repentance confronts shame with grace, restlessness with Sabbath, and fear with perfect love that casts out dread (1 John 4:18).

2.5.2. Societal Disintegration—Violence, Injustice, and Leadership Failure

Corporate sin metastasizes beyond individuals; Hosea pictures a society where murder follows murder until blood touches blood (Hosea 4:2). Violence escalates as covenant restraint disappears;

tribal factions settle disagreements with swords, echoing the concubine outrage in Judges 19. Injustice becomes structural: courts favor the wealthy, land is seized through legal loopholes, and prophets are bribed to stay silent (Micah 3:11). Leadership failure compounds chaos; kings ascend by conspiracy, reigning only months before assassination (Hosea 7:7; 10:3). Policy vacillates; some rulers appease Egypt, others Assyria, creating strategic whiplash that destabilizes economy. Social trust erodes; neighbors spy on one another, anticipating betrayal (Micah 7:5-6). Religious institutions lose credibility as priests exploit offerings, mirroring Hophni and Phinehas's corruption (1 Samuel 2:12-17). Economic disparities widen; luxurious mansions rise beside collapsing cottages, reflecting Amos's indictment of ivory houses (Amos 3:15). The poor suffer first, but disintegration eventually engulfs elites when Assyrian taxes drain treasuries. Education falters; scribal schools promote myths rather than Torah, producing a generation ignorant of covenant history. Artistic expression degenerates into propaganda for royal agendas, abandoning prophetic critique. Foreign policy failures invite invasion; finally, exile uproots the populace, scattering identity across empires (2 Kings 17:6). Hosea presents societal collapse not as random but as covenant consequence: when vertical loyalty dies, horizontal fabric unravels. Modern parallels include widening economic inequality, political instability, and institutional distrust in cultures that marginalize God. Renewal, therefore, must address root idolatry, not merely symptoms of disintegration.

2.5.3. Ecological Groaning—Land Mourns, Beasts Languish (Hosea 4:3; Romans 8:22)

Hosea declares that drought, withered vegetation, and dying animals accompany Israel's unfaithfulness (Hosea 4:3). The land is personified as a plaintiff in covenant lawsuit, underscoring creation's vested interest in human obedience. Israel's fertility cult promised agricultural bounty, yet apostasy ironically triggered barrenness, revealing idol propaganda. Torah linked ecological blessing to covenant faithfulness (Leviticus 26:3-5), so environmental crisis functions as prophetic billboard. Modern science echoes this principle: deforestation, soil erosion, and climate instability often correlate with greed, corruption, and overconsumption—forms of idolatry. Paul universalizes the pattern, describing creation groaning under human sin until liberated at Christ's return (Romans 8:22). Hosea's imagery warns against dualism that divorces spiritual life from ecological stewardship; worship choices shape watersheds. Sabbath year laws illustrate restorative ecology: allowing fields to rest honors divine ownership and preserves fertility (Leviticus 25:4). Ignoring such rhythms leads to land "enjoying its Sabbaths" through forced exile, a grim greenhouse of judgment (2 Chronicles 36:21). Prophets envision reversal—streams in desert, wolf with lamb—when covenant is restored (Isaiah 35:1-7; 11:6-9). Christian environmental action aligns with this hope, treating recycling, conservation, and clean energy as liturgies of fidelity. Churches can host tree-planting liturgies linked to repentance services, embodying Hosea's promise of cedars replacing thorns (Hosea 14:6-9). Eucharistic theology affirms material goodness; bread and wine require healthy soil, warning that polluted fields impair worship elements. Ecological crises thus signal deeper disease, inviting both environmental reform and spiritual renewal. Hosea integrates creation care into discipleship, challenging believers to repent of exploitative patterns that echo Baal worship's abuse of the earth.

2.5.4. Divine Pathos—God's Wounded Heart (Hosea 11:8-9)

Hosea offers one of Scripture's most poignant glimpses into divine emotion; God cries out, "How can I give you up?" (Hosea 11:8). This rhetorical anguish reveals covenant love feels betrayal, countering deistic images of impassible deity. Divine pathos is not volatile moodiness; it is holy attachment forged by covenant vows at Sinai, akin to marital fidelity. Prophets use anthropomorphic language not to diminish God but to communicate relational reality in human terms. Wounded love intensifies mercy: judgment is delayed, warnings multiplied, because affection restrains wrath. Yet pathos also legitimizes justice; if betrayal did not hurt, punishment would resemble bureaucratic penalty rather than moral consequence. Jesus embodies divine pathos, weeping over Jerusalem's refusal of covenant overtures (Luke 19:41-44). Gethsemane's agony echoes Hosea's wrestling between compassion and holiness, showing continuity between Testaments (Mark 14:34). Divine grief sanctifies human lament; believers may name pain without fear of faithlessness, mirroring their God's transparency. Pathos confronts cynicism that imagines God indifferent to injustice; every orphan's cry reverberates in heavenly chambers. Pastoral counseling uses this truth to assure victims that God understands betrayal trauma personally. Worship songs like "How Deep the Father's Love" derive emotional depth from Hosea's revelation. However, pathos warns against presuming upon grace; unrelenting rebellion eventually reaches a tipping point where judgment serves love by removing cancerous idolatry. Revival preaching therefore weaves tenderness and urgency, inviting response before divine anguish turns to decisive action. Ultimately, Hosea's portrait invites readers into intimate communion where God's heart, not just His law, guides repentance.

2.6. Prophetic Call and Pathways to Return

2.6.1. "Come, Let Us Return" (Hosea 6:1-3)—The Grammar of Repentance

Hosea proposes a communal liturgy of return, beginning with acknowledgment of God's rightful wounding yet confident in His healing (Hosea 6:1). Repentance grammar starts with "we," rejecting individualism for corporate solidarity; sin is communal, so restoration must be as well. The next verb is "return," denoting directional change—repentance is not mere remorse but covenant re-alignment. Time imagery—"after two days...on the third day"— anticipates resurrection hope, hinting at transformative renewal (Hosea 6:2). Knowing the Lord becomes the goal, not merely avoiding punishment; this relational target redefines repentance as intimacy restoration. Rains imagery conveys refreshing grace that follows confession, linking agricultural blessing to spiritual renewal (Hosea 6:3). The grammar includes confession of specific sins, not vague regrets, mirroring Daniel's prayer enumerating Israel's rebellion (Daniel 9:5-11). It embraces humility—fasting, sackcloth—as embodied acknowledgment of dependence. Restitution appears where harm was done; Zacchaeus's fourfold repayment exemplifies covenant justice (Luke 19:8). Repentance also involves covenant-renewal ceremony, such as reading Torah aloud, as Josiah modeled (2 Kings 23:1-3). The grammar expects opposition; pride resists exposure, so leaders model vulnerability first. Prophets facilitate with hopeful tone, avoiding despair that paralyzes; they remind people of God's character—gracious, compassionate, slow to anger (Exodus 34:6). The call includes future orientation—seeking knowledge of God implies ongoing discipleship, not one-time apology. Sacramental acts—Eucharist, baptism reaffirmations—seal repentance vows. Finally, this grammar integrates eschatology; returning prefigures ultimate reconciliation at Christ's return, infusing present repentance with eternal significance.

2.6.2. Lament as Spiritual Surgery—Tearing Clothes vs. Tearing Hearts (Joel 2:13)

Lament voices sorrow without self-pity, naming injustice and unfaithfulness before God. Ancient Israel tore garments as grief sign, yet prophets insist the true tear must slice the heart, not the wardrobe (Joel 2:13). Hosea embodies lament; his children's names are living dirges announcing covenant fracture (Hosea 1:4-9). Lament begins with honest emotion—anguish, confusion, even holy anger—rejecting stoic denial. It then recounts God's past faithfulness, creating dialectic between promise and pain, as many lament psalms do (Psalm 77). Lament absorbs communal dimension, including innocent sufferers caught in societal sin—exiled children, widows, and land itself. It refuses premature resolution, allowing grief to do its refining work; quick fixes mutter "peace, peace" where none exists (Jeremiah 6:14). In surgery terms, lament is incision, exposing infection so healing mercy can cleanse. Corporate lament services—ashes, silence, minor-key music—teach congregations to process betrayal collectively. Personal lament journaling helps individuals confront idols' devastation rather than minimize it. Spiritual directors guide lament, ensuring it moves toward hope, not cynicism. Lament also protests systemic evil—racism, exploitation—functioning as prophetic witness that things are not as God intends. When expressed faithfully, lament becomes intercession, pleading for divine intervention based on covenant love (Psalm 79:8-9). It cultivates empathy, aligning hearts with God's wounded pathos. Ultimately, lament positions the soul for the comfort promised to mourners (Matthew 5:4), catalyzing transformation rather than despair.

2.6.3. Confession, Renunciation, Renaming—Reversing Lo-Ruhamah & Lo-Ammi *(Hosea 2:23)*

Confession names sin in God's hearing, aligning human verdict with divine truth; Israel must admit, "Baal is no husband." Renunciation follows, severing ties with idols through decisive acts—destroying altars, canceling treaties, discarding amulets, paralleling Ephesus believers burning sorcery scrolls (Acts 19:19). Confession and renunciation create space for renaming, the covenant act where God reassigns identity: "No Mercy" becomes "Mercied," "Not My People" becomes "My People" (Hosea 2:23). Renaming heals shame, replacing negative labels accrued through sin with dignity grounded in divine election. Liturgically, churches may conduct renunciation rites, inviting members to verbally reject idols—materialism, lust, control—and receive new names like Beloved or Free. Baptism embodies all three; candidates confess sin, renounce Satan, and rise with new identity in Christ (Romans 6:3-4). Family systems adopt renaming by blessing children nightly, countering cultural insults with covenant titles—Chosen, Holy, Treasurer of God. Workplace believers can rename vocations—seeing teaching as disciple-making, engineering as creation care—redeeming secular labels into kingdom purpose. Confession includes restitution where idolatry harmed others, knitting justice into renaming. Spiritual warfaring prayer demolishes strongholds, recalling that behind idols lie demonic forces (1 Corinthians 10:20). Psychological healing accompanies spiritual renaming; studies show narrative reframing alters neural pathways, confirming Scripture's renewal of mind (Romans 12:2). Community affirmation stabilizes new identity; peers refer to one another by covenant descriptors, fostering culture of grace. Failure will occur, but renaming ensures relapse does not redefine redeemed people. Finally, renaming anticipates eschatological white stone with a new name (Revelation 2:17), situating present identity in future glory.

2.6.4. Restorative Practices—Corporate Worship, Communal Intercession, Acts of Justice

Restoration requires practices that stabilize renewed loyalty. Corporate worship reorients imagination weekly, rehearsing gospel storyline through song, Scripture, and sacrament, replacing Baal myths with Christ's narrative. Liturgical confession and assurance create rhythm of ongoing repentance, preventing build-up of hidden sin. Communal intercession embodies priestly vocation, standing in the gap for city and nation, mirroring Moses' mediation (Exodus 32:11-14). Intercession meetings may employ Hosea texts, appealing for mercy that heals apostasy (Hosea 14:4). Acts of justice translate liturgy into public witness—feeding programs, legal aid, environmental clean-ups—modeling Hosea 12:6's call to maintain love and justice. Restorative circles address interpersonal conflicts, seeking reconciliation rather than mere punishment, reflecting Matthew 18 principles. Economic generosity funds relief for those harmed by prior exploitation, paralleling Jubilee vision. Discipleship groups sustain accountability and scriptural grounding, ensuring new believers root habits in truth. Artistic expression—murals, music—celebrates redemption, embedding testimony in neighborhood aesthetics. Pilgrimage retreats to historical revival sites inspire hope for communal renewal, connecting past moves of God to present longing. Leadership development focuses on servant-hearted models, countering political power plays that marked Israel's kings. Sabbath celebrations provide counter-cultural rest, witnessing to freedom from productivity idolatry. Storytelling nights allow members to narrate God's intervention, strengthening faith and resilience. Missional engagement invites restored people to invite outsiders, preventing inward focus and spreading covenant blessing. These practices create a regenerative ecosystem where loyalty flourishes and spiritual adultery loses allure, fulfilling Hosea's vision of a people alive with steadfast love.

2.7. Cultivating Covenant Fidelity in Everyday Life

2.7.1 ▪ Exclusive Worship in a Pluralist World— First-Commandment Living

Covenant fidelity begins with the unwavering confession that the Lord alone is God, a claim that still sounds intolerant in cultures prizing spiritual eclecticism (Exodus 20:3). First-commandment living therefore requires more than a doctrinal nod; it asks believers to examine every sphere—music playlists, reading lists, friendship circles, career goals—for rival allegiances masquerading as harmless options. Biblical models such as Shadrach, Meshach, and

Abednego show that exclusive worship may provoke social pressure and even legal censure, yet loyalty to God protects identity even in the furnace (Daniel 3:17-18). Practically, exclusive worship involves intentional liturgies: beginning each morning by declaring, "Jesus is Lord," and ending each night with a prayer of surrender keeps the covenant center stage (Romans 10:9). Participation in inter-faith civic events can be navigated with clarity by affirming common grace while declining syncretistic rites, following Paul's pattern in Acts 17:22-31 where he commends truth yet calls for repentance. Exclusive worship also demands honesty about hidden syncretism, such as combining horoscope consultations with daily devotions or anchoring worth in national identity rather than the kingdom (Philippians 3:20). Community reinforcement is vital; small groups rehearse testimonies of divine faithfulness to remind one another that no alternative savior ultimately delivers. Corporate worship leverages ancient creeds to anchor communal memory and inoculate hearts against cultural amnesia. Moreover, public symbols—cross necklaces, Bible verses on office walls—are not talismans but conversation starters that declare covenant allegiance without apology (Deuteronomy 6:8-9). Exclusive worship shapes financial priorities: tithes leave bank accounts before entertainment spending, testifying that God receives first love (Proverbs 3:9). Decision-making processes also change; choices are prayed through discernment grids asking, "Will this enlarge Christ's honor or subtly enthrone myself?" Fasting from entertainment events that glorify violence or occult imagery breaks sentimental ties with idolatrous narratives (1 Corinthians 10:21). Finally, exclusive worship cultivates humility, for absolute loyalty to Jesus leaves no room for prideful comparison—faithfulness, not superiority, is the badge of covenant people (Micah 6:8). As pluralism intensifies, Christians who embody gentle exclusivity will shine not as culture warriors but as clear-toned witnesses whose singular devotion invites respectful curiosity (1 Peter 3:15).

2.7.2 • *Vocational Integrity—Marketplace Faithfulness as Marital Faithfulness*

Hosea links dishonest scales to spiritual prostitution (Hosea 12:7); therefore, integrity at work is covenant fidelity in business attire. Every profession offers unique temptations—doctors to overbill, marketers to manipulate, engineers to cut safety corners—and each compromise echoes Israel's flirtation with other gods for competitive advantage. Daniel's refusal to defile himself with royal delicacies illustrates vocational faithfulness that does not require exit from pagan structures but steady allegiance within them (Daniel 1:8). Christians practice integrity by adopting transparent accounting, refusing bribes, and honoring contracts even when loopholes might excuse them (Psalm 15:4). Regularly offering work to God in prayer shifts motivation from personal promotion to kingdom service (Colossians 3:23-24). Mentoring younger employees reflects covenant generosity; seasoned professionals share expertise without extracting undue credit, mirroring God's self-giving love. Sabbath observance limits endless hustle, signaling trust in divine provision above quarterly targets (Exodus 20:9-11). Vocational integrity also addresses speech; gossip and deceit poison team culture, whereas truthful, gracious communication builds communal trust (Ephesians 4:29). Performance reviews become opportunities for humility and growth rather than idolized validation. Christians advocate for equitable pay and humane scheduling, aligning corporate policy with biblical justice (James 5:4). Entrepreneurs integrate tithing into business models, viewing profits as stewardship rather than entitlement. Ethical supply-chain audits guard against hidden exploitation abroad, living out love of neighbor beyond national borders (Luke 10:36-37). When failures occur, prompt confession and restitution uphold testimony, paralleling Zacchaeus's marketplace repentance (Luke 19:8). Ultimately, vocational integrity adorns the gospel in the public square, showing colleagues that covenant loyalty produces both excellence and empathy (Titus 2:10). Such witness can open evangelistic doors far more effectively than workplace slogans, embodying Hosea's call to steadfast love in the everyday grind.

2.7.3 • *Embodied Habits—Sabbath, Simplicity, and Stewardship of Attention*

Israel's weekly Sabbath was a living protest against productivity idolatry, and its violation paralleled Baal worship in Hosea's day (Hosea 2:11). Reclaiming Sabbath now means scheduling twenty-four hours where earning, buying, and scrolling cease, allowing souls to remember they are betrothed, not bought (Mark 2:27). Simplicity complements Sabbath; decluttering wardrobes and calendars cultivates contentment, freeing resources for generosity (1

68

Timothy 6:6-8). Practically, families purge closets seasonally, donating surplus as a tangible act of dethroning material gods. Meal planning that prioritizes shared tables over fast-food runs slows life to relational pace, echoing Hosea's vineyard songs of restored intimacy (Hosea 2:15). Stewardship of attention addresses the digital onslaught: believers set "rule of life" guidelines limiting social-media minutes and turning phones to grayscale to dull addictive allure. Morning Scripture meditation precedes device activation, ensuring God's voice anchors the day (Psalm 5:3). Embodied habits also involve posture; kneeling in prayer counters self-reliant stance, while standing in worship proclaims resurrection hope. Regular exercise respects the body as temple, resisting dualistic views treating physical health as irrelevant to spirituality (1 Corinthians 6:19-20). Silence practices retrain neural circuits overstimulated by constant noise, enabling discernment of the Bridegroom's whisper (1 Kings 19:12). Financial simplicity—living below means—creates margin for crisis benevolence, modeling Hosea's redeeming generosity. Seasonal liturgies like Advent waiting and Lent fasting weave embodied rhythms through the year, tethering time itself to covenant story. When these habits falter, grace invites restart; disciplines are wedding dances, not grading rubrics. Over months, embodied habits reshape desires, making faithfulness feel less like duty and more like delight, fulfilling Hosea's prophecy that God's people will call Him "My Husband" with affection, not obligation (Hosea 2:16).

2.7.4 • Family Discipleship—Teaching Children to Spot Cultural Baals (Deuteronomy 6:4-9)

The Shema commands parents to impress covenant truth on children at home, on the road, and even in décor (Deuteronomy 6:7-9). Family discipleship therefore requires intentional conversations about media content, peer values, and advertising claims, naming idols early so kids develop discernment muscles. Parents read Hosea's narrative at age-appropriate levels, framing Gomer's betrayal as a cautionary tale about divided hearts. Bedtime blessings counter identity messages from social platforms, declaring daughters beloved beyond likes and sons valued beyond grades. Shared service projects—food banks, neighborhood cleanup—demonstrate justice as worship, inoculating against self-centered religion (Micah 6:8). Tech agreements set screen limits and

Sabbaths, modelling digital hedges of thorns (Hosea 2:6). Family budgeting meetings show how money follows worship; children help choose charitable recipients, experiencing generosity's joy. Celebrating Christian calendar events anchors time in covenant narrative—Advent wreaths and Passover-style meals bring theology to the dinner table. Parents confess their own failures promptly, teaching grace's rhythm and avoiding hypocrisy that breeds rebellion (Ephesians 6:4). Storytelling evenings invite grandparents to recount God's faithfulness across generations, weaving communal memory against amnesia. Music playlists mix hymns with quality contemporary worship, turning car rides into theology classrooms. Family goal-setting each New Year asks, "How will we love God and neighbor more this season?" pushing discipleship beyond abstract talk. Outdoor Sabbath walks train appreciation for creation, linking stewardship with gratitude (Genesis 2:15). Regular intercession circles invite children to pray aloud, normalizing dependence on the Bridegroom. As kids mature, parents discuss apologetic challenges—pluralism, sexuality, suffering—providing biblical frameworks rather than reactive fear. When children fail, restorative discipline mirrors Hosea's tender pursuit, prioritizing heart restoration over mere behavior correction.

2.8. Living Prophetically amid Cultural Seduction

2.8.1 • Counter-Cultural Loyalty—The Church as a Faithful Spouse (Ephesians 5:25-27)

Paul portrays the church as a bride being purified for Christ, a collective vocation that demands visible counter-cultural loyalty (Ephesians 5:25-27). Such loyalty starts with doctrinal unity around the gospel, but it must manifest in communal practices that critique consumerism, racism, and political idolatry. Sunday gatherings model kingdom demographics—rich and poor sharing Eucharist, diverse ethnicities singing one song—defying segregation norms (Galatians 3:28). Corporate decision-making values discernment over majority rule, symbolizing submission to the Bridegroom rather than democratic idols of autonomy. Church budgets allocate significant percentages to missions and benevolence, testifying that love gives sacrificially. Conflict resolution processes prioritize reconciliation, refusing cancel culture's quick severance (Matthew

18:15-17). Members forgo gossip, choosing Matthew 18 pathways that honor relational vows. Baptism services function as wedding ceremonies, reminding the congregation of collective identity. The table liturgy invites weekly covenant renewal, echoing Hosea's hopeful betrothal (Hosea 2:19-20). Church architecture that places the font near the entrance and the table at the center visually narrates covenant progression—entry, nourishment, sending. Public stances on hot-button issues emerge from theological reflection, not partisan echo chambers, signaling allegiance to Christ above party lines. Pastoral leadership models servant authority, washing feet literally or metaphorically to counter celebrity culture. Rhythms of fasting and prayer accompany major ministry decisions, enshrining dependence over savvy. Hospitality teams greet newcomers with familial warmth, practicing inclusive loyalty that mirrors divine welcome. By embodying these habits, the church becomes a prophetic signpost, demonstrating that monogamous devotion to Jesus is not only possible but beautiful amid cultural seduction.

2.8.2 ▪ Public Witness through Mercy & Justice—Hosea 12:6 in Action

Hosea instructs Israel to "return to love and justice," pairing vertical devotion with horizontal rectitude (Hosea 12:6). Public witness therefore extends mercy to the poor, refugee, and marginalized, not as social hobby but covenant overflow. Churches partner with local agencies to combat homelessness, providing transitional housing funded by sacrificial giving (Isaiah 58:7). Legal professionals offer pro bono services to under-resourced neighbors, translating justice into courtroom advocacy. Medical teams host free clinics, echoing Jesus' healing ministry (Matthew 4:23). Congregations sponsor refugee families, integrating language tutoring and job placement to embody hospitality. Advocacy initiatives challenge unjust zoning laws that entrench poverty, demonstrating structural mercy alongside relief. Environmental projects—river clean-ups, tree plantings—reflect the land-mending aspect of covenant obedience (Hosea 4:3). Annual budgets earmark percentages for global water wells or anti-trafficking work, ensuring compassion isn't episodic. Members write legislators on behalf of prisoners, aligning with Hebrews 13:3. Worship services weave justice testimonies between songs, preventing detachment. Youth ministries incorporate service learning, shaping disciples who equate faithfulness with neighbor

71

love. Activists receive pastoral care and theological training to avoid burnout and maintain gospel centrality. Metrics of success shift from seating capacity to sent capacity—how many servants mobilized. When media spotlight these efforts, leaders point glory to Christ's redeeming love rather than brand promotion. In this way, mercy and justice become apologetic forces, proving Hosea's message has contemporary traction.

2.8.3 · Apologetics of Integrity—Answering Cynicism with Consistent Love

Post-Christendom audiences often dismiss verbal claims until embodied consistency validates them; thus apologetics begins with integrity. Believers refrain from exaggeration on résumés, rejecting utilitarian ethics that breed public distrust. Online discourse models civility, resisting outrage algorithms and demonstrating the gentleness Peter commends (1 Peter 3:15). Financial transparency in churches combats skepticism from scandal-weary observers. Public confession of mistakes—misreported finances, leadership missteps—shows humility and accountability. Neighbourliness builds credibility; mowing an elderly neighbor's lawn opens conversational doors that cold-call evangelism may never access. Scholars engage academic debates with rigor and respect, refusing straw-man tactics. Artists produce excellent work—films, novels, music—that explores brokenness honestly while hinting redemption, mirroring Hosea's poetic realism. Social media bios link to local churches, not just personal brands, underlining communal belonging. When Christians are caught in hypocrisy, swift repentance and restitution maintain witness. Apologists develop listening skills, allowing skeptics to articulate wounds often rooted in church betrayal; empathic presence precedes intellectual rebuttal. Narrative apologetics—story of personal redemption—connects emotionally before logically. Serving alongside atheists in community projects demonstrates shared love for neighbor and challenges caricatures of insularity. Faith-and-work conferences equip professionals to articulate how biblical worldview shapes innovation and ethics. Cumulative integrity invites the curious to "come and see," echoing Philip's simple invitation to skeptical Nathanael (John 1:46). When words and deeds converge, the gospel's plausibility rises, fulfilling Jesus' prayer that unity would persuade the world of His divine mission (John 17:21).

2.8.4 • Hope-Filled Vigilance—Awaiting the Bridegroom while
Resisting New Idols (Matthew 25:1-13)

Jesus' parable of the ten virgins warns disciples to keep lamps
trimmed, balancing expectant hope with active vigilance (Matthew
25:1-13). Hope prevents vigilance from devolving into paranoia;
vigilance prevents hope from drifting into naivety. Practically,
believers cultivate eschatological imagination through regular
meditation on resurrection passages, fueling joy rather than
escapism (1 Thessalonians 4:16-18). Annual teaching on the
doctrine of new creation fortifies against despair when cultural
decline intensifies. Vigilance expresses itself by monitoring
emergent idols—cryptocurrency speculation promising utopian
wealth, AI transhumanism offering god-like enhancement, or
wellness movements spiritualizing self-optimization. Discernment
teams within churches read culture critically, producing briefing
notes for congregations so they are not caught unaware (1 Chronicles
12:32). Prayer watches intercede through the night once a month,
symbolically keeping lamps burning. Sermon series on Daniel or
Revelation explore faithfulness under empire pressures, equipping
saints for future trials. Spiritual disciplines like fasting detach hearts
from immediate gratification, mirroring virgins storing extra oil.
Community emergency funds prepare for economic shocks,
embodying prudence without hoarding. Hope-filled songs—"Even
So, Come," "King of Kings"—sustain anticipation during prolonged
delay. When new technologies emerge, ethical panels assess
implications through a biblical lens, guiding usage that honors
dignity. Vigilance includes mentoring the next generation, passing
on wisdom so lamps remain lit after current leaders sleep. Sacred art
depicting the marriage supper hangs in lobbies, keeping destiny
before the congregation's eyes (Revelation 19:7-9). Periodic retreats
for silence and prophecy create space to hear fresh direction,
preventing stale routines. Thus, the church lives like a wise
maiden—joyfully adorned yet watchfully prepared—ensuring that
when the Bridegroom arrives, faith is found burning bright, not
flickering out amid the latest cultural craze.

Conclusion Facing the mirror Hosea holds up can feel searing, yet
the reflection is not the final scene. The same voice that thunders
judgment also whispers allure, promising deserts transformed into
vineyards and estranged names rewritten with mercy (Hosea

73

2:14-23). When the sting of conviction leads to honest confession, betrayal is not the terminal chapter but the doorway to deeper covenant fidelity. Christ, the faithful Husband who absorbed every curse of our wandering, now empowers His people to exchange divided affections for undivided devotion, turning recognition into repentance and repentance into resilient love (Ephesians 5:25-27; 1 John 1:9). As you move forward, let the pain uncovered here sharpen your discernment, deepen your gratitude, and galvanize your resolve to guard the bridal loyalty that alone can satisfy the heart of God and flood your life with the wholeness His covenant intends.

Chapter 3. Relentless Pursuit— Grace That Will Not Let Go

Across the prophetic landscape of Hosea, the most arresting feature is not the magnitude of Israel's failure but the magnitude of God's determination to recover His wayward bride. From the moment the Lord whispers that He will "allure her and lead her into the wilderness" (Hosea 2:14), the narrative pivots from judgment to an almost scandalous grace that refuses rejection as the last word. This chapter traces that divine initiative as the unbroken thread linking Sinai's covenant, Hosea's marriage drama, the parables of Jesus in Luke 15, and the self-giving climax of the cross. Rather than functioning as a theological add-on, grace emerges as the very engine of redemption: a pursuing love that navigates barren deserts, pays unthinkable costs, and rewrites names once stamped with shame. By entering this story, modern disciples confront a startling truth—our deepest transformations do not originate in moral effort but in surrender to a God whose resolve outpaces our rebellion.

3.1. The Divine Allure—Wilderness Rendezvous (Hosea 2:14-15)

3.1.1. Historical echoes of Sinai courtship

God's promise to "allure" Israel into the wilderness deliberately evokes the earliest days of covenant romance when the nation, newly freed from Pharaoh, followed the Lord's pillar of cloud across an uncharted desert (Ex 19:4; Jer 2:2). In Hosea's vision the wilderness is not a prison camp but a honeymoon suite, a stripped-down environment where competing voices fall silent and the memory of first love can resurface. Israel's original journey featured manna they could not hoard, water summoned from unlikely rocks, and daily guidance they could neither predict nor control (Ex 16:4; 17:6). Each provision trained them to trust relationship over resource management, and Hosea insists the same pedagogy is still necessary when affluence has dulled dependence. Modern believers encounter analogous "wildernesses" in job loss, illness, or relocation—periods where familiar structures collapse, revealing whether faith rests on circumstance or covenant. Historical parallels extend to Elijah's flight to Horeb, where divine whisper replaced earthquake and fire, reminding readers that sacred romance often blooms in scarcity (1 Ki 19:11-13). Even Jesus reenacted the pattern, entering the Judean desert to rehearse Israel's forty-year test in forty decisive days (Mt 4:1-2). Therefore, the wilderness motif is not punitive exile alone; it is God's chosen classroom for rekindling intimacy. When contemporary disciples find themselves between jobs or on silent retreats, they participate in a formative lineage stretching back to Sinai. Remembering that history reframes hardship: what feels like abandonment may actually be the Lover's strategic relocation for undivided attention. Spiritual mentors can help seekers trace wilderness benefits by journaling answered prayers that would have gone unnoticed in busier seasons. Ultimately, the Sinai echo underscores grace's initiative; Israel did nothing to schedule this rendezvous, yet Yahweh orchestrated it to renew vows that complacency had muted.

76

3.1.2. Wilderness as detox from false lovers

The Israelites' dalliance with Baal thrived on crowded vineyards, bustling markets, and high-place pageantry; a barren expanse offers none of those stimulants (Ho 2:12; 4:13). By removing Israel from the sensory cues that triggered idolatry, God initiates a detox program far more radical than self-help renunciation. Addiction specialists observe that new environments interrupt habituated cravings; Hosea showcases the spiritual parallel centuries before neuroscience named it. The desert's monochrome landscape contrasts sharply with the colorful Baal festivals, recalibrating Israel's aesthetic palate to prize contentment over spectacle. Silence exposes inner monologues previously masked by marketplace chatter, making space for honest lament and renewed awareness of divine presence (Ps 62:1). The daily scarcity of water mirrors spiritual thirst, transforming physical need into metaphor for covenant longing (Ps 63:1). Even the desert's temperature extremes—blistering days, freezing nights—teach reliance on a cloud of protection by day and a pillar of fire by night, symbols that foreshadow Christ as shade and light (1 Co 10:1-4). In pastoral practice, digital sabbaths, urban prayer walks, or service trips to remote villages reproduce detox dynamics, distancing hearts from algorithmic flattery and consumer noise. Such practices should be framed positively—as bridal get-aways—rather than punitive austerities, preserving the romance motif. When Israel eventually re-enters fertile land, the hope is that preferences will have shifted: Baal's gaudy promises will taste stale beside Yahweh's quiet fidelity. The church can reinforce this shift by crafting liturgies that highlight simplicity—unaccompanied psalm singing, candlelit scripture readings—allowing worshipers to discover joy unmediated by production value. Detox culminates not in emptiness but in appetites re-tuned for covenant exclusivity, demonstrating that grace expels idols by satisfying deeper hungers rather than merely forbidding superficial desires.

3.1.3. Valley of Achor re-named "Door of Hope"

Achor, site of Achan's hidden theft and Israel's subsequent defeat (Jos 7:24-26), symbolizes collective shame and the memory of covenant breach with fatal consequences. Hosea's prophecy that this valley will become a portal of hope illustrates grace's alchemy:

cursed ground can host a doorway into renewed destiny (Ho 2:15). The renaming parallels Bethel's transformation from Jacob's flight venue to a house of God (Gn 28:19), revealing a pattern wherein divine encounters reframe fiascos. Theologically, this signals that God's pursuit redeems not by erasing history but by re-patterning it—turning liabilities into launchpads for testimony. Psychologically, the shift equips believers to process trauma; painful chapters are acknowledged yet recast within a larger narrative arc of restoration. Practically, churches can hold "Achor testimonies" nights where members narrate how bankruptcy, divorce, or imprisonment became thresholds to grace, dismantling stigma through communal celebration. This subverts enemy tactics that weaponize memory, transforming shame archives into praise reports (Ps 40:2-3). The future-oriented phrase "door of hope" also implies movement; covenant grace never leaves people in limbo but escorts them toward vocation and influence. Ministries that provide job training for ex-offenders or counseling for abuse survivors echo Achor's renaming by fashioning gateways where society saw only dead ends. On eschatological horizons, Revelation envisions gates of pearl—jewels formed from painful irritation—underscoring the same logic (Rev 21:21). Thus, Hosea teaches that relentless pursuit does more than forgive; it re-brands cursed spaces as seedbeds for covenant promise.

3.1.4. Modern seasons of desolation that refine desire

Twenty-first-century disciples seldom traverse literal deserts, yet vocational layoffs, relationship break-ups, or prolonged singleness function analogously, stripping life to essentials. Sociologists note rising phenomena of "quarter-life crises" and midlife loneliness; Hosea's wilderness theology offers interpretive lenses that shift these states from mere deficits to refinement zones. When promotions stall, ambition idols lose luster, inviting reflection on identity apart from achievement (Php 3:7-8). Health crises compel confrontation with mortality, echoing Israel's dependence on manna and water beyond human provision (2 Co 12:9). Geographic relocation uproots social networks, paralleling exilic grief yet enabling fresh covenant disclosures unfiltered by inherited expectations (Jer 29:11-14). Digital overwhelm leads some to technology fasts, discovering stillness scarce in algorithmic ecosystems. Therapists describe "liminal space" as crucial for transformation; Scripture anticipated this by positioning many call narratives—Moses, David, Elijah—in deserts. Churches can normalize desolation seasons by integrating lament psalms into worship and offering spiritual direction that frames loss as divine pursuit rather than punishment. Mentors encourage journaling of wilderness insights, creating spiritual memoirs akin to Israel's wilderness scrolls that later guide new generations. The refining outcome is not stoic endurance but heightened capacity for delight in God's sufficiency; re-entrance into abundance is then navigated with calibrated appetites and resilient joy. Finally, recognizing modern desolations as grace laboratories equips believers to support others who enter similar terrains, perpetuating a culture that sees every desert as potential holy ground.

3.2. Scripture's Portraits of Pursuit—Lost Yet Sought

3.2.1. The shepherd and the one stray sheep (Luke 15:4-7)

Jesus' parable opens with a shepherd noticing a numerical discrepancy—one percent of his flock missing—and responding not with pragmatic resignation but with uncalculated resolve to find the lone wanderer. This image counters utilitarian instincts that sacrifice the minority for the stability of the majority. It also reframes failure; the sheep's lostness does not nullify its value, it amplifies the shepherd's devotion. Hosea's Gomer echoed that value equation when Hosea purchased her back despite serial betrayals (Ho 3:2-3). The shepherd's pursuit involves risky geography—wilderness ravines and predator-infested hills—mirroring Christ's incarnation into a fallen world (Jn 1:14). The act of laying the sheep on his shoulders depicts restorative grace that carries the restored until it can walk again, prefiguring seasons when new believers rely entirely on spiritual scaffolding (Is 40:11). The communal rejoicing upon return reflects heaven's alignment with redemptive mission; angels celebrate rescue more than they savor perfection. Contemporary applications include pastoral emphasis on individualized discipleship, ensuring that statistical growth never overshadows personal care. Small-group leaders emulate the shepherd by tracking attendance not to enforce control but to discern early drift. Evangelism strategies prioritize marginalized demographics— runaway teens, elderly shut-ins—who often represent the "one" overlooked by market-driven ministries. The parable also challenges theological fatalism; the shepherd does not wait for the sheep to find its way back but acts decisively, safeguarding doctrines of prevenient grace. Finally, the narrative encourages believers who intercede for prodigal relatives: heaven endorses laborious search missions and promises party-level joy at every homecoming (Lk 15:7).

3.2.2. The diligent woman and the lost coin (Luke 15:8-10)

Unlike the sheep, the coin is lost within the house, suggesting the possibility of spiritual disorientation inside religious settings. The woman's lamp symbolizes revelation; Scripture study and Spirit illumination expose overlooked souls sitting in pews yet detached from gospel assurance. Her broom indicates deliberate effort— teaching classes, follow-up calls, mentorship programs—that sweeps corners where dust of neglect accumulates. The coin's monetary imprint remains intact; lost status does not diminish intrinsic imago-Dei value (Gn 1:27). The parable underscores perseverance; the search persists "until" recovery, modeling pastoral tenacity that resists burnout in volunteer follow-up. Hosea demonstrates similar diligence when he vows Gomer will dwell with him "many days" for re-orientation (Ho 3:3). In church life, child-safety protocols, accessibility ramps, and translation headsets metaphorically brighten interior spaces, ensuring no "coin" is lost due to negligence. The woman's eventual rejoicing with neighbors teaches communal celebration culture—baptism testimonies, reconciliation stories—nurturing gratitude ecosystems. Missionally, the parable invites evaluation of discipleship pipelines: do assimilation processes quickly lose people in ecclesial clutter? Spiritually, believers conduct personal inventories—examining hidden motives and dormant gifts—allowing the Spirit's lamp to reclaim neglected areas. The lost-coin portrait complements the shepherd parable by showing pursuit within as well as beyond covenant spaces, reinforcing grace's omnidirectional reach.

3.2.3. The waiting father and the prodigal son (Luke 15:11-24)

The father's posture—scanning horizon daily—illustrates anticipatory grace that prepares celebration long before repentance speech rehearsals commence. Unlike neighbors who might demand restitution, the father runs, an undignified gesture in patriarchal culture, exposing heart over reputation. Hosea embodied similar vulnerability by paying scandalous silver and barley to redeem Gomer before public eyes (Ho 3:2). The embrace interrupts the son's confession mid-sentence, signifying that persuasive contrition is not prerequisite for full acceptance. The robe, ring, and sandals restore status, authority, and dignity, paralleling Isaiah's garments of salvation and Paul's justification theme (Is 61:10; Ro 3:24). The fattened calf feast foreshadows eschatological banquet and teaches churches to invest resources in restoration parties rather than moral shaming. Yet the elder brother warns against internal legalists who begrudge grace; Hosea had contemporaries who dismissed prophetic mercy as naive (Ho 9:7-8). In counseling settings, the father's model guides parents of prodigals: maintain relational availability without funding rebellion. The story also challenges individuals harboring self-loathing; sonship is a bestowed reality, not achievement. For corporate culture, the parable invites hospitable spaces where newcomers experience immediate belonging regardless of backstory. Evangelists employ the narrative to illustrate repentance's relational orientation—returning to a person, not merely abandoning habits. Ultimately, the father's relentless pursuit underscores that grace not only seeks but also celebrates, ensuring homecoming culminates in communal joy.

3.2.4. The Risen Christ on the Emmaus road (Luke 24:13-35)

Post-resurrection pursuit extends to disillusioned disciples walking away from Jerusalem; Jesus joins unrecognized, showing that grace meets wanderers on routes of disappointment. His questions draw out lament, modeling pastoral presence that listens before correcting. Exegetical exposition follows, as He traces Messiah promises "beginning with Moses," depicting pursuit through revealed word (Lk 24:27). Table fellowship triggers recognition, teaching that sacramental moments often unveil hidden Christ. The instant vanish indicates that revelation launches mission; the disciples sprint back to community, demonstrating restored purpose. Hosea anticipated this pattern: wilderness dialogue leads to covenant renewal and public testimony (Ho 2:16-23). Emmaus narrative comforts post-crisis believers whose shattered expectations obscure divine presence; Scripture and communion remain catalytic for regained sight. It validates the vocational ministry of spiritual direction,

81

where guides accompany pilgrims in questions until hearts burn anew. Liturgically, the church reenacts Emmaus each Sunday—Word proclaimed, Bread broken—inviting renewed recognition cycle. Missiologically, the story emphasizes that pursuit includes re-evangelizing insiders drifting into cynicism. The disciples' retrospective insight—that their hearts burned—assures seekers that emotional resonance often precedes cognitive clarity. This pursuit episode completes Luke-15 triad by showing the shepherd, woman, and father motifs fulfilled in the risen Lord who walks, teaches, and hosts, sealing Hosea's relentless grace in glorified flesh.

3.3. Justice and Mercy Intersect—The Cross as Climactic Pursuit

3.3.1. Holiness that cannot overlook treachery

Scripture presents God as "of purer eyes than to look on evil" (Hab 1:13), meaning relational betrayal incurs real debt that covenant passion cannot ignore. Hosea's oracles detail impending exile as necessary surgery, not arbitrary wrath (Ho 9:7; 10:10). Yet divine holiness is not temperamental volatility; it is covenant fidelity protecting relational integrity. When humans trivialize sin, they domesticate grace into indulgence, undercutting the high cost of redemption. The cross, therefore, must be understood against the backdrop of violated vows—each untruth, lust, or exploitative act comprises spiritual adultery. Israel's sacrificial system dramatized this debt through unblemished animals (Lv 4:32-35), but the blood of bulls foreshadowed a superior payment. Holiness ensures justice: oppressor and oppressed matter to God, so wrongdoing must be addressed for victims' sake. Modern preaching that sanitizes sin inadvertently diminishes the awe of relentless pursuit; honesty about cosmic treason magnifies rescuing love. Holiness also shapes sanctification post-forgiveness; grace never excuses relapse into former lovers but empowers new obedience (Ro 6:1-2). Discipleship curricula should balance Isaiah's "woe is me" with John's assurance "we have an advocate," maintaining tension that produces worshipful reverence (Is 6:5; 1 Jn 2:1). In counseling abuse survivors, proclaiming God's intolerance of evil provides solace that their pain matters juridically. Hosea's portrayal of holiness thus sets the stage for understanding why the cross is simultaneously verdict and vindication.

3.3.2. Substitutionary love paying the bride-price

At Calvary, Jesus assumes covenant curses described in Deuteronomy 28, becoming forsaken so adulterers might be restored (Ga 3:13). Substitution is not divine child abuse but Triune conspiracy of love wherein the Son willingly bears penalty to fulfill justice while extending mercy (Jn 10:18). Hosea's fifteen shekels and barley symbolize partial cost; Christ's blood is infinite value, satisfying righteousness completely (1 Pe 1:18-19). The Greek term *hilasterion* (propitiation) in Romans 3:25 evokes mercy-seat imagery, where sacrificial blood met law's demands, now realized in Christ's self-offering. Bride-price language underscores union; the goal is not mere legal acquittal but relational closeness—"Christ loved the church and gave Himself up for her" (Eph 5:25). Substitution also dismantles shame; debts erased free consciences from endless self-payment attempts. Liturgically, the Lord's Supper commemorates this transaction, placing tangible tokens of price into believers' hands. Preaching substitution combats moralism, assuring strugglers that acceptance rests on completed work, not fluctuating zeal. Simultaneously, it refutes antinomianism by highlighting costliness; expensive grace inspires grateful obedience. Hosea's marriage finds ultimate fulfillment here—the faithful spouse pays adulterer's ransom and then clothes her in righteousness. Missionally, substitution provides universal invitation: since the price covers every tribe, the church ventures confidently to unreached peoples. Counseling addicts, mentors root sobriety in substitutionary identity, moving clients from performance anxiety to cross-anchored security.

3.3.3. "Steadfast love and truth have met" (Psalm 85:10)

Psalm 85 poetically announces the kiss of *ḥesed* (steadfast love) and *'emet* (truth), an image realized when justice and mercy converge at Golgotha. Truth acknowledges sin's gravity; love satisfies truth's demand through self-sacrifice. Hosea foreshadows this intersection when God wrestles between compassion and wrath (Ho 11:8-9). At the cross, the tension resolves without compromise:

83

righteousness is upheld, sinners are embraced. Theologians call this convergence *harmonious perfection*, demonstrating divine attributes are not competing but complementary. In apologetics, this synthesis answers dilemmas about Old Testament wrath and New Testament mercy; both stem from the same covenant heart. Worship songs that juxtapose holiness and kindness ("Holy and Anointed One") draw directly from this theme, aiding congregational theology. Disciples learn relational ethics here: truth without love becomes harsh, love without truth becomes hollow; both together reflect divine pursuit. Confession practices embody convergence—truth-telling before God invites love's assurance of pardon. Social justice ministries likewise blend advocacy (truth) with rehabilitation (love), steering clear of punitive or permissive extremes. Personal conflict resolution follows suit: honest confrontation coupled with forgiveness mirrors gospel pattern. Ultimately, Psalm 85:10 provides interpretive lens for the entire redemptive story—every page moves toward this climactic embrace where law is written on hearts now alive with grace (Jer 31:33).

3.3.4. Empty tomb as proof grace outruns judgment

Resurrection vindicates Christ's payment, declaring receipt marked "paid in full" across cosmic ledgers (Ro 4:25). If the cross settled debt, the empty tomb signals restored relationship, inaugurating new-creation life in which shame no longer defines identity (1 Co 15:17). Hosea foretold a ransom from Sheol and victory over death—promises Paul cites to celebrate resurrection's stingless defeat (Ho 13:14; 1 Co 15:54-55). Relentless pursuit thus extends beyond forgiveness into empowerment; the risen Christ breathes Spirit life, enabling fidelity that was impossible in Adamic weakness (Jn 20:22). Easter reality secures eschatological hope: because grave clothes were left behind, believers trust that future valleys of Achor will also become doors of hope on a global scale. Practically, resurrection fuels perseverance amid trials; hardships are reframed as birth pangs of glory rather than omens of abandonment (2 Co 4:17). Pastoral care leverages this truth at funerals, proclaiming death's demotion from tyrant to doorway. Sacramental baptism enacts burial and rising, integrating participants into relentless pursuit's trajectory (Ro 6:4). Mission urgency arises: a living Lord warrants witness, not mere memory, propelling gospel proclamation across cultures. Ethical implications abound; resurrection calls for

84

holistic renewal—environmental stewardship, bodily care, cultural creativity—since redemption targets physical as well as spiritual realms. Finally, the empty tomb confirms that no betrayal, however grievous, can outrun grace; the story ends not in exile but in radiant dawn where covenant love reigns unchallenged forever.

3.4. Grace that Transforms Shame—Renaming the Unloved

3.4.1. From Lo-Ruhamah to "Beloved" (Hosea 2:23)

Hosea's firstborn daughter bears the name *Lo-Ruhamah*—"Not Pitied" or "No Mercy"—a living sign of relational rupture between Yahweh and a faithless nation (Hosea 1:6). When God later promises, "I will have mercy on *Lo-Ruhamah*," He is not simply tweaking vocabulary; He is rewriting identity at its core, demonstrating that covenant grace penetrates the deepest labels of rejection (Hosea 2:23). In antiquity, names carried prophetic weight, shaping destiny; thus renaming is tantamount to resurrection for a shamed soul. The reversal echoes earlier biblical episodes—Abram to Abraham, Sarai to Sarah—where divine promise overwrote barrenness with blessing (Genesis 17:5, 15). For modern disciples, *Lo-Ruhamah* frames every experience of parental neglect, peer bullying, or systemic marginalization that whispers "unloved." God's renaming initiative counters shame narratives by announcing belovedness before moral improvement, mirroring Jesus' baptism where the Father's delight precedes public ministry (Matthew 3:17). Liturgically, the church enacts this shift in baptismal declarations— "You are sealed by the Holy Spirit and marked as Christ's own forever"—embedding new identity in communal memory. Pastoral counseling applies the renaming by inviting counselees to identify negative labels, then crossing them out and inscribing gospel names like Forgiven, Chosen, and Priest (1 Peter 2:9). In small-group settings, members speak blessings over one another, substituting sting of past epitaphs with covenant affirmations. Renaming also fuels mission; those once called "outsiders" become bridge-builders, announcing mercy they have received (2 Corinthians 1:3-4). On eschatological horizons, Revelation promises a white stone with a secret name, assuring believers their transformation story will culminate in an identity no shame can touch (Revelation 2:17). Thus,

Hosea's vow inaugurates a redemptive cascade—if God can rename *Lo-Ruhamah*, no human condition is beyond re-inscription by relentless grace.

3.4.2. Adoption motifs in Paul's epistles (Romans 8:15)

Paul builds on Hosea's renaming theme by portraying salvation as adoption, a legal act in the Roman world that granted full heir status to former outsiders (Romans 8:15). Adoption language counters the ancient patron-client system where belonging hinged on performance; instead, the Spirit of sonship secures belonging by divine decree. In Ephesians 1:5, Paul insists this adoption is rooted in God's pleasure, not human worth, echoing Hosea's unilateral mercy. Greco-Roman courts required adoptive fathers to pay debts of the adoptee; likewise, Christ's redemptive price cancels sin's ledger (Colossians 2:14). The Spirit's cry "Abba" functions as audible evidence of new status, analogous to Hosea's prediction that Israel will call God "My Husband" (Hosea 2:16). Adoption also confers inheritance—believers become co-heirs with Christ (Romans 8:17)—erasing scarcity mindsets birthed by spiritual orphanhood. The metaphor carries ethical weight: heirs reflect family likeness, so holiness becomes identity expression, not entrance fee (Ephesians 5:1). Practically, churches model adoption theology through fostering ministries and financial support for orphans, displaying the gospel in social form (James 1:27). Communal language shifts from "membership" to "family," reinforcing covenant bonds over consumer affiliation. Adoption metaphors comfort believers estranged from biological kin; spiritual family fills relational vacancies unmet by bloodlines. In cross-cultural contexts, adoption dissolves ethnocentric barriers, uniting Jew and Gentile under one Father (Galatians 3:28). The already-not-yet tension emerges: legal adoption is finalized, but experiential formation into likeness unfolds progressively—mirroring wilderness betrothal leading to marital intimacy. Paul's motif ensures that Hosea's renaming is not isolated poetry but systemic New-Testament doctrine, embedding relentless pursuit in the very structure of salvation.

3.4.3. Healing toxic narratives and inner vows

Shame crafts toxic stories—"I am unworthy, unsafe, unlovable"—while inner vows form self-protective oaths: "I'll never trust again." These psychological strongholds parallel Israel's lie that Baal, not Yahweh, secured fertility (Hosea 2:5). Healing begins by surfacing narratives through journaling or counseling, naming them like idols toppled by prophets (1 Kings 18:39). Scripture provides counter-narratives: Psalm 139 proclaims purposeful design, Ephesians 2:10 declares workmanship, and Hosea reveals divine delight amid failure. Cognitive renewal involves meditating on such texts until neural pathways of worthlessness weaken (Romans 12:2). Inner vows are renounced in prayer, much like covenant ceremonies where Israel confessed misplaced trust and renewed allegiance (Nehemiah 9:2). Community plays vital role; trusted friends echo truth, offering corrective feedback when old scripts resurface. Embodied practices—standing tall while reciting identity verses—harness somatic memory to reinforce liberation. Creative arts therapy employs painting or songwriting to externalize and re-script traumatic memories under gospel light. Sacramentally, Eucharist confronts toxic narratives with tangible grace; broken bread testifies that shame was borne and body accepted. Healing advances through incremental exposure to vulnerability: sharing testimony in small settings, then larger gatherings, testing new identity's resilience. Relapse moments are reframed not as failure but as opportunities to rehearse grace, preventing shame's resurgence. Mentors track progress, celebrating milestones to anchor joy. As narratives align with gospel truth, emotional capacity expands—fear recedes, love overflows, mirroring Israel's promised singing in restored vineyards (Hosea 2:15). Thus, relentless pursuit dismantles internalized rejection, paving paths for robust spiritual and psychological flourishing.

3.4.4. Practicing gospel self-talk and communal blessing

Gospel self-talk replaces self-critique with covenant proclamation; instead of "I'm such a failure," believers say, "I'm redeemed and under renovation" (Philippians 1:6). Daily declarations draw from scriptural "I am" statements—chosen (1 Peter 2:9), forgiven (Colossians 1:14), empowered (Acts 1:8). Writing these truths on mirrors or phone screens harnesses visual cues for neural reinforcement. Self-talk is paired with breath prayer—inhale "Loved," exhale "Forever"—linking physiology to theology. However, solitary practice risks echo chamber dynamics, so communal blessing amplifies and verifies identity. In small groups, members conclude meetings by speaking Numbers 6:24-26 over one another, transferring priestly benediction to laypeople. Parents bless children before school, shielding them from playground labels. Husbands and wives transform conflicts by ending apologies with identity affirmations: "I forgive you; you are still my covenant partner." Church services reserve space for congregants to turn and bless neighbors, embedding scriptural speech in gathered life. Corporate blessing counters cancel culture, creating prophetic communities where fault is confronted yet dignity upheld. When unbelievers visit, receiving blessing preaches gospel before sermon begins, illustrating Hosea's hospitable grace. Training workshops teach believers to discern Holy Spirit nudges—specific compliments that reflect God's heart rather than generic flattery. Over time, self-talk and communal proclamation weave protective nets that catch shame arrows before they pierce, enabling disciples to walk confidently in their renamed status.

3.5. Habits of Yielding—Living Inside the Pursuit

3.5.1. Prayer of receptivity: listening more than listing

Most prayer lists resemble vending-machine transactions; receptive prayer shifts posture from acquisition to attentive presence. Inspired by Samuel's "Speak, Lord" (1 Samuel 3:10), believers practice silence, inviting God to set the agenda. This contemplative stance acknowledges relentless pursuit: before we ask, the Father already knows (Matthew 6:8). Practical steps include centering with a breath verse—"The Lord is my shepherd" (Psalm 23:1)—allowing distractions to drift by like clouds. Five-minute listening segments can gradually extend to half-hours, training neural circuits for sustained attention. Journaling impressions prevents drift into vagueness and offers discernment checkpoints with mentors. Scripture may surface unbidden; noting references and studying them later honors the Spirit's whispers. Receptive prayer also scans bodily sensations—tight shoulders, fluttering stomach—as potential signals of unresolved issues God wants addressed. Corporate gatherings benefit from guided silence between worship songs, modeling for congregants who fear quiet. Listening posture cultivates humility, admitting that the Lover's voice interprets life better than frantic petitions. It often births prophetic insight—names to call, injustices to confront—turning receptivity into missional fuel. Moreover, receptive prayer counters idol pressure to perform; value comes from being heard, not from eloquence. Over months, practitioners report heightened peace and clarity, aligning with Hosea's promise of intimate dialogue in wilderness hush (Hosea 2:14). Thus, listening prayer becomes a daily rendezvous where grace pursues and the heart yields.

3.5.2. Contemplative scripture reading as divine embrace

Lectio divina's four movements—read, meditate, pray, contemplate—slow the mind, allowing verses to migrate from page to bloodstream. Choosing narrative texts such as Hosea's marriage story engages imagination; readers envision scenes, feeling prophetic ache and divine tenderness. Repetition shapes familiarity; the same passage over a week deepens flavor like marinating. Meditation involves savoring a phrase—"I will allure her"—until emotional resonance surfaces. Prayer flows as response, perhaps lamenting one's own wanderings or thanking God for pursuit. Contemplation then rests wordlessly, trusting Spirit assimilation. Integrating body postures—open palms symbolizing receptivity—reinforces non-striving stance. Groups can practice together, sharing gleanings to highlight scripture's multifaceted voice. Scripture artwork—illuminated verses or calligraphy—extends meditation into visual domain. Memorization cements embrace, providing portable promises when anxiety strikes. Over time, contemplative reading detoxes hurried proof-texting that treats Bible as ammunition. It births affection; Hosea's God shifts from abstract concept to audible Lover whispering across centuries. Such encounters re-script identity and align actions with interior love. Research shows slowed reading enhances comprehension and emotional impact, validating ancient practice scientifically. Ultimately, contemplative engagement turns text into touch, fulfilling Augustine's dictum that scripture is "letters from home" delivered to wandering exiles.

3.5.3. Sabbath rest as protest against striving

Sabbath observance proclaims that identity stems from being pursued, not producing output. In Egypt, Israel was valued for bricks; in covenant land, value derived from relationship, a truth Sabbath weekly dramatized (Deuteronomy 5:15). Today's hustle culture mirrors Pharaoh's quotas—emails ping at midnight, gig economy never sleeps. By ceasing paid and unpaid labor, believers erect a time-wall against idols of efficiency. Sabbath planning begins mid-week: chores pre-completed, meals prepped, digital notifications silenced. Rituals mark entry—lighting candles, praying Psalm 92, or sharing communion bread. Activities shift from utilitarian to delight-based: nature walks, leisurely meals, unhurried conversation. Family rules ban conflict-heavy topics, preserving peace atmosphere. Single adults curate "Sabbath buddies" to share meals, combating isolation. Church traditions offer corporate worship as Sabbath anchor, but personal reflection later deepens rest. Essential workers on rotating schedules creatively choose alternate twenty-four-hour windows rather than abandoning practice. Sabbath teaches trust—emails unanswered for a day won't implode livelihood—and reshapes calendar around grace rhythms. Field studies show practitioners experience lower anxiety and increased relational satisfaction, echoing promised refreshment (Exodus 23:12). Spiritually, Sabbath rehearses future rest when striving ends entirely (Hebrews 4:9). Thus, weekly cessation becomes liturgical evidence of relentless pursuit: the Bridegroom says, "Stop; let Me love you today."

3.5.4. Gratitude journals that trace daily pursuit

Noticing grace requires disciplined attention; gratitude journals function as microscopes revealing divine footprints in mundane hours. Each night, believers record three evidences of pursuit—sunrise hues, unexpected encouragement, Scripture insight. Psychological research links gratitude logging with increased well-being, aligning science with 1 Thessalonians 5:18's exhortation. Entries move beyond generic blessings to specific Lover's touch: "Received text exactly when loneliness peaked." Periodic rereading on discouraging days provides empirical data of faithfulness, countering amnesia. Family versions invite children to share "God sightings" at dinner, cultivating early attentiveness.

Small groups swap weekly highlights, turning private logs into communal praise. Digital platforms or shared docs enable dispersed friends to celebrate together, building worship ecosystems. Gratitude lists often catalyze repentance, exposing complaint patterns that mask abundance. Artists transform journal lines into poems or paintings, enhancing memory retention. At year-end, congregations compile collective gratitude chronicles, testifying like Israel's stone memorials (Joshua 4:7). Turmoil seasons—hospital stays, unemployment—widen lens to micro-mercies, sustaining hope when macro circumstances disappoint. Ultimately, gratitude journaling trains eyes to see relentless pursuit in real time, replacing coincidence theology with covenant recognition.

3.6. Pursuing Others with Grace—Missional Overflow

3.6.1. Evangelism as extending wedding invitations

If salvation culminates in the marriage supper of the Lamb (Revelation 19:9), evangelism resembles invitation distribution, not sales pitch. Ambassadors share personal stories of being courted by grace, offering authenticity over argument. Invitations highlight relational joy—"Come meet the Groom who knows your name"—rather than fear-based coercion. Contextualization matters: invitations are worded in cultural vernacular without diluting gospel content. Hospitality events—Alpha courses, backyard barbecues—set welcoming stage mirroring Hosea's allure. Pre-evangelism prayer identifies "persons of peace" (Luke 10:6) whose receptivity signals Spirit readiness. Joyful urgency drives follow-up; forgetting to RSVP risks missing feast, so ambassadors kindly remind without harassment. Printed or digital media use celebratory aesthetics—wedding imagery, feast metaphors—to capture imagination. Testimonies of transformed shame illustrate dress fitting for new garments of salvation (Isaiah 61:10). Rejection is interpreted as "not yet," preserving relationship; constant love may thaw resistance over time. Evangelists collaborate across denominations, valuing invitation reach above brand loyalty. Metrics shift from decision tallies to ongoing discipleship engagement, ensuring invitees actually arrive dressed in wedding attire (Matthew 22:11-14). Trainers mentor believers in storytelling, teaching three-minute grace narratives that fit coffee queue contexts. Evangelistic prayer

91

teams adopt Hosea's language—"allure them, Lord"—aligning intercession with divine pursuit strategy. Ultimately, the invitation paradigm frames mission as joyous matchmaking, not obligatory quota fulfillment.

3.6.2. Radical hospitality to prodigals and strangers

Relentless grace moves toward outsiders, so churches architect spaces—literal and relational—that welcome without pre-clearance. This begins at front doors: friendly greeters trained to recognize nervous newcomers and escort them to seats. Potlucks offer diverse cuisines, honoring immigrant cultures and reflecting eschatological banquet diversity. Hosts prioritize listening over lecturing, validating stories before offering advice. Spare rooms become transitional housing for refugees or recovering addicts, embodying Isaiah 58:7 hospitality. Coffee budgets are redirected to "open-table" funds, subsidizing meals with seekers. Local partnerships with shelters break silo mentalities, uniting mercy arms. Church signage avoids insider jargon, eliminating obstacle course feel. Accessibility ramps and translation headsets signal intentional inclusion of disabled and non-English speakers. Members proactively invite acquaintances, aware shamed souls rarely self-refer. Confidential small groups for ex-offenders or abuse survivors provide safe re-entry contexts. Hospitality extends online—moderated chat prayers for livestream viewers create digital porch. Annual "Homecoming Sunday" celebrates prodigals' returns with testimonies, feast, and liturgy of welcome. Budget lines allocate generous benevolence funds, trusting God to replenish through cheerful givers. Radical openness risks mess—stolen purses, relapsed addicts—but Hosea's marriage reminds leaders that covenant love bears scandal for redemption's sake. Over years, hospitality culture becomes a powerful apologetic, proving grace tangible.

3.6.3. Forgiveness "seventy-seven times" (Matthew 18:22)

Peter's inquiry about forgiveness quotas receives Jesus' hyperbolic math—limitless grace mirroring God's pursuit. Practically, forgiveness unfolds in stages: acknowledgment of harm, choice to release debt, ongoing heart alignment when memories resurface. Boundaries may remain; forgiveness is not enabling, echoing

92

Hosea's period of separation before full marital restoration (Hosea 3:3). Narrative therapy encourages writing offense accounts, then overlaying cross imagery, symbolically transferring debt to Christ. Communal liturgies on Maundy Thursday rehearse foot-washing, embodying servant forgiveness. Counselors utilize 2 Corinthians 2:7-8 protocols—comfort repentant offenders lest excessive sorrow overwhelm them. Victim advocates ensure justice systems engage, upholding Romans 13's role and preventing cheap grace. Forgiveness frees victim's psyche from bitterness captivity (Ephesians 4:31-32). Neuroscience notes decreased cortisol in forgiving individuals, illustrating physiological wisdom of Jesus' command. Reconciled relationships testify powerfully to unbelievers; former enemies worshiping together incarnate gospel credibility. Families teach children apology liturgy—"I'm sorry; will you forgive me?"—forming early muscle memory. Annual reflection on grievances ensures old wounds do not ossify. Cross-cultural churches emphasize forgiveness to navigate racial tensions, modeling kingdom unity (Colossians 3:13). The seventy-seven principle does not ignore patterns of abuse; safety plans coexist with heart posture of release. Forgiveness culture fuels revival; bitterness quenches Spirit, while mercy invites His flow. Ultimately, forgiving repetitively echoes relentless pursuit, translating received grace into relational currency.

3.6.4. Justice ministries fueled by experienced mercy

Having tasted undeserved kindness, believers channel zeal into systemic restoration, reflecting Micah 6:8's trio—justice, mercy, humility. Teams analyze local data to pinpoint injustice hotspots—food deserts, eviction rates, discriminatory policing—and develop action plans. Advocacy training equips members to draft legislation briefs and speak at council meetings. Mercy experiences guard against self-righteous activism; rescuers remember they were once Hosea's Gomer. Partnerships with secular NGOs expand reach while offering gospel witness through servant posture. Funding models include micro-grants for entrepreneurially-minded marginalized neighbors, aligning with jubilee economic reset (Leviticus 25). Education initiatives—tutoring, scholarships—address generational poverty by offering "door of hope" trajectories. Creation-care projects integrate ecological and social justice, planting community gardens in blighted areas. Prayer undergirds activism; monthly vigils lament broken systems and invite divine intervention. Storytelling events elevate voices of survivors, empowering them and educating congregation. Justice ministries practice accountability: metrics evaluate whether interventions reduce inequality rather than perpetuate dependency. Sabbath for activists prevents burn-out, acknowledging God is ultimate Redeemer. Mission trips shift from paternalistic relief to mutual learning exchanges, echoing Hosea's two-way covenant respect. Early-church precedents—Acts 6 food distribution—guide governance, ensuring equitable resource allocation. Victories are celebrated liturgically, connecting policy wins to worship. By rooting justice in mercy experienced, ministries sustain compassion without contempt, mirroring divine pursuit that weds righteousness and grace.

3.7. Corporate Renewal—Communities Shaped by Pursuing Love

3.7.1 ▪ Liturgy that rehearses the redemption story weekly

When a congregation gathers, its order of service is never neutral; every prayer, reading, or song either drifts toward amnesia or drills covenant memory deeper. A grace-shaped liturgy begins with a scriptural call to worship—"Come, let us return to the LORD" (Hosea 6:1)—inviting the assembly to acknowledge divine initiative before they utter a word. Confession follows, echoing Hosea's naming of Israel's betrayal (Hosea 4:1–2), creating safe space for honesty and leveling status distinctions that performance cultures nurture. An audible assurance of pardon—perhaps Isaiah 55:7 or Romans 8:1—replaces self-loathing with bridal confidence, reminding everyone that relentless pursuit has already outrun their failures. Public reading of both Old and New Testament texts connects Hosea's longing with its fulfillment in Christ, reinforcing a grand narrative larger than personal experience (1 Timothy 4:13). Preaching then traces themes of pursuit, justice, and mercy, not as abstract theology but as living address to that week's anxieties—job insecurity, family tension, cultural fear. The creed recited afterward unites saints across centuries, displaying that the same pursuing God who redeemed Israel now guards a global bride. Intercessory prayers widen congregational concern, teaching members to pursue cities and nations with petitions shaped by God's heart (1 Timothy 2:1–2). The passing of peace enacts reconciliation, ensuring horizontal breaches are mended before Eucharistic fellowship (Matthew 5:23–24). Communion, center-set rather than side-dish, reenacts Hosea 3:2's costly redemption; broken bread and poured wine tangibly assure worshipers they are Gomer welcomed home. An offering collected after the table turns gratitude into stewardship, challenging consumerism by funding ministries of pursuit. Benediction sends disciples into neighborhoods with words like Numbers 6:24–26, sealing the service with divine favor rather than moral pep talk. Over months, such rhythm rewires instincts: people learn to expect welcome, confess quickly, forgive freely, and live on mission. Children absorb gospel choreography before they grasp theological vocabulary, inheriting muscle memory of mercy. Visitors intuit before they understand that this community swims in grace, and the weekly rehearsal becomes both evangelistic proclamation and spiritual formation tool.

3.7.2 ▪ Church discipline framed as restorative pursuit

Discipline often evokes images of judicial hearings, yet Hosea reframes correction as wounded love pursuing restoration (Hosea 2:6–7). A grace-anchored church begins discipline privately, one-to-one, echoing Jesus' instruction in Matthew 18:15; the aim is reunion, not expulsion. Leaders approach with tears before charges, remembering they too once wandered and were found (Galatians 6:1). Procedurally, every step is saturated with prayer, seeking the Spirit's wisdom to distinguish stubborn rebellion from immature missteps. Communication avoids shaming labels—no gossiping in prayer requests—because exposing without covering contradicts the Father who clothed Adam and Eve (Genesis 3:21). When silence or defiance persists, two or three mature believers join, embodying Hosea's hedge of thorns designed to halt destructive momentum (Hosea 2:6). Even formal exclusion, if required, is portrayed as a temporary protective measure, like Paul's handing over to Satan "so that his spirit may be saved" (1 Corinthians 5:5). Throughout, the church keeps a redemption chair open—literally leaving an empty seat in meetings—to visualize anticipation of return. Restoration paths are clear: confession, agreed-upon accountability, and gradual re-immersion into ministry responsibilities, mirroring Hosea's period of abstinence before full marital intimacy (Hosea 3:3).

95

Success stories are celebrated publicly, not to spotlight past sin but to magnify pursuing grace; applause greets prodigals, teaching the body to prefer mercy over record-keeping (Luke 15:24). Records of discipline remain confidential, but testimonies of restoration, shared with permission, feed congregational hope that no case is hopeless. Over time, discipline culture matures into preventive health—members invite correction early, knowing the motive is love. Outsiders observing such redemptive processes recognize a community courageous enough to confront yet too compassionate to cancel, making discipline itself a potent apologetic.

3.7.3 • Testimony nights celebrating "found" stories

In Hosea, reversal culminates in singing: "She will respond as in the days of her youth" (Hosea 2:15). Testimony nights capture that melody, turning sanctuary into storytelling theater where grace takes the microphone. Curated diversity matters—addict, academic, immigrant, executive—so hearers see pursuit crossing social strata. Each storyteller rehearses alienation, divine interception, and ongoing transformation, keeping the spotlight on the Redeemer rather than autobiography. Hosts coach speakers to include Scripture that anchored their turning points, knitting individual arcs into the biblical tapestry (Psalm 107:2). Musicians weave reflective choruses between testimonies—"Amazing Grace" or contemporary thank-you anthems—letting song seal narrative. Visual media—before-and-after photos, creative art pieces, short films—engage multiple senses, ensuring memories lodge deeply. Children present mini-testimonies too, normalizing early awareness of God's pursuit and countering future doubt. Invitations follow each segment: prayer stations offer listeners space to respond, mirroring the father's open-armed run in Luke 15. Refreshments afterward extend celebration into fellowship, food echoing the fattened-calf motif. Those still wrestling with shame glimpse living proofs that no pit is beyond reach, sparking seeds of hope. Pastors compile stories into annual "Ebenezer journal," preserving corporate memory against future slippage into routine. Online recordings amplify impact, allowing distant seekers to overhear grace. Over months, testimony culture shifts atmosphere: cynicism melts, expectancy rises, evangelism accelerates as members realize stories are in motion all around them. In essence, testimony nights function as communal retelling of Hosea's marriage—scandalous mercy turning catastrophe into chorus.

3.7.4 ▪ *Mutual encouragement cultures vs. performance cultures*

Performance cultures grade faith by visible output—attendance, giving, stage presence—breeding competition and concealed weakness. In contrast, mutual-encouragement cultures echo Hebrews 10:24–25, where believers "spur one another on toward love and good deeds." Such churches train members to spot grace glimpses and verbalize them: "I saw Christ's courage in you today." Encouragement is fact-based, not flattery; it names specific fruit, reinforcing Spirit work rather than ego (Philippians 1:6). Institutional rhythms support this: staff meetings open with "wins" recounting God's pursuit in ministries, resetting motivation. Smaller cells adopt "high-low-hear-obey" rounds—sharing a week's highlight, struggle, Scripture heard, obedience step—distributing attention evenly. Failure is processed openly; leaders confess mistakes from pulpits, dismantling perfection myths. Feedback loops replace anonymous critique with face-to-face honesty framed by affirmation sandwiches. Volunteer appreciation is lavish: handwritten notes, spotlight videos, retreats—echoing Jesus' "Well done" preview (Matthew 25:23). Systems guard against burnout: sabbaticals granted, workloads monitored, acknowledging human limits embraced by grace. Newcomers undergo gifts discovery rather than plug-and-play conscription, ensuring service flows from design, not duty (1 Peter 4:10). Over time, KPI idols loosen; qualitative fruit—peace, joy, gentleness—earns equal celebration with numerical gains. This atmosphere makes room for prophetic risk-taking because failure isn't fatal; it's a learning lab under pursuing love. The community thus becomes self-reinforcing: encouragement births courage, which spurs witness, which sparks new stories, returning to encouragement—a virtuous cycle energized by Hosea's relentless God.

3.8. Eschatological Consummation—Pursuit Perfected

3.8.1 • Marriage Supper of the Lamb (Revelation 19:7-9)

John's apocalypse culminates in a wedding banquet where the long-pursued bride finally sits down to feast with her Groom, fulfilling Hosea's betrothal prophecy on a cosmic canvas. The "fine linen, bright and clean," worn by the bride, represents righteous deeds already prepared by grace (Ephesians 2:10), proving pursuit not only rescues but beautifies. Ancient Hebrew weddings included a *mattan* (groom's gift); at this feast, the Groom supplies his own righteousness as bridal attire (Isaiah 61:10). The announced "blessing" on those invited recalls Jesus' parables, confirming the church's evangelistic invitations were authentic previews of this ultimate RSVP (Luke 14:17). Music swells from myriad voices, echoing Hosea's vineyard songs yet amplified across galaxies. The menu symbolizes abundance—imagery of rich marrow and aged wine promised in Isaiah 25:6—declaring that scarcity and wilderness hunger are forever past. Eschatological justice is embedded: beasts and Babylon judged before the meal ensures no oppressor lurks at the table (Revelation 19:2-3). The supper fuses remembrance (like Eucharist) with anticipation; past redemption and future glory kiss just as steadfast love and truth did at the cross (Psalm 85:10). Liturgically, every earthly Communion is a dress rehearsal; lifting the cup, believers echo, "Next time with You in the kingdom" (Mark 14:25). Pastoral care uses this imagery at funerals, shifting grief toward reunion hope. Ethical implications arise: knowing a seat awaits prompts present holiness—brides keep gowns unstained (Revelation 19:8). Mission urgency intensifies: empty chairs grieve the Groom, so the church persists in invitation. Imagination fired by this feast resists nihilism—history is headed toward banquet laughter, not cosmic heat death.

3.8.2 • "God dwelling with humanity" (Revelation 21:3)

The New Jerusalem descends, not the church ascending, underlining divine initiative to consummate pursuit. The Edenic ache is healed; what began with God "walking in the garden" (Genesis 3:8) ends with God pitching His tent permanently among people. No temple is present because the Lord Himself is sanctuary, fulfilling Hosea's promise of intimate knowledge: "You shall know the LORD" (Hosea 2:20). Tears wiped away signify relational fruition—abandonment wound cured by unbroken presence (Revelation 21:4). The city's dimensions—12,000 stadia cubed—echo the Most Holy Place, expanding personal fellowship into civic architecture. Precious stones recall Gomer's dowry reversal: shame-stacked valley now paved with gold, jewels once withheld showered on the beloved (Isaiah 54:11–12). Nations bring glory, proving pursuit's multicultural reach; Hosea's "Not My People" now stream through open gates (Hosea 1:10). Light emanates from the Lamb, eliminating night and metaphorical hiddenness—every secret sin the pursuit once exposed is gone. Civic life flourishes without police or hospitals, showing shalom ecosystem stemming from Presence, not policy. Isaiah's prophecy of children playing safely is realized, indicating that vulnerability faces no threat (Isaiah 11:8–9). Eucharist finds completion: the tree of life yields monthly fruit, offering perpetual communion better than wine. For believers trudging through hostile cultures, this vision fuels endurance; present tents groan but an eternal dwelling nears (2 Corinthians 5:1).

3.8.3 ▪ How future hope energizes present perseverance

Paul links eschatology with ethics: because resurrection awaits, steadfastness abounds (1 Corinthians 15:58). Hope operates like gravitational pull from tomorrow, drawing conduct upward. Suffering saints recall that "the Judge is standing at the door" (James 5:9), deterring retaliation and sustaining patience. Missionaries endure hardship because a crown of glory, not ratings, validates labor (1 Peter 5:4). Environmental stewardship gains rationale: the earth will be renewed, so current care anticipates future harmony (Romans 8:21). Addiction recovery taps eschatological imagination—visualizing future freedom strengthens present choices. Worship music rich in future themes (e.g., "Is He Worthy?") shifts eyes from screens to skyline. Hope inoculates against escapism; knowing labor matters into eternity motivates civic engagement, echoing Jeremiah's seek-the-city mandate (Jeremiah 29:7). Small groups perform "future audits," asking how goals align with coming kingdom, adjusting budgets and calendars accordingly. Persecuted believers draw courage: martyr blood is not wasted but seeds banquet rejoicing (Revelation 6:11). Parenting priorities shift from résumé building to soul forming, confident that children's ultimate story outlasts college admissions. Thus, eschatology is pastoral dynamite, detonating despair and launching resilient obedience in Hosea's pursued people.

3.8.4 • Eternal security: grace that will never let go, forever

Jesus promises, "No one will snatch them out of My hand" (John 10:28), echoing Hosea's assurance that God's betrothal is "forever" (Hosea 2:19). Eternal security rests not on believer grip strength but on divine covenant oath sealed in blood (Hebrews 6:17–18). Critics fear this breeds laxity; Paul anticipates and counters—grace trains us to renounce ungodliness (Titus 2:11–12). Security fosters honesty; believers confess quickly, knowing relationship is not at risk. Prayer boldness rises—adopted heirs approach throne without fear of eviction (Hebrews 4:16). In suffering, security comforts: cancer or persecution cannot annul adoption papers (Romans 8:38–39). At deathbeds, pastors articulate security, helping saints cross rivers with songs rather than doubt. Spiritual warfare leans on security: accusation loses teeth when verdict is irrevocable (Revelation 12:10–11). Worship erupts from safe hearts; secure children sing louder than anxious servants. The doctrine propels generosity—possessions lose grip when future inheritance is untouchable (1 Peter 1:4). Even discipline is viewed through security lens: pruning proves sonship, not rejection (Hebrews 12:6–8). Eternal security also fuels plural cultures; converts risking family ostracism need assurance pursuit will never cease. Finally, security guarantees eschatological praise: endless ages will not exhaust God's commitment—love that would not let go in Hosea will never let go in glory.

Conclusion Standing at the far side of Hosea's testimony and the empty tomb's vindication, we discover that relentless pursuit is not merely an attribute of God; it is the atmosphere in which the believer now lives and breathes. Every wilderness detour, every prodigal chapter, and every lingering vestige of self-condemnation is met by a grace that closes the distance before we can finish plotting an escape. Far from encouraging passivity, this discovery animates mission: those who have been found become seekers, those who have been renamed become namers of others, and those who have tasted covenant security extend invitations to the coming wedding feast (Revelation 19:7-9). As the story rushes toward its eschatological consummation—when the pursuing Shepherd will lose none of His flock (John 10:28)—our calling is clear: rest in the embrace that will not release us, and let its power reshape every pursuit of our own until His relentless grace is unmistakable in the world we touch.

Chapter 4. Tough Love—Divine Discipline That Restores

Every great love story includes moments of confrontation—scenes where devotion refuses to stand idle while the beloved wanders toward ruin. In Hosea, those confrontations arrive as crop failure, political shocks, and prophetic rebukes, yet beneath each hard edge pulses a covenant heartbeat determined to reclaim rather than discard. Divine discipline is the thread that binds holy passion to human waywardness, transforming judgment from a terminal verdict into a surgical grace. To understand this "tough love," we must step behind the raw imagery of withered vines and foreign invaders and listen for the voice of a Father who "wounds that He may heal" (Hosea 6:1). This chapter explores why God disciplines, how He weaves correction through providence, and what posture of heart turns chastening into restoration. By tracing the logic of discipline from Sinai's warnings through Hosea's oracles to the cross where the Son bore our ultimate penalty, we will discover that every divine rebuke is an invitation back to joy.

4.1. Purpose of Divine Discipline—Covenant Loyalty through Correction

4.1.1 ▪ Holiness over Happiness—Why Love Sometimes Wounds

Divine discipline begins with God's unwavering commitment to His own character; because He is holy, He cannot tolerate in His people what would ultimately destroy them (Leviticus 19:2). The purpose is therefore not to diminish joy but to direct it along paths that will actually satisfy. Just as a surgeon risks pain to excise a tumor, the Lord permits discomfort to remove soul-killing idols (Hosea 2:10). Scripture repeatedly connects chastening with affectionate concern: "Those whom I love I reprove and discipline" (Revelation 3:19). If happiness is defined as the absence of pain, discipline feels cruel; but if happiness is union with God, then temporary wounding is a severe mercy. Moses warned Israel that prosperity would tempt them to forget the covenant (Deuteronomy 8:10-14); Hosea confirms the prophecy as wealth fuels Baal worship, necessitating divine intervention. Hardship thus exposes false definitions of the good life, revealing that comfort without communion is a sophisticated form of poverty. The psalmist admits, "Before I was afflicted I went astray, but now I keep Your word" (Psalm 119:67), showing hindsight gratitude for painful tutoring. Parents intuitively understand this logic—time-outs and revoked privileges aim at mature flourishing, not perpetual restriction. Likewise, God's holiness is not an icy perfection but a blazing love that refuses to watch beloved children self-destruct. When trials strike, believers can ask, "What deeper joy is God guarding on the other side of this pain?" rather than "Why is God against me?" Even Jesus "learned obedience through what He suffered" (Hebrews 5:8), underscoring that discipline is not punitive for the sinless but formative for the obedient. Holiness over happiness is therefore gospel logic: the cross inflicts unimaginable agony to secure eternal delight. Accepting this paradigm liberates disciples from chasing painless Christianity and invites them into life abundant through sanctified wounds.

4.1.2 • Fatherly Formation—Hebrews 12 and the Training of Sons and Daughters

Hebrews 12:5-11 paints a household scene in which God is not a distant principal issuing detentions but a Father raising heirs for glory. The writer recalls Proverbs 3:11-12, reminding weary believers that chastening is evidence, not absence, of sonship. Earthly parents discipline for limited years and with mixed motives, yet they still produce tangible fruit; how much more will perfect discipline yield "the peaceful fruit of righteousness" (Hebrews 12:11). The Greek word *paideia* refers to holistic education— intellectual, moral, and physical—implying that God's corrective work shapes every dimension of personality. Athletes submit to draining drills so they might win perishable wreaths; Christians endure divine workouts for imperishable crowns (1 Corinthians 9:25). The author urges readers to "strengthen weak knees," linking acceptance of discipline to renewed vigor for the race (Hebrews 12:12-13). Spiritual lethargy often signals resistance to training, whereas surrendered hearts find hardship sharpening discernment. Adoption theology reinforces the picture: because believers are legally brought into God's family (Romans 8:15), discipline functions as family privilege, not outsider's penalty. The Father never disciplines to exact payment—that was finished at Calvary— but to cultivate resemblance to the Firstborn Son. In practice, this means setbacks can be reinterpreted as customized lessons: financial strain teaches stewardship, relational conflict hones humility, illness deepens empathy. Small groups can explore connection points by mapping life trials alongside character growth, tracing the Father's hand. Gratitude for discipline may feel counter-intuitive, yet Hebrews commands it, seeing beyond the sting to the harvest. Ultimately, fatherly formation assures believers that nothing is wasted; every tear waters seeds of Christ-likeness, preparing children for the family business of reigning with Him (2 Timothy 2:12).

4.1.3 • Discipline vs. Condemnation—Key Differences in Scripture (Romans 8:1)

Romans 8:1 declares, "There is therefore now no condemnation for those who are in Christ Jesus," establishing a bright line between punitive judgment and restorative discipline. Condemnation flows from law violated without atonement; discipline flows from relationship secured by atonement. Condemnation ends in separation—Adam and Eve driven from Eden—whereas discipline aims at deeper intimacy, as Hosea lures Israel into the wilderness for renewed vows (Hosea 2:14). The courtroom imagery of condemnation features a gavel; the family-room scene of discipline features a shepherd's staff. Emotions differ: condemnation breeds shame and dread (1 John 4:18), discipline, though painful, carries undertones of hope because love remains intact. Timing differs too—condemnation awaits final judgment day for unbelievers, but discipline operates in the present age for believers' sanctification. The cross absorbed wrath, so any hardship believers face cannot be retributive payment; that theological settlement changes the emotional atmosphere of trials. Therefore, when a Christian loses employment, the question shifts from "Is God punishing me?" to "How is God fathering me through this?" Shame whispers generalized guilt—"I'm bad"—while discipline pinpoints specific growth areas—"I overspent; God is teaching me budgeting." Condemnation isolates, pushing sufferers into hiding; discipline invites community, as James 5:16 encourages confession within the body. Worship songs can reinforce the distinction by celebrating forgiveness before requesting refinement, sequencing identity before improvement. Counseling ministries help disciples discern Satan's accusing voice from the Spirit's convicting nudge (John 16:8). Ultimately, understanding this difference breaks legalistic fear and fosters courageous repentance—believers run toward correction knowing no condemnation awaits on arrival.

4.1.4 • Love's Protective Jealousy—Guarding Hearts from Self-Destruction

Biblical jealousy is not insecure envy but covenant passion that will not share rightful affection with destructive rivals. Yahweh identifies Himself as "a jealous God" within the Ten Commandments, directly linking jealousy to exclusive love (Exodus 20:5). Hosea dramatizes this by marrying Gomer and then intervening when her lovers exploit her (Hosea 2:7). Protective jealousy explains why God blocks idols: idolatry is spiritual adultery that harms both relationship and worshiper. Proverbs 6:27 asks, "Can a man carry fire next to his chest and his clothes not be burned?"—discipline is the hand that removes smoldering coals before flesh ignites. Parents confiscate dangerous toys; similarly, God may remove a lucrative job that fuels pride or a toxic romance that derails destiny. Paul echoes this divine jealousy when he says he feels "a divine jealousy" for the Corinthians, wanting to present them as a pure bride (2 Corinthians 11:2). Protective jealousy also guards witness; a compromised church cannot display gospel beauty, so God purifies to protect mission. Jealousy motivates boundaries: hedge of thorns in Hosea 2:6 limits Israel's access to paramours, paralleling modern spiritual disciplines that fence sin opportunities—internet filters, accountability partners, financial budgets. Far from being oppressive, such hedges create freedom by keeping wolves out of the pasture. In worship, songs that celebrate God's jealousy remind believers that they are passionately desired, combating feelings of abandonment. Ultimately, love's jealousy assures disciples that God is not indifferent; He will confront, block, and break counterfeit affections to secure their eternal joy.

4.2. Instruments of Discipline in Hosea

4.2.1 • Withheld Harvests—Drought, Famine, and Economic Wake-Up Calls (Hosea 2:9)

Agrarian Israel viewed bumper crops as covenant blessing (Deuteronomy 28:11-12); thus, when God vows to "take back My grain in its time" (Hosea 2:9), He strikes at the theological epicenter of security. Drought in Scripture often signals covenant breach, as in Elijah's three-year famine confronting Baal worship (1 Kings 17:1). Withheld harvests unmask idols promising fertility; when rains stop, Baal's impotence is exposed. Economically, scarcity pressures budgets, revealing whether hearts trust Providence or profit margins. Families revisiting spending habits may discover tithes neglected, mirroring Israel's robbed offerings (Malachi 3:8-10). Modern equivalents include market crashes, job layoffs, or unexpected medical bills—economic tremors that challenge financial idolatry. Hosea's contemporaries faced failing vineyards; today's disciples might face vanishing retirement accounts—both invite reconsideration of stewardship. Scarcity also re-humanizes community: neighbors share resources, echoing Acts 2:45 generosity catalyzed by need. Theologically, God's ownership of harvest reframes labor; farmers sow but Yahweh sends rain (Psalm 147:8). Prayer meetings during recessions become practical confession services: "We trusted in savings, not the Savior." Stories of miraculous provision—groceries on doorsteps, anonymous rent checks—teach children that Jehovah-Jireh still sees (Genesis 22:14). By ending famine when repentance dawns, God underscores that discipline is reversible; the same hand that withheld grain can restore double (Joel 2:25). Churches can preach stewardship series in downturns, guiding congregations from panic to principle. In all, drought operates as megaphone to deafened hearts, amplifying God's call back to covenant dependence.

4.2.2 ▪ Political Turmoil—Assyrian Pressure as Rod of Correction (Hosea 5:13)

Northern Israel treated geopolitical alliances like insurance policies, paying tribute to Assyria while flirting with Egypt. Hosea labels this diplomacy "a silly dove without sense" (Hosea 7:11), and Yahweh turns the chosen partner—Assyria—into disciplinary rod. Tiglath-Pileser III's campaigns devastate Galilean territories, shrinking borders and puncturing national pride (2 Kings 15:29). Political instability, assassinations, and puppet kings ensue, fulfilling Hosea's prediction that they "set up kings, but not by Me" (Hosea 8:4). In modern contexts, God may use governmental upheaval—pandemics exposing weak infrastructures, elections revealing moral divides—to jolt churches from nationalism back to kingdom allegiance. Political idols promise security, but when policies fail or leaders fall, believers confront misplaced trust (Psalm 146:3-4). Prophetic voices today, like Hosea, warn against equating partisan agendas with God's purposes. Turmoil also drives diaspora; exiles carry witness into new regions, as Assyrian scattering later seeds Samaria for Jesus' outreach (John 4). Intercessory ministries arise during crises, giving the church prophetic role rather than partisan panic. Tours through history—Rome's collapse sparking monastic renewal, China's revolutions fueling underground church growth—illustrate discipline morphing into expansion. For Israel, Assyrian pressure ended autonomy but initiated heart-searching; likewise, societal shake-ups invite the global church to examine loyalties and re-embrace pilgrim identity (Hebrews 11:13). Political discipline, then, is not divine endorsement of tyrants but sovereign leverage to dismantle false confidences and redirect hope toward unshakable kingdom.

4.2.3 • Social Disintegration—Violence and Leadership Collapse (Hosea 4:2; 7:3-7)

Hosea catalogs societal decay: "There is swearing, lying, murder, stealing, and committing adultery; they break all bounds" (Hosea 4:2). Corrupt leaders rejoice in wickedness, "all of them hot as an oven" plotting coups (Hosea 7:6-7). Social disintegration serves as mirror showing covenant breach's relational fallout. When violence escalates, citizens yearn for justice, subconsciously crying for righteous reign. The prophet Micah, contemporary to Hosea, links injustice to idolatry, reinforcing that broken vertical relationship fractures horizontal structures (Micah 6:13). Modern parallels abound: soaring homicide rates, corporate scandals, and distrust in institutions reflect moral foundations eroded by secular caricatures of freedom. God allows systems to buckle so that reform movements birthed from prayer may emerge—William Wilberforce's abolition, Martin Luther King Jr.'s civil rights, all catalyzed amid societal fractures. Congregations witnessing civic chaos should interpret headlines as calls to repentance and engagement, not resignation. Church leadership failure—abuse scandals, embezzlement—functions likewise: painful exposure intended to purify bride's witness (1 Peter 4:17). Lament liturgies help communities process collective trauma without cynicism; prophets grieved before they preached. Restorative justice programs, birthed from Christian ethos, demonstrate alternate society under Christ's lordship. Finally, Hosea anticipates eventual healing: when God restores covenant, "sword shall be no more" (Hosea 2:18), pointing to eschatological shalom that present disciples can preview through peacemaking initiatives.

4.2.4 • Wilderness Exile—Corporate Detox from Idolatry (Hosea 2:14; 9:3)

Exile is discipline's severest form—a forced relocation disconnecting Israel from polluted rhythms of land and liturgy. Removed from fertile Canaan to Assyrian provinces, they lose access to high places and harvest festivals that fueled Baalism. The wilderness motif reappears: diaspora fields become spaces for re-learning dependence. Psalm 137 captures exile's sting—harps hung on willows, memories mocked—yet grief fertilizes longing for Zion. Captivity also democratizes hardship; princes and peasants alike feel loss, leveling pride. Exile spreads Yahweh's fame as scattered Israelites witness in foreign courts—Daniel in Babylon, Esther in Persia—turning punishment into platform. Theologically, exile reinforces God's sovereignty over geography; His presence travels, contradicting pagan territorial gods (Ezekiel 1). Modern church experiences "cultural exile" in post-Christian societies—loss of privilege and marginal status press believers to authenticity. Detox occurs when popularity idol dies, sparking creativity in mission: house churches, workplace fellowships, digital prayer rooms. Exilic literature—Lamentations, 1 Peter—equips saints to suffer without assimilation. Hope surfaces: Jeremiah's letter promises future homecoming after seventy years (Jeremiah 29:10-14). Hosea echoes, envisioning Israel seeking Davidic king "in the latter days" (Hosea 3:5). Thus, exile, though severe, is a grace instrument resetting worship and propelling redemptive history toward Messiah.

4.3. Reading Providence—Discerning Discipline vs. Random Suffering

4.3.1 ▪ Biblical Criteria—Prophetic Diagnosis, Conscience, and Community Witness

Determining whether hardship is divine discipline or common-groaning suffering requires multilayered discernment. First, Scripture provides covenant benchmarks: willful idolatry aligned with Deuteronomy curses likely invites corrective measures. Prophets historically delivered explicit oracles—Nathan to David (2 Samuel 12:7-12), Hosea to Israel—clarifying causation. Absent prophetic clarity, believers examine conscience; the Spirit convicts of specific sin rather than vague dread (John 16:8). Community witness adds objectivity; trusted leaders test impressions against biblical truth and broader patterns. Circumstances aligning with clear disobedience (e.g., secret affair followed by family fracture) often signal discipline, while suffering unrelated to sin (John 9:3) may be venue for glory. Patterns matter: recurring trials in the same area might indicate unaddressed roots. Dreams or impressions are weighed, never sole determinants. Scripture warns against presumptuous attribution—Job's friends misread righteous suffering, proving criteria must be holistic (Job 42:7). Pastoral teams may call corporate fasts to seek understanding, echoing Acts 13:2 discernment process. Journaling events and heart responses over time exposes links between rebellion and repercussions. Discernment ultimately aims at repentance or perseverance; mislabeling can paralyze. Therefore, biblical data, Spirit conviction, communal counsel, and humble reflection form a grid preventing both denial and undue guilt.

4.3.2 ▪ *Avoiding Simplistic Blame—Lessons from Job's Comforters*

Job's friends embody reductionism: they equate tragedy with specific sin, weaponizing theology against a suffering innocent (Job 8:4). God rebukes them, highlighting complexity in providence. Their mistake lies in collapsing multifaceted sovereignty into karma-like formulas, ignoring spiritual warfare, testing, and mystery. Modern parallels emerge when Christians claim every disaster—hurricanes, pandemics—is direct punishment for societal sin, risking slander against God's compassionate nature (Luke 13:1-5). Simplistic blame also wounds victims, compounding grief with shame. Hosea shows nuance: some calamities are discipline, yet even then, motivation is restorative love, not retributive glee. Pastors must teach lament and inquiry instead of glib explanations, allowing space for unanswered questions. The book of Ruth demonstrates famine not explicitly tied to sin but becomes redemptive thread leading to David. Jesus wept at Lazarus's tomb without attributing blame, showing empathy precedes analysis (John 11:35). Blame culture breeds self-righteous distance—"I'm safe because I'm obedient"—contradicting gospel humility. Therefore, discernment balances prophetic courage with compassionate restraint, acknowledging fog while pursuing light. Ultimately, Job's restoration reveals that God can vindicate sufferers and instruct counselors, urging careful speech about divine motives.

4.3.3 • *Testing the Fruit—Does the Trial Invite Repentance or Merely Produce Despair?*

Jesus teaches that trees are known by fruit (Matthew 7:17); likewise, discipline yields identifiable outcomes. Hebrews 12 promises "peaceful fruit of righteousness" when training is accepted, whereas random suffering may tempt toward nihilism. Evaluate responses: is the heart softened, sin renounced, prayer life deepened? Hosea anticipates this fruit: "In their affliction they will earnestly seek Me" (Hosea 5:15). Conversely, if hardship spawns bitterness, isolation, or cynicism, guidance is needed to redirect perspective. Paul's thorn drove him to dependence, evidencing beneficial fruit despite Satanic origin (2 Corinthians 12:7-10). Leaders can help congregants catalogue growth—instances of humility, compassion—affirming discipline's positive yield. Spiritual inventory questions—"What is God teaching me? Where do I see transformation?"—function as orchard inspection. However, early stages may look barren; seed germination requires time. Community encouragement prevents premature verdicts of futility. Despair indicates misinterpretation or enemy condemnation; counselors combat with Romans 8:28 assurance. Ultimately, fruit testing provides pragmatic gauge: authentic discipline, though painful, moves believers closer to Christ and community, not away.

4.3.4 • *Practices of Corporate Discernment—Fasting, Prayer, and Wise Counsel*

Acts 13 portrays leaders fasting and praying until the Spirit directs mission, offering template for collective guidance. Fasting quiets appetites, amplifying spiritual sensitivity similar to Hosea's wilderness hush. Corporate prayer meetings invite diverse gifts—prophetic insight, pastoral wisdom—so no single voice monopolizes interpretation. Elders weigh impressions against Scripture, sustaining doctrinal safety. Listening circles allow affected members to share experiences, fostering empathy. Historical reflection—looking at church minutes, financial trends—can uncover systemic sins requiring repentance. Outside mentors provide objectivity, as Paul consulted Jerusalem pillars (Galatians 2:2). Once consensus forms, leaders communicate findings transparently, outlining repentance steps or comfort emphasis. Sacramental acts—

communion, foot-washing—seal unity and dependence on grace. Follow-up reviews track progress, adjusting course if fruit eludes. Such communal discernment transforms crises into bonding catalysts, mirroring Hosea's vision of corporate return: "Come, let us return to the LORD" (Hosea 6:1). The process embodies humility, guarding against autocratic decrees or passive fatalism. In a world craving quick answers, disciplined listening showcases body life shaped by the pursuing, correcting, and guiding God.

4.4. Responding to Discipline—Pathway to Restoration

4.4.1 ▪ *Honest Confession—Owning Sin without Excuse (Hosea 5:15; 6:1)*

The first step out of divine discipline is candor before God—"I will return again to My place until they acknowledge their guilt" (Hosea 5:15). Confession in Scripture is never a perfunctory checklist; it is truth telling that aligns the sinner's verdict with God's. David models it in Psalm 32:5, refusing to cloak transgression once the Spirit's hand grew heavy. Hosea echoes this movement by urging, "Come, let us return to the LORD, for He has torn us, that He may heal us" (Hosea 6:1). Genuine confession avoids blame-shifting ("The woman You gave me," Genesis 3:12) or minimization ("We only kissed"), and instead names attitudes, actions, and root idols. It includes specific language—"envy," "pornography," "dishonest weights"—so that darkness loses camouflage (1 John 1:7-9). Public dimension sometimes follows: Daniel confessed national sins despite personal integrity, interceding on behalf of a people (Daniel 9:4-5). In corporate worship, responsive readings of penitential psalms cultivate a culture where admitting failure is normal, not scandalous. Confession also listens—allowing the Spirit and trusted community to identify blind spots we cannot see (Psalm 139:23-24). The posture is humility, face to the ground, yet hope glimmers because exposure occurs before a Father, not a firing squad (Luke 15:21-22). Practically, journaling sins and then writing a cross over the page enacts Isaiah 43:25's promise that God blots out transgressions. Small-group confessions framed by James 5:16 bring healing, breaking secrecy's stranglehold. Regular examination—daily examen or weekly Sabbath reflection—pre-empts protracted rebellion. Honest confession reverses Hosea's indictment that Israel "did not consider in their hearts" (Hosea 7:2), transforming foggy self-deceit into clear-eyed repentance that opens prison doors.

4.4.2 • *Humility and Fasts—Embodied Repentance that Softens Hearts (Joel 2:12-13)*

Biblical repentance recruits the body; "return to Me with fasting, weeping, and mourning" (Joel 2:12) indicates that inner contrition manifests in outward practice. Fasting weakens fleshly appetites that often fuel rebellion, creating space to hunger for righteousness (Matthew 5:6). In Hosea's context, abstaining from food and drink directly confronted fertility-cult feasts, signaling divorce from Baal's table. Humility also expresses itself in posture—sackcloth, ashes, kneeling—reminding worshipers of creaturely fragility (Jonah 3:6-10). Modern equivalents might include digital fasts that unhook dopamine cycles, financial fasts (no discretionary spending) that expose consumer idols, or silence retreats that unmask hurried pride. The goal is not ascetic showmanship (Matthew 6:16-18) but a softened heart God can mold. Acts 13:2-3 shows the early church fasting before mission decisions, illustrating that humility invites fresh guidance. Couples can fast together when marriage conflict reveals entrenched self-will, modeling mutual submission. Congregational fast calendars—Advent hunger for Christ's coming or Lenten repentance—create communal rhythm aligning appetite with the gospel story. Physiologically, fasting lowers blood sugar, often heightening emotional awareness, which the Spirit can redirect to lament or intercession. Joel promises God will leave behind a blessing after heartfelt fasts (Joel 2:14); Hosea echoes with restored grain and wine (Hosea 2:21-22). Thus, embodied repentance becomes fertile soil where divine tenderness germinates.

4.4.3 • *Making Amends—Practical Fruits of Repentance (Luke 3:8-14)*

John the Baptist demands fruit in keeping with repentance—tangible changes, not sentimental regret (Luke 3:8). Hosea links spiritual adultery to social injustice; therefore, restoration must include restitution. The Mosaic Law prescribed four- or fivefold repayment for theft (Exodus 22:1); Zacchaeus outdid the law by restoring four times and giving half to the poor (Luke 19:8). Making amends reconciles relationships: apology letters, repaid debts, public corrections of slander. It can involve dismantling structures—dissolving unethical business partnerships or deleting pirated software. Corporate repentance might see churches funding counseling for abuse victims or reforming governance after leadership failure. Amends intentionally cost; the silver and barley Hosea paid showed love's willingness to absorb loss for another's gain (Hosea 3:2). They also protect against relapse—returning what was wrongfully gained severs economic incentive to repeat sin. Guidance from mentors or legal advisors ensures amends are wise, not impulsive. Where direct repayment is impossible, symbolic reparations like charitable donations can honor justice principles. Testimonies of restitution glorify Christ more than vague "past mistakes" narratives, showcasing power to right wrongs. Ultimately, deeds verify that confession has reached the will, mirroring Paul's charge, "let the thief labor, doing honest work…so that he may have something to share" (Ephesians 4:28).

4.4.4 ▪ Receiving Mercy—Faith that Grabs Hold of God's Promise to Heal (Hosea 14:4)

After confession and corrective action, believers must actively receive mercy, or else discipline results in perpetual penance rather than joy. Hosea closes with divine assurance: "I will heal their apostasy; I will love them freely" (Hosea 14:4). Receiving implies trust that God's character outweighs our failure, echoing Hebrews 4:16's call to "approach the throne of grace with confidence." Faith draws water from wells of salvation—if shame barricades the heart, healing stalls. Rituals like Eucharist function as mercy conduits, letting taste buds verify pardon. Personalizing promises—reading Hosea 14 aloud in first person—anchors grace deeply. Psychological studies show self-compassion fosters resilience; gospel mercy is holy self-compassion rooted in Christ's blood. Spiritual directors may lead penitents in imaginative prayer, picturing Jesus clothing them anew (Zechariah 3:4). Worship that lingers in adoration ("Amazing Grace," "He Loves Us") helps emotions catch up with theological reality. Receiving mercy also means dropping self-punishment behaviors—excessive busyness, emotional withdrawal—that secretly atone for guilt. Community affirmation, as James 5:16 suggests, re-voices mercy until it sinks in. Finally, mercy propels mission: forgiven people become conduits of forgiveness, proving God's embrace by how widely they open their arms (Colossians 3:13).

4.5. The Cross—Ultimate Discipline Borne by the Son

4.5.1 ▪ *"Pierced for Our Transgressions"—Isaiah 53 and Substitutionary Suffering*

Isaiah's Servant is "pierced for our transgressions" (Isaiah 53:5), absorbing covenant curses deserved by Israel's spiritual adultery. This substitution fulfills Hosea's shadowed promise of ransom (Hosea 13:14). Roman nails and thorns externalize what sin merited—exile, death, divine abandonment. 1 Peter 2:24 confirms the linkage, stating Christ "bore our sins in His body on the tree." The Hebrew term for "pierced" (*chalal*) conveys violent penetration, underscoring cost. Substitution guards two truths: God's holiness is satisfied, and sinners are spared condemnation. Early church fathers saw Genesis 22's ram caught in thicket as typological preview of Christ caught in judgment in Isaac's place. At Golgotha, darkness and earthquake mirror Sinai tremors, signaling covenant judgment concentrated on one man. This act silences Satanic accusation—legal demands met, certificates canceled (Colossians 2:14-15). Substitution also dismantles self-justification; if a sinless Savior died, moral improvement is no rescue. Emotionally, contemplating pierced love melts resistance, drawing hearts with cords stronger than Hosea's wilderness allure. Preaching substitution therefore remains central; Paul determined to know nothing but "Christ crucified" (1 Corinthians 2:2) because every pastoral issue roots in believing or forgetting that exchange.

4.5.2 ▪ *Justice Satisfied—Divine Righteousness Upheld without Losing the Beloved (Romans 3:25-26)*

Romans 3 presents the cross as *hilasterion*—mercy-seat where God demonstrates justice while justifying the ungodly. Without this, discipline risks caricature: either sentimental (justice sidelined) or wrathful (mercy eclipsed). Propitiation means God's wrath, rightfully aroused by covenant betrayal, is quenched in Christ, freeing Him to pursue without violating his moral nature. Hosea's internal debate—"How can I give you up?" (Hosea 11:8)—finds

115

resolution at Calvary, where giving up His Son preserves Israel. The veil tearing from top down signals legal barriers removed (Matthew 27:51). Paul celebrates a "new and living way" (Hebrews 10:20), granting disciplined sinners access beyond courtroom into Father's presence. Cosmic implications abound: principalities cannot claim God is lax, for justice is displayed publicly. In evangelism, this answers objections about arbitrary forgiveness—God does not sweep evil under the rug; He shoulders it. Social justice advocates likewise see model: wrongs require redress, yet mercy can flourish when price is paid. Thus, crucifixion is both gavel and embrace, showcasing perfect integration of attributes.

4.5.3 • From Penalty to Pedagogy—How Christ's Work Transforms Punishment into Training

Because Christ exhausted penal wrath, remaining trials shift category from retribution to pedagogy. Paul calls them "light momentary afflictions preparing an eternal weight of glory" (2 Corinthians 4:17). Discipline now refines rather than condemns, like heat on gold post-smelting (1 Peter 1:6-7). The Greek *paideia* (education) in Hebrews 12 presupposes Calvary; God is not double-charging sin. This paradigm frees believers from interpreting every hardship as payback; instead, they ask, "What lesson?" rather than "What penalty?" Luther likened trials to a gymnasium for faith muscles. Spiritual gifts also transition—prophetic rebuke, church discipline—into coaching rather than sentencing. Sacraments serve similarly: baptism symbolizes burial of penalty, raising to new life of training (Romans 6:4). Guilt-ridden perseverance mutates into hope-filled endurance, knowing chastening is purposeful. Testimonies of persecuted saints—Corrie ten Boom, Chinese house churches—confirm that imprisoned faith often shines brighter, validating pedagogical design. Pastors should therefore shepherd sufferers toward growth objectives, not merely escape strategies, echoing James 1:2-4's exhortation to count it joy when tested because maturity is maturing.

4.5.4 ▪ *Grace-Empowered Obedience—The Spirit as Internal Tutor (Ezekiel 36:26-27)*

The new covenant promises a heart transplant—stone to flesh—and Spirit indwelling that causes obedience (Ezekiel 36:26-27). Post-cross discipline collaborates with this internal tutor, moving morality from external compulsion to intrinsic delight. Romans 8:13 says the Spirit enables believers to put deeds of flesh to death, functioning like internal accountability software. He convicts, comforts, and reminds disciples of Jesus' words (John 14:26). Spiritual formation practices—solitude, Scripture memory—tune ears to His coaching voice. Unlike schoolteachers who clock out, the Spirit monitors 24/7, turning ordinary irritations into tutorials: traffic produces patience lessons, toddler tantrums refine gentleness. Galatians 5 fruit list reveals character syllabus; discipline sessions target deficits in love, joy, peace. Cooperative obedience requires yielding; quenching the Spirit resists tutoring (1 Thessalonians 5:19). The Spirit also gifts power for obedience: resurrection energy inside mortal bodies (Romans 8:11). Thus, grace is not lenient permissiveness but dynamic empowerment, fulfilling Augustine's prayer, "Command what You will and give what You command." Hosea foresaw this when prophesying Israel would "blossom like the lily" under divine care (Hosea 14:5). Obedience becomes relational reciprocity, not legal fulfillment—children delighting the Father who delights in them.

4.6. Communal Discipline within the Church

4.6.1 ▪ *Matthew 18 Process—Private Appeal, Shared Witness, Covenantal Accountability*

Jesus outlines a graduated pathway: go alone, then with two or three, then tell the church (Matthew 18:15-17). This protects reputations while prioritizing rescue. Private approach respects dignity, giving space for Spirit-led conviction. If resistance stiffens, adding witnesses fulfills Deuteronomy 19:15 jurisprudence, ensuring fairness. Only after persistent refusal does matter escalate to the whole assembly, emphasizing corporate responsibility rather than clerical authoritarianism. The goal is always "winning the brother," not winning the argument. Churches train members in conflict resolution skills—active listening, "I" language—to maximize first-step success. Documentation prevents gossip; facts replace rumors. When the case reaches leadership, elders weigh evidence prayerfully, mindful of their own frailty (Galatians 6:1). Public communication balances transparency with confidentiality, informing congregation enough to pray, not to judge. If the final step—treating as tax collector—occurs, it signifies relational boundaries, yet hope for repentance remains; Jesus dined with tax collectors, modeling ongoing gospel invitation. Reinstatement procedures are predetermined, avoiding ad-hoc bias. This covenantal accountability counters consumer church mentality, fostering depth of belonging akin to family discipline. Healthy Matthew 18 cultures reduce pastoral burnout; conflicts resolved peer-to-peer seldom overrun elder bandwidth. Ultimately, the process embodies Hosea's layered pursuit—warnings escalated yet love persistent.

4.6.2 • Galatians 6:1 Tone—Gentleness, Self-Watch, and Aim of Restoration

Paul commands that those "who are spiritual" restore the fallen in a spirit of gentleness, coupling skill with temperament. Gentleness disarms defensiveness, resembling Jesus' restoration of Peter with breakfast before challenge (John 21:9-17). Self-watch prevents superiority; confrontors remember potential for identical sin. Practical training includes reflective statements—"I could be wrong, help me understand"—rather than accusatory "you always." Body language—open hands, soft eyes—communicates safety. Timing matters; discussions occur in private neutral spaces, not public lobbies. Prayer precedes confrontation, inviting Spirit's presence. The Greek katartizo (restore) pictures mending nets; discipline aims to repair, not discard. Restorers provide follow-up: accountability plans, counseling referrals, spiritual disciplines. They celebrate incremental wins, reinforcing identity over performance. Gentleness doesn't negate firmness; boundaries may include temporary ministry pause. Leaders model tone by publicly repenting when they err, normalizing humility. Congregations that master this tone radiate attractiveness, turning conflict into gospel display. Galatians 6:1 thus functions as emotional thermostat regulating Matthew 18 machinery.

118

4.6.3 • When Exclusion Is Love—1 Corinthians 5 and the Hope of Repentance

Paul instructs Corinth to remove a man sleeping with stepmother, "deliver him to Satan for the destruction of the flesh" (1 Corinthians 5:5). Such exclusion, though severe, targets repentance and eventual salvation. The action protects community from leaven of blatant sin, safeguarding weaker believers. It also jolts sinner from complacency by confronting the reality of covenant breach. Modern churches rarely excommunicate, fearing legalism, yet permissive tolerance breeds hypocrisy. Exclusion follows due process, clear evidence, and pastoral anguish. Practical steps: membership covenant outlines expectations upfront; elders issue formal letters citing sin and gospel call. Removal means barred leadership, withheld communion, and honest explanation to congregation to prevent speculation. Loving contact remains—texts expressing prayer, invitations to counsel—distinct from social shunning. The church prays for brokenness, not downfall. Paul's later joy at offender's sorrow (2 Corinthians 2:7) shows exclusion can succeed. Leaders review cases periodically, ready to welcome back at first fruit of repentance. This practice clarifies gospel seriousness: grace is free but not cheap; covenant demands loyalty for communal health. When executed biblically, exclusion becomes prodigal pigsty moment hastening return.

4.6.4 • Celebrating Return—Public Reaffirmation and Healing Liturgies (2 Corinthians 2:6-8)

Paul urges Corinthians to "reaffirm your love" for the repentant brother, lest excessive sorrow swallow him (2 Corinthians 2:7-8). Celebration solidifies restoration, preventing stigma. Liturgies may include reading confession, elder declaration of forgiveness, and congregational applause echoing Luke 15's party. Reinstating communion publicly visualizes table fellowship renewed. Restored individuals share testimony, converting failure into edification. Symbolic acts—robe over shoulders, ring handed like father to prodigal—incarnate acceptance. Follow-up discipleship pairs returnee with mentor, safeguarding against relapse. Congregations learn mercy culture: they witness discipline's redemptive arc, balancing necessary firmness with overflowing joy. Worship songs pivot from lament to praise, mirroring transition in Psalm 51.

119

Celebration also heals victims; they see justice and mercy intertwine, building trust. Documentation updates membership status, closing disciplinary file. Annual "jubilee service" may showcase multiple restorations, underscoring ongoing grace. In doing so, the church images Hosea buying back Gomer in town square—public disgrace reversed by public love (Hosea 3:2-3).

4.7. Personal Spiritual Formation—Embracing Pruning

4.7.1 ▪ John 15 Imagery—The Vinedresser Cuts to Multiply Fruit

Jesus' teaching in John 15 locates discipline in the vineyard, where the Father personally trims every branch "that it may bear more fruit" (John 15:2). The knife is not punitive but purposeful; a viticulturist removes suckers and deadwood because unchecked growth diverts sap away from clusters. Spiritual suckers—time-wasting habits, ego projects, even overcrowded ministry calendars—consume energy that could ripen character. When God curtails these pursuits through closed doors or deprioritized influence, He is channeling life toward love, joy, peace, and patience (Galatians 5:22-23). Pruning seasons feel like loss: social platforms shrink, dreams stall, comfort rhythms disappear. Yet viticulture notes that the deepest cuts often precede the sweetest harvests, a truth mirrored in Paul's imprisonment producing letters still feeding the church (Philippians 1:12-14). The Vinedresser also lifts drooping branches from the mud, washing them before tying them to trellises; so discipline sometimes elevates discouraged believers through counsel and community, enabling exposure to Son-light rather than additional hacking. The process requires proximity—God's hand steady and tender—reminding disciples that they are not abandoned during pain. Abiding, not striving, is the branch's role; the sap of the Spirit keeps nutrients flowing even when outer structures feel reduced (John 15:4). Pruning realigns priorities toward eternal fruit that remains, such as transformed lives rather than padded résumés. Reflection questions—"What activity drains life without bearing fruit?"—help identify areas God might target next. Seasonal rhythms show God's wisdom: pruning in winter protects plants from infection; likewise, God often disciplines in hidden seasons when public scrutiny is low. Accepting this rhythm cultivates trust that silence and subtraction signal care, not neglect. Ultimately, the vineyard metaphor reframes discipline as artisanal craftsmanship, producing vintage faith capable of intoxicating the world with Christ's aroma.

4.7.2 ▪ *Co-operating with Discipline—Silence, Scripture, and Self-Examination*

While pruning is God's initiative, branches co-operate by positioning themselves for optimal growth. Silence is the first cooperative practice, echoing Habakkuk's hush before the Lord in His holy temple (Habakkuk 2:20). Exterior quiet exposes interior noise—worry, resentment, ambition—that the Spirit highlights for confession. Scripture then enters as pruning shears; Hebrews 4:12 describes the Word slicing between soul and spirit, discerning motives hidden even from the self. Lectio divina slows reading pace, allowing verses like Psalm 139:23-24 to probe unexamined attitudes. Self-examination borrows from the Ignatian *examen*, asking where consolation and desolation appeared each day, mapping patterns in need of trimming. Journaling observations transforms vague conviction into concrete transformation plans. Accountability partners function as fellow gardeners, spotting blind-spots and affirming progress. Retreat days—digital sabbaths spent in nature—amplify receptivity to God's corrective whispers. Memorizing passages about God's fatherly heart (Hebrews 12:6) keeps pruning linked to love, not rejection. Periodic solitude with communion elements reenacts submission to the knife: believers break bread, acknowledging areas that must die with Christ to rise again. Spiritual direction offers skilled accompaniment, ensuring cuts do not become self-harm through legalistic excess. Co-operation also includes obedience in small nudges—returning overcharged money, deleting unclean playlists—so larger surgeries become unnecessary. When resistance flares, breath prayers—"Not my will, prune Me"—re-align stubborn will with Spirit's blade. The synergy of silence, Scripture, and self-examination gradually fashions a supple branch ready for sustained fruitfulness.

4.7.3 • Contentment and Perseverance—Learning Paul's Secret in All Circumstances (Philippians 4:11-13)

Paul confesses he "learned the secret" of contentment through abundance and lack (Philippians 4:11-13). That secret is not stoic indifference but Christ-sufficiency—"I can do all things through Him who strengthens me." Discipline classrooms life into this secret by cycling believers through varied conditions. Job knew prosperity then bankruptcy, developing a theology that blesses God on both sides of loss (Job 1:21). Contentment is cultivated, not innate; repeated exposure to shifting seasons stretches trust muscles. Practical exercises include gratitude listing in scarcity and humility practices in abundance (e.g., choosing economy travel though funds allow first-class). Budgeting aligns with contentment, teaching hearts to live below means as a discipline against covetousness (1 Timothy 6:6-8). Perseverance grows simultaneously; trials produce endurance, which matures character (James 1:2-4). Athletes maintain form when fatigued; believers maintain obedience when discouraged, revealing gospel power. Mentors tell stories of decades-long faithfulness, modelling slow-burn spirituality rather than flash-in-pan zeal. Sabbath rest paradoxically fuels perseverance by preventing burnout, demonstrating that God can sustain work we pause. Suffering communities—Persecuted Church testimonies, chronic-illness saints—become living commentaries on contentment, inspiring global body. Ultimately, discipline presses disciples into the secret until they echo Paul: "Whether in lockdown or on mission field, Christ is enough."

4.7.4 • Witness through Weakness—How Refined Lives Display Gospel Beauty (2 Corinthians 4:7-10)

Paul calls believers "jars of clay" carrying treasure so surpassing greatness is seen to be God's (2 Corinthians 4:7). Discipline intentionally cracks pottery, letting light spill through fissures. Weakness, therefore, is not ministry disqualification but amplification. Hosea's public humiliation as betrayed husband became prophetic billboard of divine fidelity; likewise, modern Christians' refined weaknesses preach louder than unblemished facades. Cancer patients radiating joy, widows offering hospitality, and paraplegic theologians writing hope confound worldly logic.

122

Audience observes suffering and asks for the reason of hope (1 Peter 3:15). God's strength made perfect in weakness (2 Corinthians 12:9) dethrones human boasting cultures. Ministry teams openly acknowledge mental-health struggles, modeling authenticity over curated perfection. Social media testimonies of failure-to-freedom rebut influencer gloss, pointing followers to Christ, not lifestyle hacks. Artists incorporate scars into art—Kintsugi pottery mended with gold—parallel to redeemed cracks. Cruciform witness undermines prosperity gospels; it says, "God is good even when life is not." Ethically, weakness sensitizes to others' pain, fueling justice engagement. Heavenly reward calculus flips—last are first, meek inherit earth—validating present losses (Matthew 5:5; 19:30). Therefore, discipline, by refining weakness, equips saints to display a kingdom upside-down in which fragile vessels carry immortal narrative.

4.8. Eschatological Hope—Discipline Ends in Glory

4.8.1 • From Exile to Return—Previewing the Final Homecoming (Hosea 3:5)

Hosea envisions days when Israel will "return and seek the LORD their God and David their king" (Hosea 3:5). Post-exilic history partially fulfills this via remnant return, yet ultimate homecoming awaits the multi-ethnic bride gathered to New Jerusalem. Exile-return arc frames Christian pilgrimage: strangers and exiles on earth (Hebrews 11:13) moving toward a better country. Every smaller restoration—prodigal back home, addict sober—previews the grand return. Feasts like Passover and, in Christianity, Easter rehearse liberation narratives, fueling anticipation. Teaching eschatology through exile lens avoids date-setting sensationalism; it roots hope in relational reunion rather than speculative charts. Psalms of ascent (120-134) become soundtrack for journey, reminding hearts of Zion nearing. Church architecture sometimes symbolizes pilgrimage—central aisle representing path to altar—to embody forward motion. The sacraments hold exilic tension: we eat in foreign lands, proclaiming Lord's death "until He comes" (1 Corinthians 11:26). Endure discipline, therefore, because the trek has destination; suffering is mile marker, not terminus. Mission expands horizon—inviting nations to join caravan home, reversing Babel exile. Thus, homecoming hope re-contextualizes chastening: God's rod redirects feet toward Zion gates.

4.8.2 • New Covenant Promise—Hearts of Flesh and Spirit-Written Law (Jeremiah 31:31-34)

Jeremiah foretells a covenant unlike Sinai, internalizing Torah so obedience flows from desire, not external compulsion. Ezekiel adds the Spirit-infused heart transplant (Ezekiel 36:26). This promise, inaugurated at Pentecost (Acts 2), means discipline increasingly works from inside out: conscience pricks before circumstances crash. Sanctification is progressive writing of law on neural pathways; spiritual disciplines are pens, Spirit the ink. New covenant also guarantees unbreakable relationship—God swears, "I will be their God," ensuring end of exile cycles. Hebrews 8 cites this to show why old system faded; sacrifices of bulls could not re-write desires. Counseling leverages promise during relapse: "Sin felt natural yesterday; today, new heart means sin contradicts your truest self." Corporate worship celebrates by reading Ten Commandments, then singing grace songs, integrating law and Spirit. Sacramental wine symbolizes covenant blood sealing heart work. Thus, eschatological hope is not only spatial (heaven) but ontological— our very nature permanently aligned with holiness. Discipline now confirms upgrade in progress; glitches get patched until final release.

4.8.3 • "No More Curse"—Heaven as the Land Where Discipline Is Finished (Revelation 22:3-5)

Revelation ends with startling phrase: "No longer will there be anything accursed." The ground once plagued by thorns (Genesis 3:17-18) and Hosea's wilderness thistles (Hosea 10:8) is healed. Discipline's temporal necessity ceases because perfected saints require no further correction. Leaves of the tree of life heal nations, removing political rods of judgment. Face-to-face vision replaces mediated faith, erasing doubt-driven chastening. Time's cycle of night ends, precluding seasons of pruning; uninterrupted light from God's presence sustains growth. Work continues—servants reign (Revelation 22:5)—but toil lacks frustration. Memory of discipline fuels eternal gratitude; scars become testimonies like Jesus' glorified wounds. Heaven's culture thus sings two songs: Lamb's redemption

124

and Vinedresser's faithfulness through discipline. Children once fathered by correction now walk mature, echoing C. S. Lewis: "School is over; summer has begun." Contemplating this removes sting from current trials—if discipline has an expiry date, endurance has proportionate gain (2 Corinthians 4:17).

4.8.4 ▪ *Living Today in Future Light—Encouragement, Holiness, and Resilient Mission*

John writes, "Everyone who thus hopes in Him purifies himself" (1 John 3:3). Eschatological vision fuels present holiness; visionary athletes train harder. Churches preach second coming not to terrify but to motivate ethical vigilance—servants stay awake because master may return tonight (Matthew 24:42-46). Hope also encourages: Thessalonians grieved, yet not without hope, because resurrection waits (1 Thessalonians 4:13-18). Mission thrives: Revelation's people from every tribe call believers to cross cultures now. Future light reframes suffering; hospital rooms become sanctuaries of future healing rehearsal. Environmental care aligns with coming new earth, witnessing against escapist abandon. Justice work perseveres because ultimate Judge guarantees vindication. Daily decisions—finances, sexuality, screen time—get filtered: "Will this endure the fire?" (1 Corinthians 3:13-14). Communion ends with "Until He comes," anchoring liturgy in anticipation. Artistic expressions—music, poetry—paint hope, discipling imagination. Parents instill eschatological worldview, reading Chronicles of Narnia finale to kids to depict "further up and further in." As discipline prunes, hope fertilizes, creating balanced growth. Thus, believers live as dawn people, shadows behind, sun rising, embodying resilient joy that declares: tough love is temporary; unbreakable glory is forever.

Conclusion When the curtain falls on Hosea's narrative, the last word is not exile but embrace, not devastation but "I will heal their apostasy" (Hosea 14:4). Such an ending reframes every instance of divine correction we have examined: the drought becomes a ploughed field ready for new seed, the wilderness a classroom of intimacy, even the cross a place where judgment and mercy kiss. For the believer, accepting discipline is not passive resignation but active cooperation—confessing without excuse, receiving forgiveness without self-punishment, and leaning into the Spirit's pruning so that

125

richer fruit can grow. At the communal level, churches that practice restorative accountability mirror the Father's heart and offer a living apologetic to a culture versed in either harsh cancellation or sentimental permissiveness. And on the horizon of hope stands the day when discipline's work is complete, when every tear has been wiped away and love's tough edges are sheathed forever in glory (Revelation 21:4). Until then, we submit to the Vinedresser's skilled hands, trusting that every cut is calibrated for flourishing and that the God who corrects is the same God who sings over His people with delight.

Chapter 5. Knowing God— Intimacy over Ritual

A heartbreaking refrain runs through Hosea's prophecy: Israel was rigorously religious yet relationally estranged. Altars were crowded, calendars crammed with feast days, but heaven heard hollow echoes because the worshipers no longer knew the One they addressed. In a single searing sentence God unveils His priority—"I desire steadfast love and not sacrifice, the knowledge of God rather than burnt offerings" (Hos 6:6). That collision of terms—love versus ritual, knowledge versus routine—still reverberates in contemporary churches where smart phones track devotional streaks while hearts drift on autopilot. This chapter therefore invites us to move from performance to presence, from information about God to communion with God. Drawing on the whole sweep of Scripture— from Eden's evening walks to Christ's upper-room prayer—we will explore what it means to *know* the Lord in the Hebrew sense of shared life, mutual delight, and covenant loyalty. Our goal is not to abandon external practices but to allow them to become living conduits of encounter, re-infusing worship, work, and witness with relational fire.

5.1. Defining "Knowledge of God" in Scripture

5.1.1 ▪ Hebrew yadaʿ—Relational Covenant Term, Not Data Download

The Hebrew verb *yada*ʿ appears almost 950 times in the Old Testament and rarely functions as mere mental cognition; it points to personal involvement and often covenant loyalty. When Genesis 4:1 says, "Adam *knew* Eve," the term describes marital intimacy that produces life, not an intellectual biography. Exodus 6:7 shows God pledging that Israel will "know" He is the LORD through deliverance, meaning salvation would stamp divine character onto communal memory. Conversely, Hosea indicts Israel for lacking *daʿat Elohim* ("knowledge of God," Hosea 4:1), exposing that statistical temple attendance does not equal covenant awareness. The word also frames prophetic vocation—Jeremiah 22:16 praises Josiah because he "defended the cause of the needy… Wasn't that to know Me?"—tying relational knowledge to social justice. *Yada*ʿ can even reference God's initiative, as in Exodus 33:17 where He says, "I know you by name," signaling elective affection. Thus, biblical knowledge is mutual—God knows, invites, and transforms; humans respond in trust, obedience, and delight. Reducing *yada*ʿ to theology notes strips it of covenant electricity, like reducing a marriage to a résumé. The term carries emotional valence—joy, jealousy, grief—because it is embedded in relationship, not clinical observation. Modern parallels include knowing a friend's heartbeat versus reading their medical chart: same subject, different realms. In Hosea, the absence of *yada*ʿ explains why rituals collapse; without relational core they become empty husks. Therefore, the chapter's pursuit is not adding data but recovering the original relational density of *yada*ʿ.

5.1.2 • *Experiential vs. Conceptual Knowledge—Head, Heart, and Hands Integrated*

Scripture depicts knowledge as a three-strand cord: conceptual truth (head), affective response (heart), and faithful practice (hands). Deuteronomy 6:4-6 commands Israel to recite, love, and obey, proving orthodoxy, orthopathy, and orthopraxy belong together. Jesus critiques Pharisees who catalogued scriptural minutiae yet lacked mercy (Matthew 23:23), exposing cerebral mastery divorced from compassion. Paul prays that the Ephesians would "know the love of Christ that surpasses knowledge" (Ephesians 3:19), paradoxically marrying cognitive grasp with experiential overflow. James 2 warns that demons possess orthodox facts but no covenant loyalty, underscoring that bare information is insufficient. Conversely, zeal without accurate gospel (Romans 10:2) can persecute truth, revealing emotion unhitched from sound doctrine. Genuine knowledge integrates all three: Thomas' confession, "My Lord and my God" (John 20:28), merges head revelation of resurrection, heart wonder, and implied lifelong allegiance. Hosea's audience excelled in sacrificial choreography but neglected justice and fidelity, illustrating fractured integration. Neural studies confirm that repeated embodied practice (hands) rewires affections (heart) and cements beliefs (head), matching biblical anthropology. Therefore, small-group curricula should couple study questions with worship response and service application, preventing lopsided formation. Personal devotions can integrate by meditating (head), journaling emotions (heart), and planning obedience (hands). Whole-person knowledge resists both sterile academia and anti-intellectual activism, embracing the integrated vision of Shema spirituality.

5.1.3 • *From Eden to New Jerusalem—A Survey of Knowing in the Biblical Story*

The Bible's narrative arc presents knowing God as humanity's original vocation, lost in the fracture of Genesis 3 and progressively restored. In Eden, Adam and Eve walk with God "in the cool of the day," enjoying unmediated fellowship (Genesis 3:8). Sin corrupts perception—fig leaves and hiding testify to distorted knowledge. Patriarchal stories show partial restorations: Abraham hears God, builds altars, and is called "friend of God" (Isaiah 41:8). Sinai codifies knowledge through covenant law and tabernacle presence, yet golden-calf relapse reveals persistent relational sabotage. Prophets, especially Hosea and Jeremiah, lament the gap between ritual and reality but also foresee a day when "they shall all know Me" from least to greatest (Jeremiah 31:34). The incarnation climaxes the quest: Jesus declares, "Whoever has seen Me has seen the Father" (John 14:9), embodying accessible deity. Pentecost internalizes presence; the Spirit enables continuous communion, fulfilling Ezekiel's heart-of-flesh prophecy. The story consummates in Revelation 21-22 where God dwells among His people, they see His face, and night is no more—a full circle to Edenic immediacy. Thus, Hosea's call sits within a grand trajectory, and our practices of intimacy anticipate eschatological completion.

5.1.4 • Jesus' High Priestly Prayer—Eternal Life as Knowing the Father (John 17:3)

In John 17 Jesus defines eternal life not as unending duration but as relational quality: "that they know You, the only true God, and Jesus Christ whom You have sent." This reorients salvation from ticket-to-heaven to covenant experience starting now. The Greek *ginosko* mirrors Hebrew *yada'*—relational knowledge proven in ongoing encounter. Jesus prays this hours before the cross, implying that His atonement removes barriers to such knowledge. The prayer ties Trinitarian intimacy ("You, Father, are in Me and I in You") to believer participation, extending intra-Trinitarian fellowship outward (John 17:21). Eternal life, then, is shared divine family life; it saturates mundane moments with transcendence. New-Testament writers echo this: Peter says believers "become partakers of the divine nature" (2 Peter 1:4), and John insists abiding in love equals abiding in God (1 John 4:16). Practically, believers taste eternal life each time they sense Spirit witness, respond to Scripture's voice, or serve neighbor in Christ's strength. This present foretaste fuels mission—evangelism invites others into life now, not mere afterlife security. Knowing God, therefore, is both the means and end of redemptive history, vindicating Hosea's assertion that rituals without relational knowledge miss the entire point.

5.2. Hosea's Indictment—Ritual Without Relationship

5.2.1 ▪ Empty Festivals and Orphaned Sacrifices (Hosea 6:6; 8:11-13)

Hosea's generation maintained a bustling liturgical calendar: new moons, Sabbaths, and harvest celebrations filled the year (Hosea 2:11). Yet God rejects their offerings, declaring He delights in steadfast love, not sacrifices (Hosea 6:6). Israel multiplied altars like "stone heaps" (Hosea 10:1), thinking quantity compensated for quality. The prophetic oracle "They love sacrifice; therefore they sacrifice" (Hosea 8:13) satirizes addiction to religious activity detached from obedience. Isaiah, Amos, and Micah echo this critique, forming a chorus across eighth-century prophecy. Jesus later quotes Hosea 6:6 twice (Matthew 9:13; 12:7), rebuking Pharisees who weaponized ritual to exclude sinners. Empty festivals today appear as packed church calendars lacking justice engagement, communion services void of reconciliation, or streaming worship consumed like entertainment. Hosea teaches that God can sanctify secular farmers' markets more than perfunctory temple liturgies. The solution isn't abandoning forms but reinfusing them with covenant affection—fasts that share bread with hungry, feasts that honor the Lord of harvest (Isaiah 58:6-7). Evaluating worship by transformed lives, not production value, realigns metrics with Hosea's prophetic plumb line.

5.2.2 ▪ Priests Who Forgot Torah—Leadership Failure (Hosea 4:6)

"My people are destroyed for lack of knowledge; because you have rejected knowledge, I reject you from being priest," laments Hosea 4:6. Priests, guardians of Torah, had embraced cultural popularity over covenant fidelity. Instead of teaching Yahweh's statutes, they "feed on the sin of My people" (Hosea 4:8), profiting from sacrificial volume. Leadership amnesia trickled down: if the pulpit grows cold, the pews will freeze. Scripture warns that stricter judgment awaits teachers (James 3:1); Hosea demonstrates consequences when shepherds sleep. Modern parallels include leaders prioritizing branding over biblical literacy, or sermon series shaped more by trending hashtags than scriptural exegesis. The cure involves re-anchoring pulpits in the whole counsel of God, cultivating Berean congregations testing messages against scripture (Acts 17:11). Leadership training must marry academic rigor with personal holiness, preventing credentialed wolves. Hosea's indictment compels boards to evaluate success by spiritual health, not just attendance graphs. Repentant priests can rebuild trust through transparent confession and covenant recommitment, proving restoration is possible.

5.2.3 • Syncretistic Liturgies—Baal Forms with Yahweh Labels (Hosea 2:11-13)

Israel's worship blended Yahweh's name with Baal's fertility rites—wheat and wine offerings dedicated to the wrong source (Hosea 2:5). God vows to remove festival mirth because the gifts were credited to lovers, not Him (Hosea 2:12-13). Syncretism appeals because it offers spiritual expediency—hedging bets across deities. Contemporary syncretism surfaces when churches conflate nationalism with gospel, self-help clichés with biblical discipleship, or prosperity slogans with sacrificial cross. Architecture of worship may mimic celebrity concerts, reinforcing consumer identity rather than covenant servant-hood. Hosea exposes that label changes cannot sanctify pagan substance. Genuine liturgy re-narrates identity: Exodus-Passover reminds slaves of liberation by grace, not technique. Churches counter syncretism by catechesis, creeds, and historic prayers anchoring worship in apostolic faith. Table and font stand as boundary markers, refusing to host foreign gods. Prophetic preaching names modern Baals—success, sexuality, security—calling congregations to wholehearted allegiance lest God dismantle counterfeit altars again.

5.2.4 • Consequences of Hollow Worship—Social Injustice and Ecological Collapse

Hosea links ritual emptiness to societal fracture: "There is no faithfulness...therefore the land mourns" (Hosea 4:1-3). Broken covenant horizontally produces lying, murder, theft, and adultery, while earth itself withers—beasts, birds, fish perish. Worship shapes ethics; when God is treated like vending machine, neighbors become disposable. Modern data echo prophecy: religious hypocrisy correlates with youth apostasy, and environmental degradation often

132

accompanies exploitative economies. Amos underscores similar logic—songs drowned out by injustice (Amos 5:23-24). Jesus condemns temple corruption feeding widows' houses (Mark 12:40). Therefore, revitalizing intimacy with God has public ramifications—justice flows when worship is true. Eco-theology draws on Hosea to promote creation care as covenant fidelity. Churches in polluted neighborhoods can lead cleanup efforts as acts of repentance. Social enterprise ministries emerge, turning tithes into micro-loans reversing generational poverty. Thus, hollow worship's curse can be reversed when intimacy births mercy and creation stewardship.

5.3. Pathways to Intimacy—Rekindling Covenant Passion

5.3.1 ▪ Awe and Reverence—Recovering Fear of the Lord (Proverbs 9:10)

"The fear of the LORD is the beginning of wisdom," yet modern spirituality often swaps reverence for casual familiarity. Awe is not terror that repels but wonder that magnetizes; Isaiah trembles, then is commissioned (Isaiah 6:5-8). Hosea balances tenderness with dread, portraying God as both lion and lover (Hosea 11:10). Practices to cultivate awe include meditating on transcendence passages (Job 38-41), stargazing while reciting Psalm 8, or visiting historical cathedrals where architecture dwarfs ego. Corporate worship can re-introduce silence after Scripture readings, allowing grandeur to settle. Preachers avoid flippant jokes about holy matters, embedding sacred weight without joylessness. Creation documentaries showcase cosmic scale, prompting "Who is man?" humility. Fasting fosters dependency, reminding bodies of Creator-creature distinction. Fear of God detoxes fear of people, empowering prophetic obedience. Wisdom decisions emerge when choices are filtered through question: "Does this honor His holiness?" Recovering awe guards intimacy from sentimentality, rooting affection in reality of majesty.

5.3.2 ▪ Vulnerable Prayer—Psalms of Lament, Joy, and Examen

Intimacy grows where masks drop. The Psalms model naked soul language—rage (Psalm 137), despair (Psalm 88), ecstasy (Psalm

103). Hosea's call to "take words with you and return" (Hosea 14:2) invites honest articulation. Lament prayer gives voice to injustice survivors, preventing polite suppression that stunts relationship. Joyful praise counters cynicism, training hearts to notice goodness. The *examen* reviews day with gratitude and sorrow, spotlighting God's footprints and personal drift. Prayer journals record dialogues, enabling retrospective faith. Breath prayers—"Jesus, Son of David, have mercy"—inject vulnerability into daily routines. Corporate services can include open-mic petition segments, welcoming raw words. Spiritual friendships practice "listening prayer," holding silence after sharing to discern God's reply. Such practices dismantle performance pressure, allowing God to meet real persons, not edited avatars.

5.3.3 ▪ *Scripture as Dialogue, Not Mere Study—Lectio & Imaginative Reading*

Bible intimacy arises when text becomes conversation rather than academic specimen. *Lectio divina*'s four movements—read, meditate, pray, contemplate—transform passages into personal address. Imaginative reading places disciples in narrative scenes: smelling sea spray with Peter (Luke 5), feeling dust underfoot in Hosea's Israel. This engages right brain, enabling encounter beyond analysis. Study notes remain valuable, but dialogue invites questioning back—"Lord, why did You phrase it this way?" Margins fill with prayers, not just outlines. Group lectio fosters communal discernment; diverse insights surfacing reveal Spirit's multi-coloured voice. Memorization internalizes dialogue cues; verses surface in traffic or board meetings, continuing conversation. Digital lectio apps prompt daily, integrating scripture with modern rhythms. Scholars attest neuroplastic benefits: slow repetitive reading increases empathy and reflection. Thus, scripture becomes meeting place, not museum exhibit.

5.3.4 ▪ *Practicing Presence—Brother Lawrence, Breath Prayer, and Micro-Moments*

Brother Lawrence washed dishes "for the love of God," proving ordinary tasks can host extraordinary communion. Practicing presence means intentional awareness of God's nearness throughout day, not merely during devotions. Breath prayers synchronize inhalation-exhalation with phrases like "Abba...I belong to You." Smartphone reminders—"Pause"—cue 60-second reorientation at work. Walking mindfulness: each footstep a silent Kyrie eleison. Before email, whisper "Speak, Lord" to remember ultimate audience. Set "doorway triggers"—every threshold crossed evokes blessing prayer for occupants. Presence practice redeems idle moments: elevator rides, red lights, diaper changes become altars. Neuroscience shows such micro-pauses reset stress, aligning physiology with peace (Philippians 4:6-7). Failures to remain aware are opportunities, not defeats—simple return echoing prodigal's homecoming. Over time, constant communion dethrones compartmentalization; boardroom and prayer closet feel alike under God's gaze. Presence saturates ethics: you cannot exploit client while conscious of Christ nearby. Thus, micro-moments stitch intimacy into daily fabric, fulfilling Hosea's longing for knowledge as lived reality, not liturgical cameo.

5.4. From Symbol to Substance—Sacrament as Encounter

5.4.1 ▪ *Baptismal Identity—Remembering the Beloved Voice (Matthew 3:17)*

Christian initiation does more than mark church membership; it plunges disciples into Trinitarian life. At Jesus' baptism the heavens open, the Spirit descends, and the Father's declaration—"This is My beloved Son, with whom I am well pleased" (Mt 3:17)—establishes identity before achievement. Paul insists our baptism unites us to that same death-and-life narrative (Rom 6:3-5), so the Father's voice now envelopes every son and daughter. Early church liturgies amplified the drama: candidates faced west to renounce the devil, turned east to confess Christ, and emerged from water wrapped in white, echoing new-creation garments (Gal 3:27). Remembering baptism, then, combats the amnesia Hosea lamented; when shame mocks—"Not My People"—the font whispers, "Beloved, chosen, washed" (Hos 1:10; 1 Pet 2:10). Practically, believers can trace the cross on foreheads during morning showers, rehearse Romans 8:1 while drying off, or celebrate baptism anniversaries with candle-lit meals. Pastors might sprinkle congregants during renewal services, letting droplets preach incarnational grace. In counseling, baptismal

135

identity anchors recovery; addicts learn that relapse cannot erase divine naming, though it calls for fresh repentance. For global missionaries, baptism becomes prophetic witness: public water grave defies ancestral spirits and state ideologies. Thus, baptism is not past tense ceremony but present-tense identity marker—a living sacrament that keeps intimacy louder than accusation.

5.4.2 ▪ Eucharist as Covenant Meal—Realigning Desire and Memory

The table where bread is broken and wine poured is Hosea's reversal of Israel's miscredited harvests (Hos 2:8–9). Jesus takes Passover symbols and reframes them around His own body and blood (Lk 22:19–20), offering more than remembrance—He offers participation in the New Covenant reality (1 Cor 10:16). Weekly, fortnightly, or even daily celebration recalibrates appetites: consumer cravings meet Sabbath rest as believers receive rather than achieve. The liturgy retells the gospel in four verbs—take, bless, break, give—forming disciples into Eucharistic people who expect their lives to be similarly broken and given for the world. Early Christians called the cup *pharmakon athanasias*—medicine of immortality—expecting tangible grace, not bare symbolism. Fencing the table with self-examination (1 Cor 11:28) maintains relational integrity; yet exclusion is temporary and aims at restored fellowship, echoing Hosea's tough love (Hos 5:15; 6:1). Multi-ethnic congregations embody eschatological banquet previews (Rev 7:9), proving that intimacy with God levels social hierarchies. Families can extend table theology by praying, "Remember Jesus," before ordinary meals, fusing daily bread with sacramental imagination. When pandemic restrictions halted physical gatherings, many rediscovered fasting-for-longing, illustrating that absence can intensify hunger for presence. The Eucharist ultimately trains memory: instead of replaying sin loops, minds rehearse cruciform love until forgiveness feels more real than failure.

5.4.3 ▪ Corporate Worship Design—Curating Spaces for Genuine Encounter

Sanctuaries preach before sermons start. Lighting, seating, and symbols either foreground God's transcendence or showcase

136

performers. A cross-centered focal point reminds worshipers they are participants around the Lamb, not spectators at a show (Rev 5:6-14). Call-to-worship passages shift attention from weekday chaos to divine address (Ps 95:1-7). Liturgy that moves through adoration, confession, assurance, Word, table, and sending choreographs Hosea 6:1-3's rhythm of return, healing, and going. Acoustic design—voices loud enough to drown self-consciousness yet soft enough to hear congregation—embodies church as choir. Visual art from varied cultures resists monocultural myopia, affirming global bride. When technology serves rather than dominates—screens enhancing text for inclusion, not laser shows—it underscores presence over performance. Silence moments after readings let Scripture settle; prayer kneelers invite bodily humility. Accessibility ramps and braille bulletins preach hospitality, revealing a God who knows every sheep. Feedback loops (surveys, testimonies) keep designers responsive to Spirit fruit, not trendy metrics. Ultimately, space becomes sacrament: our architecture of worship incubates architecture of the heart.

5.4.4 ▪ Avoiding Liturgical Consumerism—Participatory vs. Spectator Modes

In consumer culture, worship risks becoming religious entertainment. Hosea watched Israel "love the sacrifice" itself (Hos 8:13)—a dynamic alive in playlist-driven attendance where song selection dictates church choice. Counter-formation begins by emphasizing congregational voice over amplified stage. Rotating lay readers, intercessors, and Communion servers decentralize platform power (1 Cor 14:26). Testimony slots interrupt polished flow, reminding assembly that real lives, not production value, are the fruit Jesus seeks. Offering liturgies that dedicate salary slips, volunteer hours, and even ecological pledges expand giving beyond money. Children's contributions—art displays, scripture memory recitations—teach full-body ecclesiology. Digital streaming retains interactive chat prayers and post-service Zoom rooms, resisting passive "church-flix" bingeing. Metrics shift: leaders celebrate baptisms, reconciled relationships, and mission engagement over attendance spikes. Teaching dismantles celebrity myths by spotlighting unsung saints—janitors, caregivers—who embody Jesus during weekdays. Questions for reflection ("What word stood out?") at sermon end cue dialogical posture. Over time, consumers

137

morph into co-lovers of God, fulfilling Hosea's vision of knowledge expressed in community fidelity.

5.5. Ethics Flowing from Intimacy—Love, Justice, and Mercy

5.5.1 ▪ Knowing God and Loving Neighbor—1 John 4 Integration

John declares, "Whoever loves is born of God and knows God" (1 Jn 4:7), making neighbor-love diagnostic of Divine acquaintance. Hosea perceived the same: absence of *hesed* among people signaled bankruptcy toward God (Hos 4:1). Intimacy produces ethical overflow; sap determines fruit. Practical outworking includes forgiveness rhythms—daily releasing grievances as reminder of personal absolution (Mt 6:12). It spawns advocacy: those ravished by grace defend immigrants (Dt 10:18-19) and unborn alike, refusing partisan selectivity. Hospitality to "the least of these" (Mt 25:40) becomes sacramental handshake with Christ Himself. Love also corrects; admonishing wandering siblings (Jas 5:19-20) guards family integrity. Urban churches mentor youth, cutting violence through presence. Rural congregations share harvest with foodbanks, living out gleaning laws (Lev 19:9-10). Government petitions and fair-trade shopping practices utilize civic levers. Annual "Love Our City" weekends mobilize thousands for cleanup and free medical clinics. As saints practice neighbor-love, confidence before God grows (1 Jn 4:17-18), illustrating ethics' feedback loop into intimacy.

5.5.2 ▪ Compassion as Covenant Reflex—Hosea 11 and the Prodigal Father

Hosea 11 paints God teaching Israel to walk, a parent cradling stubborn toddlers, while Luke 15's father sprints toward returning son. Both texts reveal covenant compassion that acts before apology. For disciples, mercy becomes reflexive rather than occasional project: noticing tears, they instinctively offer comfort (Rom 12:15). Churches establish benevolence funds disbursing aid within 48 hours, mirroring swift hug of prodigal dad. Counseling ministries extend sliding-scale therapy, acknowledging emotional poverty. Prison-letter writing teams reflect God visiting captives (Mt 25:36).

138

Compassion also means truth-telling—interventions for addicts prevent greater ruin, echoing father's earlier release of prodigal to pigsty. Refugee sponsorship embodies embrace across borders. Story-sharing nights invite marginalized voices to center mic, dignifying humanity as image-bearers. Compassion fatigue is countered by Sabbath and shared leadership, sustaining long-term tenderness. Thus, intimacy transforms reaction time: grace moves first, just as Father ran.

5.5.3 • Vocational Holiness—Marketplace Witness Rooted in Relationship

When people know God, Monday cubicles become altars. Daniel's prayer habits (Dan 6:10) birthed ethical excellence in governance; likewise believers calibrate spreadsheets by truth, not loopholes. Intimacy fuels transparency—honest bids, wage equity, environmental stewardship—as offerings to Bridegroom. Teachers pray over seating charts, seeking Spirit insight for traumatized students. Nurses view every bed as Gethsemane, staying awake with suffering ones (Mk 14:37). Artists reject plagiarism and create culture that hints resurrection beauty. Entrepreneurs tithe company profit and embed justice clauses in supply chains. Performance reviews include character metrics: kindness, collaboration. Work prayers such as "Lord, partner with me in this email" maintain presence awareness. Sabbath boundaries declare dependency; refusing 24/7 hustle confesses God's providence. Vocational holiness evangelizes silently—colleagues ask for reasons behind peace, opening 1 Pet 3:15 conversations. Hosea's marketplace corruption indictment is thus reversed by Spirit-empowered labor.

5.5.4 • Generosity and Hospitality—Tangible Proofs of Interior Knowledge

Intimate knowledge dethrones scarcity; one who hears Father's "all I have is yours" (Lk 15:31) can share without fear. Early believers sold property to meet needs (Acts 4:34-35), displaying gospel arithmetic where love multiplies resources. Regular tithing disciplines supply lines of mercy, funding local missions and global church planting. Budget audits identifying "luxury creep" free funds for scholarships. Hospitality extends generosity into time and space—dining tables become micro-Eucharists where strangers taste the Kingdom. Diverse menus honor guests' cultures, reenacting Revelation's multi-ethnic feast. Spare bedrooms host foster children or international students, embodying adoption gospel. Digital hospitality includes listening on video calls, bridging pandemic isolation. Generosity also addresses systemic issues: churches partner with credit unions for fair lending, fight food deserts with community gardens. Giving testimonies inspire others, countering consumer narrative. Gratitude journaling fuels cheerful giving; awareness of received grace begets outgoing flow. Thus, stewardship becomes sacrament of intimacy, visible answer to Hosea's plea for *steadfast love*.

5.6. Barriers to Knowing—Idols, Distraction, and Religious Performance

5.6.1 ▪ Modern Baals—Success, Security, and Spectacle

Ancient Baal promised rain; modern equivalents promise fulfillment through metrics—likes, income, influence. Success idol whispers, "You are what you achieve," hijacking identity formation. Security idol hoards savings, firearms, or gated communities, denying Fatherly care (Mt 6:26). Spectacle idol seeks constant novelty, making boredom intolerable, thus sabotaging contemplative prayer. Indicators of captivity include anxiety spikes when market drops, envy over colleagues' promotions, or compulsive event-hopping. Hosea shows God stripping resources to expose impotence of such gods (Hos 2:9). Detox involves Sabbath rest, anonymity seasons (serving offstage), and generosity that pries fingers off security blankets. Biographical study of biblical figures—Joseph in prison, Hannah before miracle—show intimacy forged in apparent failure. Fasting from news cycles undercuts spectacle addiction. As idols lose grip, knowledge of God fills vacuum, echoing Hosea 14:8: "What have I to do with idols? I am like a flourishing pine."

5.6.2 ▪ Digital Overload—Attention Economy vs. Undivided Heart

Smart phones deliver Bacchanal buffet of stimuli 24/7, fragmenting focus essential for deep communion. Studies show average user taps phone 2,600 times daily. Push notifications become pseudo-prayer bells, discipling reflexes toward distraction. The psalmist's one-thing desire (Ps 27:4) feels impossible amid infinite scroll. Digital rule of life introduces boundaries: scheduled check-ins, grayscale mode, notification culling, and device curfews. Contemplative practices reclaim neural pathways: 20-minute scripture meditation rewires default toward stillness. Sabbatical days offline re-sensitize to birdsong and Spirit whispers. Families establish charging stations outside bedrooms, promoting sleep and marital intimacy. Churches designate "digital detox" retreats mirroring Hosea's wilderness wooing. Tech stewardship, not demonization, is goal—apps can also cue prayer or track gratitude. When attention re-centralizes on God, presence thickens; multitasking soul regains singular gaze.

5.6.3 ▪ Perfectionism in Devotions—When Quiet-Time Metrics Replace Communion

Spiritual disciplines easily morph into scorecards: chapters read, minutes prayed, journals filled. Hosea's Israel multiplied sacrifices; modern counterparts multiply checkboxes. Perfectionism breeds guilt on skipped days, making God a disappointed taskmaster. Grace reframes disciplines as dates, not duties. Jesus commends Mary's one thing over Martha's many (Lk 10:42). Practical shift: set relational intention ("to enjoy You") before opening Bible. Vary forms—walk-prayer, art meditation—to escape rut. Missed time becomes opportunity for mercy practice—confess, restart, not self-flagellate. Accountability partners ask about delight, not numbers. Spiritual directors help tailor rhythms to personality and season of life. Children or caregiving responsibilities demand flexibility; God meets in diapers changed for love's sake. Perfectionism hides pride—earning favor—so gospel assurance must saturate. When metrics submit to friendship, disciplines blossom as conduits, not cages.

5.6.4 ▪ Healing Shame and Fear—Psychological Obstacles to Divine Proximity

Many avoid intimacy because early wounds project onto God—a harsh father, fickle caregiver. Adam's fig leaves persist as chronic church busyness. Hosea depicts this dynamic: Israel flees when guilt exposed (Hos 6:1). Healing begins by naming emotions in safe community; psalms validate anguish (Ps 13). Theology of adoption (Rom 8:15) replaces orphan scripts. Trauma-informed prayer invites Jesus into memory scenes, rewriting narratives with comfort. Christian counseling integrates EMDR and scripture to desensitize triggers. Regular Eucharist counters body shame by welcoming embodied participation. Acceptance imagery—Father running, robe covering—anchors imagination. Fear of judgment dissolves under perfect love (1 Jn 4:18), enabling honest examination without terror. Testimonies of healed shame cultivate hope contagion. As emotional barricades lower, knowledge of God flows unhindered, fulfilling Hosea's promise "they shall blossom like the vine" (Hos 14:7).

5.7. Cultivating Communal Cultures of Intimacy

5.7.1 ▪ Small Groups as Spiritual Greenhouses—Shared Practices & Mutual Care

Small groups function like climate-controlled hothouses in which fragile seedlings of intimacy grow sturdy before being transplanted into the harsher climates of everyday life. Acts 2:42-47 sketches just such micro-communities—people devoting themselves to apostolic teaching, table fellowship, prayers, and joyful generosity—so the Spirit's warmth is distributed evenly across the body. For modern congregations, a "greenhouse rule of life" clarifies rhythms: a weekly gathering that features lectio divina, confession rounds, shared intercession, and a practical service plan. Breaking bread in living rooms dissolves stage-audience dynamics, allowing gifts hidden on Sunday mornings—like compassion, hospitality, or prophetic insight—to emerge. Each member is encouraged to articulate a "God-sighting" from the week, training collective eyes to recognize Emmanuel in mundane hours (Matthew 28:20). Accountability happens gently: partners text a midday reminder of agreed-upon disciplines, turning phones from distractors to discipleship tools. When crises strike—a lost job, mental-health flare, sudden grief—the group mobilizes meal trains, childcare, and financial relief faster than centralized benevolence funds, embodying Galatians 6:2's command to bear one another's burdens. Multiplication, however, is built in; once a group exceeds twelve adults, two co-leaders apprentice under the original host, preparing to "plant" a new greenhouse so intimacy doesn't evaporate into anonymity. Curriculum cycles through head, heart, and hands content to avoid Bible-study monotony: eight weeks in a gospel, six in a lament psalm, four doing neighborhood prayer-walking. Regular "story nights" let one member share a spiritual autobiography, forging empathetic bonds that outlast petty offenses. Annual retreats create immersive space for extended silence, bonfire confession, and covenant renewal. When small groups adopt local projects—school-mentoring or elder-care visits—they translate greenhouse growth into missional fruit, proving knowledge of God issues in love of neighbor. Thus, by intentional design and Spirit dependence, small groups incubate covenant intimacy large gatherings can only preview.

5.7.2 • *Intergenerational Storytelling—Passing Down Testimonies of Knowing*

Psalm 145:4 commands, "One generation shall commend Your works to another," establishing legacy as a communal discipline rather than sentimental hobby. Hosea himself is evidence: the prophet's marriage and his children's renamed identities became a living parable for subsequent generations wrestling with idolatry. Churches nurture this hand-off through "Remember Nights," where retirees share faith milestones next to teens fresh from mission trips, echoing Israel's corporate rehearsal of Exodus at Passover. Digital archives collect video testimonies categorized by theme—financial miracle, healing, perseverance through doubt—forming an on-demand cloud of witnesses (Hebrews 12:1). Children's ministries invite elders to tell how they first sensed God's call, turning Sunday-school classrooms into miniature Hebrews 11 galleries. Family-style services once a quarter scrap age-segregated programming; toddlers wave flags during worship while grandparents speak blessings, blending generational scents into fragrant incense. Storytelling is honest about valleys: miscarriages, bankruptcies, and prodigal seasons are narrated alongside breakthroughs, safeguarding youths from prosperity illusions. Home groups adopt nursing-home residents as honorary grandparents, swapping letters that become spiritual heirlooms. Parents practice Deuteronomy 6:7 at dinner tables, prompting kids, "Where did you notice God today?" and sharing their own answers. Annual church calendars include "Ebenezer Sunday," where stones inscribed with answered prayers are stacked near the altar, giving tactile memory aids. Listening

143

seminars train members to ask open questions—"What was hardest in that season?"—so that storytellers feel valued, not rushed. Reciprocal mentoring flips hierarchy: a tech-savvy 16-year-old helps an octogenarian with email, while receiving wisdom on prayer. Such narratives weave a tapestry where intimacy with God is seen as attainable across life stages, dissolving youth-culture bias and ageist dismissal simultaneously.

5.7.3 ▪ Prophetic and Contemplative Streams—Balancing Word and Spirit

Healthy communities breathe with two lungs: prophetic edge and contemplative depth. The prophetic stream prioritizes bold declaration—calling injustice to account like Hosea, speaking timely encouragements (1 Corinthians 14:3), and discerning cultural idols. The contemplative stream cultivates interior stillness—desert fathers' silence, Ignatian imagination, and lectio divina rhythms. Without the prophetic, spirituality can settle into introspective cocoon; without the contemplative, activism can fray into burnout or shrillness. Practically, leadership teams allocate rhythms: Monday night intercession laced with prophetic listening, Tuesday morning centering-prayer circle open to all ages. Training equips members to test prophecy via Scripture, community affirmation, and fruit inspection (1 Thessalonians 5:19-22), ensuring charismatic fire does not scorch. Silent retreats include debrief time where participants share insights that may carry prophetic weight, integrating streams. Sermon prep teams use contemplative exegesis, sitting with the text before outlining points, so proclamations rise from pregnant silence rather than content factories. Artists collaborate with justice committees—painting lament murals after local tragedies and facilitating healing vigils—merging contemplation with witness. Conflict-resolution processes begin with two minutes of centering prayer, inviting Spirit discernment before dialogue. Annual vision meetings pair strategic plans with extended worship night, acknowledging plans prosper only under divine gaze (Psalm 127:1). The synergy of streams nurtures balanced intimacy: knowing God in both whispered encounters and courageous proclamation.

Israel's priests failed because they "forgot" God amid busy altar traffic (Hosea 4:6). Modern ministers risk similar amnesia when calendars overflow with meetings, metrics, and marketing. Cultivating intimacy starts at the top: leaders live as presence carriers before program architects. Rule of life covenants require daily silence, weekly Sabbath, quarterly retreat, and annual study leave—guardrails that keep souls ahead of sermons. Elders pool continuing-education funds not only for conferences but for spiritual-direction cohorts. Staff meetings open with 20-minute lectio or examen, so decisions grow from communion. Metrics widen: board dashboards now track conversational prayer hours and lay-leader multiplication alongside budget lines. Leadership reviews ask, "How is your love for Jesus?" before "What are your KPIs?"—mirroring Jesus' breakfast question to Peter (John 21:15). Succession planning includes character apprenticeship, ensuring next generation inherits presence priorities. Pastors model vulnerability by naming their counselors or sharing spiritual struggles judiciously, normalizing dependence. Email curfews and tech-free staff lunches protect attentiveness. Sermon series on intimacy are paired with leaders demonstrating it—inviting congregants into prayer retreats or phone-free pilgrimages. When emergencies erupt, leaders respond first with collective prayer, then action, showing trust precedes strategy. Over time, organizational culture shifts: volunteers sign up not to fill slots but to join relational mission; budgets flow toward formation spaces, not just stage upgrades. Program excellence remains, but it is animated by the aroma of leaders who have been with Jesus (Acts 4:13).

5.8. Eschatological Consummation—Face-to-Face Knowledge Forever

5.8.1 ▪ "Then I Shall Know Fully"—1 Corinthians 13:12 and Beatific Vision

Paul likens current revelation to a dim mirror of polished bronze; one day, clarity will eclipse every theological debate. In the beatific vision—beholding God unveiled—intimacy reaches incandescent plenitude. This hope stands on the resurrected Christ's promise that "the pure in heart will see God" (Matthew 5:8). Seeing is knowing: the Greek *epignōsomai* underscores full experiential awareness. Such vision is transformative; "we shall be like Him because we shall see Him as He is" (1 John 3:2). Thus sanctification is telescopic: present glimpses pull character into future glory. Mystics like Julian of Norwich and Jonathan Edwards anchor their writings in this promise, fueling present affection. Meditation on beatific hope stabilizes saints amid obscurity—suffering loses sting when ultimate unveiling is assured (Romans 8:18). Teaching on heaven must transcend harp clichés, painting relational fulfillment where infinite facets of divine beauty unfold eternally (Ephesians 2:7). Art—icons, music—serves as appetizer, hinting at forthcoming feast. Spiritual disciplines are now re-interpreted as rehearsal for face-to-face communion, diminishing legalism. In pastoral care, dying believers are reminded of approaching clarity, turning fear into anticipation. Ultimately, the beatific horizon dignifies every partial knowledge pursuit, assuring faithful interpreters their questions will one day be answered in person.

5.8.2 ▪ The Wedding of the Lamb—Ultimate Union (Revelation 19:7-9)

Revelation's climactic metaphor swaps throne-room courtroom for wedding aisle: history ends not with mere acquittal but with covenant consummation. The bride's linen, "the righteous deeds of the saints," reveals that intimacy produces attire suitable for union. Echoes of Hosea abound—the betrothal vows ("I will betroth you to Me forever," Hos 2:19) find cosmic scale. Eucharist is the appetizer; the marriage supper is main course. Invitations are issued broadly ("Blessed are those invited"), underscoring evangelism's urgency— who would hoard RSVPs? The scene marries transcendence and tenderness: thunderous hallelujahs surround the Lamb, yet focus is relational union. Preaching this wedding inoculates against cynical end-times terror; believers anticipate celebration, not mere survival bunker. Earthly nuptials become prophetic symbols; faithful spouses mirror anticipated union, offering living apologetic. Single Christians glean hope that ultimate romance transcends temporal marital status, validating their vocation. Liturgies might incorporate bridegroom/wedding language, reminding congregations each gathering is rehearsal dinner. In suffering, the promise that "He will wipe every tear" (Rev 21:4) positions God as intimate spouse, not distant deity. Finally, wedding eschatology energizes holiness: brides keep lamps trimmed (Matthew 25:1-13), churches guard purity, and justice work arranges feast tables for future guests.

5.8.3 • *No Temple Needed—God as Immediate Light (Revelation 21:22-23)*

John's final vision shocks first-century readers: a city without temple is unthinkable. The absence signals fulfilled purpose— mediating structures obsolete because God's presence permeates every cubic inch. This contrasts Hosea's era, where priests monopolized access; future intimacy is democratized. The Lamb's glory replaces sun and moon, suggesting perpetual enlightenment— no dark nights of the soul. Sacred-secular divide evaporates; cooking pots become holy (Zechariah 14:20-21). Architecture of daily life— commerce, art, governance—operates in transparent light, negating corruption. Worship is continuous yet effortless; there's no "going to church," only living before unveiled face. Mission ceases—glory covers earth as waters sea (Habakkuk 2:14)—but creativity continues, nations bring cultural treasures into the city. Temporal sacraments like baptism and Eucharist retire, their reality absorbed in direct fellowship. This vision motivates urban theology: church plants pursue city renewal as foretaste. Environmental ethics emerge; if future earth is radiant with glory, stewardship now anticipates then. Prayer shifts from plea for presence to celebration of forthcoming omnipresence. Pain of absence many feel in spiritual dryness is met with promise of everlasting saturation.

5.8.4 • *Living the Preview—How Future Intimacy Shapes Present Pursuit*

Eschatology is not escapist day-dreaming but practical fuel for discipleship. John writes, "Everyone who has this hope purifies himself" (1 John 3:3); vision of seeing God propels ethical tightening. Hope produces resilience: martyrs endure because crown awaits (2 Timothy 4:8). Sabbath becomes weekly dress rehearsal for eternal rest, teaching ceasing and delight. Generosity flows when treasures are stored where moth and rust cannot destroy (Matthew 6:19-21). Evangelism adopts invitational tone—"Come join the approaching wedding feast"—rather than fearmongering. Artists paint Revelation's imagery, catechizing imagination. Counselors use future hope to treat despair; cognitive therapy anchored in new-creation narrative re-scripts hopeless thoughts. Conflict resolution leverages horizon: opponents destined to worship side-by-side learn to forgive now (Ephesians 4:32). Vocation reorients—work today practices skills useful in renewed earth craftsmanship. Creation care intensifies, understanding cosmos is not disposable backdrop but future dwelling. Spiritual warfare acknowledges victory secured; resistance becomes enforcement of Christ's triumph. Finally, liturgy ends with eschatological charge—"Go in peace to love and serve the Lord," sending believers as emissaries of coming kingdom. Thus, knowing God eschatologically loops back to intimacy now; rehearsal and premiere inform one another until curtain rises on unending communion.

Conclusion When rituals become windows instead of walls, a quiet revolution unfolds. Study turns into dialogue, prayer becomes shared breath, sacraments taste like home-cooked grace. The fruit proliferates outward: mercy for neighbor, integrity in vocation, resilient hope in suffering. And all of it is only the first flutter of eternity's promise, for a day is coming when faith will give way to face-to-face knowing and the dim glass will shatter in the light of the Lamb. Until that unveiling, the Spirit whispers Hosea's ancient plea into every distracted soul: *Come back to love; press on to know the Lord.* May every practice, every silence, every act of justice in our lives answer that invitation, so the world can see a people whose rituals pulse with the unmistakable presence of their God.

Chapter 6. Sowing Righteousness—Daily Habits of Holiness

Stand in an autumn field at dusk and you will feel Hosea's sermon beneath your feet. Grain stubble rustles in the wind, reminders that months earlier invisible seeds were pressed into dark soil and trusted to a process no human could speed up. *"Sow righteousness for yourselves; reap the fruit of steadfast love"* (Hosea 10:12) is the prophet's invitation to a similar, slow miracle in the soul. Holiness, he insists, is not a weekend conference or a single heroic decision; it is agriculture—a succession of deliberate habits, hidden seasons, and patient waits that eventually swell into harvest. This chapter explores that earthy spirituality: how confession loosens compacted ground, how ordinary prayers fall like nightly dew, how Sabbath functions as crop rotation, and how every small act of integrity deposits another kernel in God's furrowed field. We will trace the seed principle from Genesis gardens to Jesus' parables, discovering that the Spirit supplies both the life within the seed and the weather that ripens it. Our aim is to replace hurried perfectionism with faithful planting, knowing that the One who calls us also guarantees the yield.

6.1. The Seed Principle—Why Holiness Grows Slowly

6.1.1 ▪ Hosea's Agricultural Imagery—Ploughing Fallow Ground (Hosea 10:12)

Hosea is preaching to farmers, so he chooses a verb they feel in their lower backs: *plough*. Every spring the Galilean peasant walked behind an iron-shod wooden beam that tore open crusted terrain. In spiritual terms, unploughed fields picture hearts that prefer comfort to cultivation; soil becomes hard through neglect, not malevolence. The prophet's command, "Break up your fallow ground," implies intentional disruption of habits calcified by routine. Genuine repentance resembles that blade—sharp, intrusive, but ultimately life-producing. The plough never passes only once; farmers make successive furrows, teaching us that conviction must penetrate layers of rationalization. Hosea links ploughing to *time*—"for it is time to seek the Lord"—reminding disciples that seasons of opportunity can be missed if soil stays untouched. Jesus extends the metaphor when He explains the parable of the sower; seed that lands on a trampled path cannot germinate (Matthew 13:4, 19), underscoring Hosea's warning. Modern ploughing may involve digital detox, financial transparency, or counseling sessions where denial finally cracks. It feels violent because it is: sin's grip tightens like packed earth, and the Spirit's blade must break it open. Yet every slice makes room for oxygen, rainfall, and root systems. Farmers know that deeper furrows mean stronger stalks able to withstand wind; likewise, thorough repentance creates resilience against future temptation. Ploughing is noisy, messy, and public—neighbors see dust clouds— but harvest later vindicates the spectacle. Refusing the plough invites weeds, erosion, and starvation; embracing it inaugurates hope. Ultimately, Hosea's imagery corrects microwave spirituality by celebrating the holy ache of preparation.

6.1.2 ▪ Jesus' Parables of the Soil—Hidden Growth and Sure Harvest (Mark 4:26-29)

Jesus advances Hosea's lesson with a kingdom vignette: a farmer scatters seed, sleeps, wakes, and "the earth produces by itself" (Mark 4:28). The Greek *automátē* suggests innate power; holiness sprouts because divine life pulses inside gospel seed. Growth is hidden—

150

germination happens underground beyond the farmer's analytics—teaching disciples to trust unseen processes. The blade, ear, and full grain appear in sequence, mirroring incremental sanctification outlined by Paul: first babes in Christ, then mature (1 Corinthians 3:1). Anxiety about speed cannot accelerate photosynthesis; likewise, self-condemnation cannot force spiritual fruit. Faithful sowers maintain two tasks: spread seed broadly and guard optimism while waiting. The parable counters perfectionism: the field looks barren for days, yet invisible roots prepare visible shoots. Jesus' subsequent mustard-seed story magnifies disproportionate outcomes—tiny beginnings yield expansive shade (Mark 4:30-32)—so no habit is trivial. A single practice of thanking God in morning traffic could one day mature into stable joy under persecution. Hiddenness protects tender sprouts from trampling eyes seeking instant results. Community plays the role of patient watchers, celebrating small green tips rather than demanding golden sheaves prematurely. The Spirit choreographs sunlight-scripture, rainfall-prayer, and nutrient-fellowship in perfect proportion. Eventually, "the harvest has come," and the sickle is wielded—a picture of both seasonal breakthrough and final eschatological gathering. Therefore, daily holiness embraces obscurity, trusting that what germinates in private will, in God's timing, bless the public square.

6.1.3 ▪ From Genesis Gardens to Revelation Trees—A Canon-Wide Farming Motif

Scripture opens in a garden and closes in a garden-city, framing redemption as horticultural enterprise. Genesis 2:8 depicts the Lord planting Eden, placing humanity as caretakers—not mere consumers—highlighting vocational dignity. After the fall, thorns curse the ground (Genesis 3:17-18), introducing resistance that mirrors spiritual struggle. Prophets envision reversal: deserts blooming like crocus (Isaiah 35:1) and ploughshares replacing swords (Micah 4:3). Jesus resurrects in a garden and is mistaken for a gardener (John 20:15), a subtle signal that new creation tilling has begun. Revelation 22:2 shows the tree of life yielding fruit monthly, healing nations—agricultural productivity perfected. This canonical sweep anchors Hosea's metaphor in salvation history; our daily habits participate in cosmic reclamation of wilderness. Gardening requires partnership: humans sow, God gives increase (1 Corinthians

3:7). Adam's failure to guard Eden contrasts with believers' call to guard heart gardens (Proverbs 4:23). Biblical feasts tied to harvest—Firstfruits, Pentecost, Tabernacles—rhythmically rehearse dependence on divine agronomy. Thus, sowing righteousness taps into an ancient storyline: tending soil anticipates eschatological orchards. Each journaled gratitude, each resisted resentment, is a shovel of compost on kingdom rows, cooperating with the Gardener who promises blooms beyond curse.

6.1.4 ▪ Patience and Process—Rejecting Instant-Spirituality Myths

Modern culture microwaves everything—meals, news cycles, even dating. Holiness, however, resists acceleration. James exhorts farmers to "be patient until the Lord's coming" (James 5:7), linking eschatological hope to agrarian waiting. Impatience tempts shortcuts: legalism (spray-painted fruit) or burnout (constant striving). Hebrews 6:12 urges imitators of those who inherit promises "through faith and patience," pairing trust with time. Sanctification resembles strength training; muscles tear before growing, and rest days catalyze repair. Spiritual disciplines likewise need recovery—Sabbath breathes between weekdays of sowing. Patience is not passive; farmers weed, irrigate, and fend off pests, illustrating active participation without obsession over growth metrics. Social media testimonies of instant deliverance encourage but cannot define normative pace; even Paul spent silent years in Arabia (Galatians 1:17-18). Church cultures that celebrate incremental victories—one less anxious reaction, one honest confession—cultivate sustainable disciples. Patience also nurtures compassion toward others' unfinished stories; seeing yourself as slow-growing grain curbs judgmental pruning of neighbors' sprouts. Waiting seasons teach lament and trust—spiritual muscles absent in quick-fix religiosity. Ultimately, rejecting instant-spirituality myths frees believers to enjoy the journey, marveling at each shoot while celebrating certain harvest secured by the faithful Farmer (Philippians 1:6).

6.2. Preparing the Heart-Soil—Repentance and Identity

6.2.1 ▪ Breaking Up Hard Ground—Confession as Spiritual Tilling

Confession is spiritual agriculture's first mechanical act; it fractures the crust of denial covering hidden sin. David's imagery in Psalm 32:3-4 likens unconfessed transgression to drought that saps vitality, proving hardened soil starves roots. True confession names specifics—Bartimaeus didn't ask for "stuff"; he asked for sight (Mark 10:51). Vague apologies—"Sorry if I did anything"—are like shallow scratches, not deep furrows. Hosea models corporate confession: "Assyria cannot save us...we will say no more 'Our God' to what our hands have made" (Hosea 14:3). Writing sins on paper and burning them at the foot of a cross sculpture offers tangible release, engaging kinesthetic learners. Public confession, wisely guided, dismantles isolation; hearing another's vulnerability emboldens honesty, fostering James 5:16 healing. Confession also includes listening: inviting the Spirit to spotlight blind spots (Psalm 139:23-24) prevents selective tilling. Timing matters—daily examen keeps soil soft, averting deep compaction requiring heavy machinery later. Confession ends not in shame trenches but in tilled rows ready for gospel seed; assurance of pardon (1 John 1:9) rains grace, preventing legalistic dust storms. Over years, habitual confession forms humility reflexes, making repentance quicker and recovery swifter, much like seasoned farmers adjusting to soil feedback instinctively.

6.2.2 ▪ Root Removal—Forgiving Others to Make Space for Grace

Unforgiveness embeds like taproots; surface weeding leaves bitterness regenerating. Hebrews 12:15 warns of roots of bitterness defiling many, indicating communal contagion. Jesus uses agricultural hyperbole—uprooting mulberry trees by faith (Luke 17:6)—to describe forgiveness's power. Practical root removal starts with naming offenders and the debts owed, mirroring ledger language in Matthew 18:24-27. Emotional honesty precedes pardon; denial cements roots deeper. Forgiveness is decision and process: a legal cancellation followed by seasons of emotional weeding when memories sprout resentment shoots. Visualizing placing debts at the cross links forgiveness to Christ's payment (Ephesians 4:32).

153

Counseling tools like imagined chair dialogues can release stored anger. Corporate liturgies such as passing the peace rehabilitate relational soil each Sunday. Forgiven ground receives nutrients; studies show reduced stress and improved cardiovascular health among forgivers, echoing Proverbs 14:30. Communities practicing mutual forgiveness cultivate trust, enabling seeds of exhortation to germinate without fear. Ultimately, root-free soil welcomes gospel rain; where grudges linger, holiness withers.

6.2.3 • Baptismal Identity as Fertile Base—Beloved Before Productive

Before Jesus performed miracles, the Father affirmed Him as beloved (Matthew 3:17); identity precedes productivity. Paul grounds moral exhortations in positional truth—"since you are chosen, holy, beloved" (Colossians 3:12). Baptism signifies burial of performance-based righteousness and resurrection into grace fields (Romans 6:4). Farmers know soil composition matters; baptismal identity enriches heart-soil with nutrients of acceptance, freeing seedlings from striving for worth. Daily affirmation—"I am God's child, dearly loved"—acts like fertilizer spikes. When temptation whispers, "Prove yourself," identity answers, "It is written—I already am His." Community reminders—addressing one another as "brother, sister"—echo this status. Failure thus becomes setback, not ejection; seedlings bend but roots remain secure. Identity also fuels risk: beloved children experiment in obedience without terror of rejection. Hosea, renaming Lo-Ammi to "My People" (Hosea 2:23), illustrates identity fertilizer reversing sterility. Saturating in baptismal reality—through creed recitation, cross-signing, communion—maintains nutrient levels that legalism or shame would leach.

6.2.4 • Guarding the Seedbed—Monitoring Thought-Weeds and Toxic Narratives

Jesus warns that enemy sows weeds among wheat (Matthew 13:24-25), a strategy paralleled by intrusive thoughts that choke holiness. Cognitive neuroscience confirms: unattended mental scripts strengthen neural pathways. Paul prescribes vigilance—"take every thought captive" (2 Corinthians 10:5)—turning believers into field

154

scouts. Practical weeding involves identifying distorted narratives: "I'm alone," "Change is impossible," "God's holding out." Scripture counter-narratives uproot lies; Romans 8 demolishes abandonment fears. Journaling exposes repetitive weed patterns; prayer partners assist in spot-spraying truth. Media discernment prevents seedbed contamination—constant doom-scrolling plants anxiety seeds. Gratitude practice competes with complaint weeds, as Colossians 3:15 connects thankfulness to peace. Sleep hygiene matters; exhausted soil succumbs to invasive species of irritability. Sabbath acts as herbicide, disrupting productivity weeds that strangle serenity. Mental health professionals can help dismantle trauma-rooted brambles. Guarded seedbeds raise yield capacity; holiness flourishes when thought ecology is intentionally curated.

6.3. Rhythms of Word and Prayer—Daily Watering Practices

6.3.1 • Morning Lectio—Scripture as Dew (Deuteronomy 32:2)

Moses likens Torah to dew, gentle moisture that prevents seedlings from scorching in early heat (Deuteronomy 32:2). Morning lectio divina positions hearts to receive that dew before emails sun-blast attention. Four movements frame the practice: *lectio* (read slowly), *meditatio* (ponder phrases), *oratio* (respond in prayer), and *contemplatio* (rest). Selecting short passages—five to ten verses—avoids information overload. Reading aloud engages auditory senses; underlining verbs spotlights divine action. Silence between readings soaks soul-soil. Journaling a sentence distills essence into portable nourishment. Over weeks, themes recur, weaving a tapestry of divine conversation. Aligning lectio with church calendar—Gospels in Advent, Psalms in Lent—syncs personal rhythm with global body. Even five-minute sessions outweigh sporadic marathons; consistency saturates like daily dew. When travel disrupts routine, audio scripture on earbuds recreates moisture in transit. Dew vanishes by midday, reminding disciples to carry memorized droplets into tasks.

6.3.2 • Mid-Day Examen—Checking Soil Moisture of the Soul

Farmers inspect fields midday to adjust irrigation; likewise, the Ignatian *examen* at lunch recalibrates interior climate. Five steps guide: presence invite, gratitude recall, review of feelings, confession, and forward look. Gratitude first acknowledges morning dew effects; review identifies pests—envy at a meeting, impatience in traffic. Confession pulls weeds before roots deepen. Forward look asks Spirit for grace in pending afternoon challenges. A two-minute version—breathe, name one gift, one glitch, receive mercy—fits busy schedules. Smartphone alarms labeled "heart check" prompt practice. Sharing examen insights weekly with mentor fosters accountability. Mid-day prayers echo Psalm 55:17 rhythm—morning, noon, evening petitions. They convert slump hour into sacred hinge, preventing drift.

6.3.3 • Nighttime Psalm-Praying—Closing the Day in Trust (Psalm 4:8)

Bedtime is sowing time for tomorrow's peace; Psalm 4:8 promises sleep for those dwelling secure in God. Reciting compline psalms (4, 91, 134) releases anxieties accumulated. Parents blessing children mirror Aaronic benediction, planting seeds of identity. Journaling day's highlights cements gratitude neuro pathways, shown to improve REM quality. Candle-lit prayer corners signal brain to wind down, replacing blue-light cortisol spikes. Confessing failures prevents rumination; assurance sentences like Romans 8:1 tuck conscience in. Visualization of handing worries to Jesus (1 Peter 5:7) quiets racing thoughts. Some play gentle worship instrumental tracks, mimicking ancient lullabies. Husbands and wives holding hands to pray knit marital field rows. Nightly routine acts as irrigation timer, ensuring roots drink before dark dryness.

6.3.4 • Weekly Scripture Memory and Group Reflection

Memorization stores water reservoirs for drought days; Jesus quoted Deuteronomy in wilderness combat (Matthew 4:4-10). Choosing one verse weekly—written on cards, phone lock-screens, or sticky notes—focuses attention. Repetition during mundane tasks—dishwashing, jogging—cements neural networks. Group reflection sessions every week test recall and explore application, fostering communal scaffold. Creative methods—song lyrics, hand motions—aid diverse learners. Memory challenges across small groups spark holy competition, raising participation. Verses selected follow sermon series, integrating corporate teaching. Testimonies of on-the-spot recall during crises encourage perseverance. Over a year, 50 verses equip minds with doctrinal anchors and pastoral comfort. Internalized Word turns heart into self-watering planter; even if external disciplines falter, reservoir releases life.

6.4. Embodied Disciplines—Holiness in Habits

6.4.1 ▪ Sabbath Rest—Letting the Field Lie Fallow for Renewal

Ancient farmers rotated fields or left them fallow every seventh year so soil microorganisms could recharge; Sabbath embodies this agronomic wisdom for the soul (Ex 20:8-11; Lev 25:4). One day of ceasing reminds us that God's provision predates our productivity, echoing manna rhythms where double supply on day six liberated day seven (Ex 16:22-30). Sabbath begins with stop, not slow; turning off devices, closing laptops, and storing to-do lists signals trust. Prayer of release—"I resign as general manager of the universe"—prepares heart-soil for divine rain. Celebration, not dour asceticism, characterizes biblical rest: good meals, laughter, and unhurried walks mirror Edenic delight (Gen 2:2-3). Families can light candles Friday evening, read Psalm 92, and bless children, weaving identity into weekly cadence. Singles craft communal Sabbaths—brunch with friends, nature hikes—avoiding isolation's trap. Social justice dimension emerges when employers honor employees' rest, breaking Pharaoh's brick quota mentality (Deut 5:14-15). The day also functions as prophetic signpost; against hustle culture, it preaches that human worth exceeds output. Sabbath can include examen: reviewing week's grace and grief, then casting cares onto Jesus (1 Pet 5:7). Resistance will arise—urgent emails, internal guilt—but discipline trains nerves to embrace liberation. Over time, Sabbaths accumulate like crop rotation, boosting long-term fruitfulness and preventing burnout soil erosion. Jesus practiced restorative rest by retreating to solitary places despite crowds (Mk 1:35), showing rest fuels subsequent mercy. Ultimately, Sabbath is

157

eschatological rehearsal; weekly cease-fires anticipate eternal rest where toil's curse is lifted (Heb 4:9-11).

6.4.2 • Fasting and Simplicity—Pruning Excess for Fruitfulness

Pruning shears remove living branches to enhance yield; fasting snips appetites so spiritual sap flows to essential fruit (Jn 15:2). Biblical fasting spans food (Mt 4:2), drink (Est 4:16), entertainment (Dan 10:2-3), and even sexual intimacy by mutual consent (1 Cor 7:5). Hosea's Israel gorged on grain and wine yet credited Baal; fasting re-centers hunger on true Source (Hos 2:8). Begin with sunset-to-sunset fast once a month, coupling mealtimes with Psalm 63 meditation. Simplicity partners fasting daily: curated wardrobes, minimalist budgets, and decluttered schedules free bandwidth for prayer. John the Baptist's camel-hair ethic confronted consumerist Judea, while Jesus warned against barns that eclipse kingdom generosity (Lk 12:16-21). Financial simplicity reallocates tithe to mercy projects, uprooting greed. Environmental simplicity— reducing plastic, driving less—honors Creator and neighbor. Fasting is incomplete without feasting; breaks should involve Eucharistic gratitude, not binge relapse. Corporate fasts—Lent, crisis intercession—unite body in collective repentance (Joel 2:15-17). Journaling hunger pang reflections surfaces idol dependencies: caffeine for mood, streaming for escape. Medical conditions need adjustments—fasting social media can prune just as effectively. As branches lighten, prayer acuity sharpens; Isaiah 58 links true fasting to justice rivers, proving pruning is missional.

6.4.3 • Stewarding the Body—Sleep, Exercise, and the Temple Metaphor (1 Cor 6:19-20)

Paul names bodies "temples of the Holy Spirit," elevating physical stewardship to spiritual obedience (1 Cor 6:19). Sleep is temple maintenance: research shows seven-to-nine hours restores cognitive soil, reducing irritability that chokes relational fruit (Ps 127:2). Create wind-down rituals—dim lights, read a Psalm, pray compline—to reinforce circadian rhythm. Exercise mirrors Paul's athletic analogies (1 Cor 9:24-27); moderate routines—walking, swimming, resistance bands—circulate oxygen to brain for sharper scriptural meditation. Nutrition choices—whole grains, fruits, water—feed microbial allies shaping mood; Daniel's vegetable fast demonstrates dietary discipleship (Dan 1:12-15). Posture matters: stretching breaks during desk work prevent tension that distracts from prayer. Sexual purity respects temple boundaries; fleeing immorality preserves neural wiring for covenant intimacy (1 Thess 4:3-5). Sabbath includes body delight—naps, leisurely cycling—countering Gnosticism that devalues flesh. Illness seasons call for compassionate pacing; Paul told Timothy to take wine for stomach, affirming holistic care (1 Tim 5:23). Medical appointments and therapy sessions are stewardship acts, not faithlessness. When bodies falter, weakness witnesses Christ's power (2 Cor 4:7); stewardship is faithfulness, not idolization.

6.4.4 ▪ Digital Rule of Life—Attention as Fertilizer or Pest

In attention economy, algorithms plough mind-fields for profit; disciples must erect trellises guiding digital vines toward fruit. Begin by auditing screen-time stats—awareness precedes change. Craft boundaries: phone sleeps outside bedroom, news limited to two check-ins, social media sabbatical one weekend monthly. Use grayscale mode to dull dopamine colors (Mt 5:29 principle of radical removal). Replace doom-scroll with lectio-scroll—Bible app upon unlock. Curate feeds following theologians, justice advocates, and encouragement pages, turning algorithm into ally. Tech Sabbath policies for families—stack devices during meals—restore table fellowship. Notification triage reserves badges for relational essentials. Digital silence hours invite imaginative play, reading, or neighborhood walks, fertilizing creativity. Accountability apps report browsing to partner, deterring secret weeds. Email disciplines—batch processing twice daily—recover deep-work focus for lectio or study. Celebrate victories; share testimonies during small group, reinforcing communal norms. When relapse occurs, apply gospel not guilt: confess, recalibrate, continue. Ultimately, attention stewarded becomes irrigation channel for Spirit whispers instead of pest infestation.

6.5. Relational Righteousness—Community as Shared Garden

6.5.1 • Accountability Partnerships—Iron Sharpening Iron (Prov 27:17)

Iron sparks fly when blades rub; accountability's friction hones discipleship edge. Partnerships start with covenant commitments: confidentiality, honesty, Scripture centrality. Weekly check-ins cover rhythms—prayer, Word, thought life, emotional health. Specific, not vague, questions pierce armor: "Did you view pornography?" "How did you steward influence at work?" Mutuality prevents hierarchy; each partner both confesses and exhorts, mirroring Christ-centered equality. Text reminders midday provide real-time guardrails. Celebrating wins—sending gif or voice note—builds culture of grace, not inspection. Scripture memorization together (e.g., Titus 2:11-12) arms both for temptation. When lapses happen, quick confession short-circuits shame spirals; partners pray restoration, not impose penance (Gal 6:1). Triads add stability if one partner travels. Technology aids: shared habit-tracker apps log disciplines. Over time, dull corners vanish; speech purified, generosity widened, courage strengthened. Pastor involvement offers oversight but not micro-control. Accountability expands into communal ethos where disciples expect loving inquiry, fulfilling Hebrews 3:13's daily encouragement command.

6.5.2 • Peacemaking and Conflict Repair—Pulling Bitter Roots (Heb 12:15)

Conflict left untended becomes invasive thistle, absorbing relational nutrients. Jesus outlines a three-step weed-pulling in Matthew 18:15-17—private conversation, one or two witnesses, entire church if needed. Private dialog aims at "you gained your brother," valuing restoration over vindication. Non-violent communication techniques—using "I feel" statements, reflective listening—prevent defense. Confession of personal contribution softens soil. If impasse persists, impartial mediators apply biblical wisdom. Forgiveness is decision and process: cancel debt, then re-negotiate trust boundaries. Apology formula—"I was wrong, I'm sorry, will you forgive me?"—releases healing water. Peacemaking anticipates communion; unresolved grudges obstruct Eucharist flow (Mt 5:23-24). Public acknowledgment of systemic wrongs (racism, sexism) extends weeding beyond individuals. Prayer walks through neighborhoods previously sites of division model spiritual landscaping. Annual reconciliation services, foot-washing across cultures, demonstrate visible unity. Peacemaking training equips youth, diffusing school conflicts. Churches collaborating across denominations uproot competitive jealousy. These habits keep relational garden weed-free, enabling shared righteousness harvest.

6.5.3 • *Hospitality Rhythms—Open Tables, Open Hearts*

Abraham's tent flaps open to strangers birthed covenant blessing (Gen 18:1-8); Jesus' ministry consisted of eating and teaching at tables (Lk 7:34). Regular communal meals host kingdom presence. Practice "Friday soup night"—large pot, open invitation, no RSVP. Intentional seat-mixing avoids clique monoculture. Include silence moments for gratitude: guests name one thing God did that week. Story-prompt cards coax quieter attendees. Hospitality extends to exterior: porch lights, communal gardens, lending libraries seed neighborhood trust. Digital hospitality—Zoom coffee with distant member—supplements physical. Economic sharing emerges: fridge stocked for student tenants, emergency micro-grants pooled. Hospitality counters loneliness epidemic, a spiritual drought. Refugee resettlement teams furnish apartments, embodying Matthew 25 welcome. Rule: if you have two lasagnas, invite someone hungry. Table becomes catechesis; prayers, stories, and laughter communicate gospel more palatably than sermon alone. As Hebrews 13:2 notes, angels may be undercover guests, so every meal could entertain heaven.

6.5.4 • *Generational Mentoring—Passing Down Tried-and-True Farming Tools*

Paul tells Timothy to entrust teaching to faithful people who will teach others (2 Tim 2:2), illustrating four generational links. Mentoring pairs seasoned saints with novices: retirees meet young professionals monthly over breakfast. Curriculum flexible—life stories, financial stewardship, spiritual disciplines. Reverse mentoring allows younger tech-savvy believers to help elders, fostering mutual honor. Older women train younger in Titus 2 virtues—household management, kindness, self-control. Mentoring agreements set expectations: confidentiality, frequency, prayer coverage. Skills transferred: how to budget, conflict manage, lead devotion. Intergenerational mission trips bond across ages. Grandparent ministry teams read Bible stories in kids' church. Graduation blessings gift symbolic tools—study Bible, journal—signifying inheritance of craftsmanship. Digital library of testimonies archives legacy wisdom. This flow keeps garden tools sharp and avoids each generation reinventing hoe. Communities thus become multi-aged orchards where sap of intimacy nourishes every ring of growth.

6.6. Missional Fruit—Holiness Turned Outward

6.6.1 • Vocational Integrity—Sowing Righteousness at Work

Colossians 3:23 commands labor "as for the Lord," relocating holiness from pew to office cubicle. Integrity begins with punctuality, honoring employer time. Transparent expense reports, fair pricing, and refusal of bribes root righteousness in economic soil (Prov 11:1). Christians advocate for equitable wages, mirroring Mosaic gleaning laws protecting laborers. Workplace excellence—code review diligence, patient bedside manner—testifies that shoddy work misrepresents the Creator. Prayer teams meet before shifts, sowing peace over stress-heavy environments. Witness often arises from crisis competence; colleagues notice calm anchored in unseen reservoir. Ethics training utilizes Daniel's Babylon story to discuss negotiation between conscience and corporate pressure. Vocational calling language replaces secular/sacred split—plumbers fixing leaks participate in creational stewardship. Performance reviews reference character metrics, rewarding empathy and collaboration. Failures handled with confession, restitution, and process improvement reflect gospel cycle. Tax season becomes worship as honest filings resist culture of evasion. Over careers, vocational integrity yields credibility fields fertile for evangelistic seed.

6.6.2 ▪ *Justice and Mercy Initiatives—Harvest That Feeds the Poor (Isa 58:7-12)*

Isaiah connects true fasting to loosing injustice chains; Hosea echoes concern for widows and fatherless. Church gardens grow produce for food banks, literalizing fruit metaphors. Legal clinics run pro bono, defending tenants against exploitation. Budget line designates 10% to benevolence, mirroring tithe to Levites. Advocacy teams draft letters supporting criminal justice reform. Mercy might mean rotating spare cars for families in transition. Partnership with government programs leverages expertise, avoiding paternalism. Metrics include poverty-reduction data, not just volunteer hours. Storytelling nights platform beneficiaries turned co-leaders, ensuring dignity. Compassion fatigue addressed by Sabbath for volunteers, counseling access. Justice preaching expounds Old Testament jubilee and Jesus' Nazareth manifesto (Lk 4:18). Mercy is not charity alone; systems change aim uproots cyclical poverty. Thus, righteousness harvest becomes real bread on neighbor's table.

6.6.3 ▪ *Evangelism as Seed-Scattering—Trusting God for Germination*

Jesus likens kingdom advance to sowing indiscriminately (Mk 4:14). Personal evangelism adopts conversational storytelling: sharing testimonies not arguments. Prayer-walking sows presence; tract distribution may feel outdated, but digital tracts—links to testimonies—adapt method. Alpha courses, discovery Bible studies, and home dinners create safe soil. Evangelists trust Spirit timing: some soils require ploughing of prayer years before seed sprout. Celebrate sowing, not just conversions, preventing outcome idolatry. Workplace faith flags—desk verse, integrity—spark curiosity like sprouting shoots. Short-term mission trips partner with local churches, sowing mutual encouragement. Follow-up ensures seedlings receive discipleship water—new-believer groups meet weekly. Re-evangelism of church-hurt individuals requires patient listening, re-sowing trust. The harvest belongs to the Lord; our joy is scattering from full bags daily (Ps 126:6).

Romans 8 groans for redemption; disciples respond by stewarding earth entrusted in Genesis 2:15. Community composting diverts waste, enriching gardens. Church buildings add solar panels, reducing carbon witness. Stream clean-ups alongside local environmental groups open relational doors. Preachers include eco-justice in sermons, connecting pollution to love of neighbor. Youth groups plant trees on Arbor Day, learning Hosea's promise of cedars (Hos 14:6). Liturgical calendar marks "Season of Creation" with prayers for endangered species. Financial stewardship includes divesting from exploitative industries. Retreats in wilderness teach awe, restoring ecological imagination. Urban congregations install rooftops beehives, producing honey for communion bread. Simple choices—reusable cups at coffee hour—model holiness in mundane. Creation care ties back to eschatology: Revelation's healed river motivates present river cleanup. By cultivating literal soil, believers enact prophetic sign that new creation is sprouting already.

6.7. Seasons of the Soul—Persevering through Drought and Storm

6.7.1 ▪ Dry Times: Watering by Faith, Not Feeling (Jeremiah 17:7-8)

Spiritual drought arrives when prayer feels like voicemail and scripture loses its savor, yet the prophet promises that the tree "planted by water" keeps green leaves even in heat because its roots have tapped unseen streams. Those subterranean aquifers symbolize covenant realities that do not fluctuate with mood: adoption (Rom 8:15), justification (Rom 5:1), and the indwelling Spirit (John 14:17). During dryness, disciples shift from sensation-based metrics to faith-based irrigation, rehearsing promises aloud the way farmers run drip lines under cracked soil. They borrow psalmist language— "O God, You are my God; earnestly I seek You in a dry land" (Ps 63:1)—knowing honesty itself opens fissures where grace can seep. Practical strategies include "anchor texts," a short list of verses memorized for recitation when motivation tanks; Jeremiah 31:3 ("I have loved you with an everlasting love") is a common lifeline. Communal rhythms help: attending worship even when goosebumps are absent places oneself beneath corporate sprinklers of truth. Journaling evidence of God's past faithfulness provides historical moisture; reading prior entries reveals patterns of God showing up after earlier arid seasons. Body stewardship matters—sleep deprivation mimics spiritual drought, so eight hours may be the most godly act of the night. Mini-Sabbaths—ten-minute walks without earbuds—let creation's oxygen feed flagging spirits. Spiritual directors counsel against drastic life changes during drought; root systems should stay in familiar soil until rains return. Intercessors stand in gap, praying "cloud the size of a man's hand" (1 Ki 18:44) over drought victims. Eventually drizzle comes—an unexpected lyric pierces numbness—and gratitude erupts precisely because absence heightened thirst. Thus, dry times, far from evidencing divine rejection, often deepen root reach, preparing for future fruit that flashy showers could never sustain.

6.7.2 ▪ Unexpected Storms: Trials that Aerate Compacted Hearts (James 1:2-4)

Just as thunderstorms fracture hardpan and drive nitrogen into ground, life's sudden trials—job loss, betrayal, diagnosis—crack self-reliant shells and oxygenate faith. James urges believers to "count it all joy" because storms test and strengthen perseverance, the spiritual equivalent of deeper topsoil. Biblical landscapes are storm-rich: Job loses everything in a single day, disciples face a Galilean squall (Mk 4:37), and Paul's missionary voyage wrecks off Malta (Acts 27). Each event dislodges assumptions about control, pushing saints toward raw dependence. Practical aeration involves lament prayers that refuse cliché optimism; Psalm 22 models how to scream "Why?" while remaining tethered. Community acts as windbreaks: small-group members deliver meals, babysit kids, or simply sit in hospital hallways—presence that keeps the uprooted from blowing away. Storm journaling captures real-time thoughts, preventing revisionist history that later minimizes pain and stunts empathy for others. Wise counselors help identify theological lightning rods—false beliefs like "God owes me safety"—that attract excessive fear. After the tempest, reflective debrief gathers insight: Which virtues sprouted? Which idols washed downstream? Insurance adjusters count financial loss; believers count character gain (Rom 5:3-5). Storm scars can become prophetic witness— Paul's shipwreck story converts Publius's island (Acts 28:7-10).

Weather apps predict physical storms, but spiritual vigilance—daily examen—spots barometric drops of pride or complacency that invite future gales. Ultimately, storms remind gardens they are not greenhouses; exposure to elements, under the Vinedresser's supervision, produces resilient harvest able to nourish others in their own crises.

6.7.3 ▪ Dormant Winters: Hidden Roots and Quiet Growth

In temperate zones, winter fields look dead, yet root systems thicken underground, storing carbohydrates for spring burst. Spiritual winters manifest as plateau seasons—no new ministry doors, familiar disciplines feel routine, communal applause quiets. The temptation is to uproot in search of perpetual summer, but Isaiah notes that "those who wait on the LORD shall renew strength" (Is 40:31). Waiting is not idleness; it's subterranean activity: deeper reading in classic theology, slow memorization of long passages like Romans 8, and relational investment with family often sidelined by busy harvest months. Winter invites rest—extended Sabbaths or sabbaticals that heal micro-tears in emotional muscle. Retreat centers function like insulated cold frames, offering reflective environments to notice subtle root expansion. Holy Spirit uses obscurity to purify motive; when affirmation hibernates, service becomes love offering rather than résumé building (Col 3:23). Nature walks during snowfall teach hush; crunching steps mirror Lectio pauses between scriptures. Liturgical calendar reinforces rhythm—Advent's quiet longing, Lent's contemplative austerity—countering culture's endless summer of consumption. Spiritual mentors reassure: bulbs require chill hours to bloom; likewise, certain callings germinate only after protracted dormancy (Moses' Midian decades, Ex 3). Winters often precede directional clarity—Jesus spent thirty silent years before three public. Tracking subtle joys—a child's question, an insight during dishes—keeps hope embers glowing. When spring finally arrives—fresh vision, renewed energy—it carries authority authenticated by subterranean depth.

6.7.4 ▪ Celebratory Harvests: Practicing Gratitude Festivals

Harvest in Israel meant songs, dances, and firstfruits waving (Lev 23:9-22). Psalm 126 captures laughter of captives returned, sowers who "went out weeping" now carrying sheaves. Modern disciples need embodied thanksgiving to seal gains and prevent pride. Family "Ebenezer jars" collect weekly answered prayers; on Thanksgiving each slip is read aloud, recreating Feast of Booths nostalgia under living-room ceilings. Small groups host potluck testimonies, pairing each dish with a story of God's provision—financial rice, reconciliation soup—engraining narrative in taste buds. Tithing raises are firstfruits acts: before upgrading lifestyle, believers allocate harvest to kingdom projects (Prov 3:9). Creative liturgies invite congregants to write blessings on grain stalks pinned to sanctuary walls, visual crescendo of gratitude. Celebration includes rest—post-harvest farmers hold barn dances, while churches sponsor retreats treating volunteers to nature and naps. Musical playlists shift from lament minor keys to jubilee major chords, echoing Miriam's timbrel (Ex 15:20). Yet humility checks remain: Deuteronomy 8 warns abundance can birth amnesia; therefore, harvest festivals incorporate confession of dependence. Sharing surplus guards against hoarding; gleaning events invite marginalized neighbors to partake, fulfilling Ruth-Boaz precedent. Photographs catalog milestones, later fueling faith during next drought. Ultimately, well-celebrated harvests become seed for future sowing—gratitude motivates renewed obedience, ensuring righteousness cycle continues.

6.8. Eschatological Harvest—Final Rewards of Faithful Sowing

6.8.1 ▪ "Those Who Sow in Tears…"—Psalm 126 and Ultimate Joy

Psalm 126 frames exile as tearful seeding and restoration as mouth-filling laughter; eschatology universalizes that pattern. Every hidden intercession, unnoticed act of righteousness, or sacrificial gift—often accompanied by tears—drops into God's eternal acreage. Revelation 7:17 promises the Lamb will wipe tears, not because memories vanish, but because grief is transmuted into grain. Jesus uses childbirth metaphor—anguish turning to joy when life appears (John 16:20-22)—illustrating eschatological harvest. Paul assures Galatians they will reap "at the proper time" if they don't give up (Gal 6:9); that proper time may outlive earthly calendars. Martyrs' blood, like seed, sprouted exponential church growth and will be publicly honored (Rev 6:9-11). Hope of ultimate joy fortifies perseverance amid injustice delays; farmers endure long night watches believing dawn will reveal green shoots. Imagination of reversal fuels lament integrity: tears become irrigation, not futility. Psalm 56:8 says God stores tears in a bottle—inventory for future celebration. Thus eschatology validates emotional honesty and energizes steadfast sowing.

6.8.2 ▪ Bema-Seat Evaluation—Wood, Hay, or Precious Grain? (1 Cor 3:12-14)

Paul envisions believers standing before Christ's judgment seat where fire tests work quality. Holiness habits are construction materials—self-promotion posts equal hay, secret generosity equals gold. Sowing righteousness with eternal motives ensures harvest survives Eschaton flames. Awareness of evaluation is motivational, not paralyzing; grace secures identity, reward accents faithfulness. Daily decisions—whether to plagiarize, gossip, or shade taxes—take on cosmic weight. Leaders must build on Christ, not charisma; megachurch size may vanish if discipleship depth is shallow. Ordinary saints gain surprising honor—cup-of-water givers (Mt 10:42) perhaps shine brighter than conference headliners. Teaching on rewards corrects nihilism; effort matters though salvation is gift. Spiritual disciplines become investment, not legalistic chore—compound interest awaits. Fear of loss keeps complacency at bay; yet even workers whose projects burn "will be saved" (1 Cor 3:15), highlighting mercy's floor beneath reward's ceiling. Conversation about bema seat in small groups spurs accountability, sharpening kingdom priorities. Living for applause of nail-scarred hands dethrones addiction to likes.

6.8.3 ▪ New-Creation Agriculture—Trees Bearing Fruit Every Month (Revelation 22:2)

John's finale pictures river-lined trees yielding twelve crops yearly—perpetual abundance without seasonal scarcity. This imagery fulfills Ezekiel 47 and Hosea 14:7 promise that Israel will "blossom like the vine." Agricultural cycles merge: sowing and reaping co-exist in synchrony, hinting at redeemed time. Leaves heal nations, indicating ecological and relational wholeness; racism, pollution, pandemics cease under chlorophyll of grace. City-garden synthesis means holiness and culture integrate: art galleries beside orchards, work as worship. Gardening vocation continues—humans still "reign," suggesting ongoing stewardship. No curse means no thorns; effort enjoyable, productivity unfrustrated. Present creation care rehearses future caretaking, aligning eschatological hope with ecological ethic. Prophets' dream of beating swords into ploughshares actualized; budgets shift from weapons to tractors. Eternal fruit implies learning and growth don't stagnate—new flavors of righteousness expand forever. Hints of this appear when churches feed hungry or restore habitats, previewing healing leaves. Thus, sowing righteousness now harmonizes with cosmic horticulture slated for Revelation's city.

6.8.4 ▪ Living Today with Tomorrow's Harvest in View

Eschatology bends time backward, letting future certainty influence present choices. Hebrews 11 heroes acted on promises unfulfilled, greeting them from afar; we have clearer sight of the coming garden-city. Budget lines, career paths, and leisure activities undergo harvest audit: "Will this decision yield eternal grain?" Hope tempers suffering; light momentary afflictions work "an eternal weight of glory" (2 Cor 4:17). Ethical integrity becomes logical—why sow weeds that eternal fire will burn? Generosity makes sense—treasures wired ahead cannot depreciate (Mt 6:19-21). Mission gains urgency; guest list for Lamb's supper drives evangelistic creativity. Worship warms; songs of New Jerusalem out-sing dirges of cultural despair. Family discipleship highlights harvest—bedtime blessings include "May you shine like stars forever" (Dan 12:3). Sabbath foreshadows rest, fasting foreshadows feasting, lament foreshadows comfort, embedding eschatology into weekly liturgy. Even recreation shifts: hiking becomes rehearsal for new-earth exploration; art previews endless creativity. Living future-first cultivates resilience, generosity, and purpose—fruits that verify Hosea's sow-now, reap-later gospel.

Conclusion The combine does not roll through the field the day after planting, nor will the full stature of Christ be visible in us overnight. Yet the laws of the kingdom are as sure as the laws of botany: *"in due season we will reap, if we do not give up"* (Galatians 6:9). Every overlooked apology, every screen switched off for prayer, every quiet act of generosity is a seed sown into God's perennial acreage.

169

There will be dry spells that test resolve and storms that threaten tender shoots, but the Farmer is skilled at bringing beauty from buried beginnings. One day—perhaps in a sudden breakthrough, certainly in the age to come—the field will whiten with a harvest that makes every small obedience shine like wheat under a noonday sun. Until then, keep your hand on the gospel plough, your eyes on the promised horizon, and your heart open to the gentle rain of the Spirit. Sow, water, wait—and watch steadfast love rise from the furrows.

Chapter 7. Broken Cisterns—Misplaced Trust in Human Power

Stand on a Judean hillside in midsummer and you will understand why ancient people carved cisterns into limestone. Rain falls only a few months each year; the rest of the calendar is dust and thirst. A cracked reservoir, however, is worse than no reservoir at all: it lures you into false security, then abandons you when you most need water. Hosea and his contemporary Jeremiah seized that image to expose a deeper crisis. Israel had not become irreligious—its altars bustled—but it had become self-reliant, patching political pacts, economic schemes, and designer worship into a watertight future that proved anything but. Our century knows the drill. We stockpile credentials, followers, and mutual funds, certain they will slake the next drought. Yet the harder we pump, the faster the bottom drops out. This chapter traces the anatomy of cracked cisterns—how they are built, why they leak, and what happens when an entire culture drinks their dust. More crucially, it shows the way back to the only spring that never runs dry, the covenant God who still invites the parched to "incline your ear and come to Me; hear, that your soul may live" (Isa 55:3).

7.1. The Cracked-Cistern Metaphor—Sources, Symptoms, and Substitutes

7.1.1 • *Jeremiah 2:13 and Hosea's Parallels—Diagnosing Leaky Sources*

Jeremiah distills the human problem into a dual indictment: God's people have forsaken the spring of living water and then expended immense effort digging cisterns that cannot even hold what little rainfall they collect (Jer 2:13). Hosea supplies the case-study evidence. Israel's frantic courtship of Egypt and Assyria, the money spent on calf-shrines in Bethel, and the proliferation of dishonest trade (Hos 5:13; 8:4-6; 12:7-8) each represent a different shovel stroke in the same doomed project. The prophets' brilliance lies in moving idolatry from the realm of exotic statues to the ordinary choices of real economies and foreign policy. A cracked cistern, by definition, leaks slowly; the water line recedes almost imperceptibly, lulling users into a cycle of topping up rather than replacing the system. Spiritually, the first symptom is anxiety—an unrelenting need to refresh a feed, rerun budget projections, or check polls. The second is numbness; brackish leftovers breed bacteria, dulling taste for living water. Jeremiah's phrase "my people have committed two evils" signals that idolatry is not just subtraction (leaving God) but multiplication of effort elsewhere, a double energy drain. Hosea echoes the diagnosis by calling Israel "a silly dove without sense" (Hos 7:11), flapping from branch to branch when a fresh fountain flows a few meters away. The synergy of the two prophets offers a diagnostic tool: trace where energy, money, and emotional bandwidth hemorrhage, and you will likely find a leaking cistern. Finally, both prophets insist the problem is not ignorance of Yahweh's existence but distrust of His sufficiency. The cracked-cistern metaphor therefore exposes unbelief in God's character rather than atheism; the heart silently concludes that Yahweh is either unwilling or unable to satisfy, so contingency plans are dug in limestone. Until this lie is confronted, no amount of moral patchwork will hold.

7.1.2 • Ancient Water Technology—Why Cisterns Seemed a Smart Bet

In a semi-arid land where most rain falls between November and March, storing runoff was a civil-engineering marvel. Israelites carved bell-shaped cavities into soft chalk, plastered walls with hydraulic lime, and directed roof channels into these subterranean vaults. Archaeologists estimate Jerusalem's first-century cistern network held more water per capita than modern Manhattan reservoirs. From a purely pragmatic standpoint, trusting cisterns made sense: they were visible, quantifiable, and, most of the year, full. Springs, by contrast, could be capped by enemies or diverted by earthquakes. Spiritually, the contrast illustrates why tangible strategies—military treaties, cash reserves, charismatic leaders—feel safer than unseen reliance on God. Yet engineers knew plaster cracks under thermal expansion; one seismic tremor could spider-web the lining, and water would disappear overnight. Jeremiah and Hosea exploit that vulnerability: any security system reliant on human maintenance is inherently brittle. Moreover, cisterns hold stagnant water; without inflow, algae multiply and pathogens bloom—apt imagery for spiritual systems that collect yesterday's revelation but receive no fresh word. The prophets are not anti-technology; they are anti-illusion. They remind hearers that even perfect masonry cannot compensate for absence of rain, just as flawless strategy cannot conjure divine blessing. Every cracked cistern therefore becomes a monument to misplaced confidence: an empty cathedral of human ingenuity baking under the sun.

7.1.3 • Functional Idolatry Defined—Good Gifts Turned Ultimate

Idolatry rarely begins with a golden calf; it usually starts with a good gift elevated to ultimate status. Hosea's Israel adored grain and new wine—legitimate blessings of covenant land (Hos 2:8)—but credited Baal, turning provision into deity. Modern believers replicate the pattern when they transform employment into identity, family into salvation project, or wellness into eschatology. Functional idols operate Monday through Saturday while lips sing "Great Is Thy Faithfulness" on Sunday. They demand sacrifices—overtime hours, relational absenteeism, hidden debt—mirroring ancient altars. Like cracked cisterns, these idols require constant topping up yet never satisfy; the moment a KPI is met, the benchmark shifts. Diagnostic questions expose them: What triggers panic when threatened? What justifies moral compromise? Where does the mind drift in spare moments? Hosea labels such pursuits "wind" (Hos 12:1)—frenetic motion, zero hydration. Importantly, functional idolatry distorts perception; blessings appear as wages earned rather than gifts received, hardening entitlement. Recovery begins by re-naming gifts as gifts and re-enthroning the Giver. Thus, the remedy is not ascetic disdain for work or relationship but re-ordering loves so that cisterns become conduits, not containers.

7.1.4 ▪ Modern Cisterns Catalogued—Career, Politics, Platforms, and Pills

If Hosea preached today, he might swap "Assyria" for "401(k)," "Baal shrine" for "Instagram metrics," and "Egyptian chariots" for "legislative majority." Career cisterns leak when layoffs, automation, or plain retirement puncture the identity muffled in job titles. Political cisterns promise salvation every election cycle, yet partisanship fractures families and still leaves potholes in streets. Platform cisterns—follower counts, viral posts—offer dopamine shots but demand constant content sacrifice; one algorithm tweak and influence evaporates. Pharmaceutical cisterns—whether anti-anxiety meds misused or supplement stacks—mask thirst rather than quench it. Even theological systems can calcify into cisterns if they substitute concept mastery for relational reliance. Each modern reservoir shares two traits: maintenance cost inflates over time, and leakage becomes evident only when crisis reveals emptiness. The antidote is not Luddite withdrawal or civic apathy but re-embedding each arena inside first-love devotion to God. Careers become callings, politics becomes neighbor-love conduit, platforms become testimonies, medicine becomes stewardship—channels, never sources.

7.2. Geo-Political Dependence—Trusting Egypt and Assyria Instead of Yahweh

7.2.1 ▪ Hosea 5:13; 7:11—"A Silly Dove" Diplomacy Explained

Hosea likens Israel to a fluttering dove—symbol of naïveté—darting between Egypt and Assyria without landing in Yahweh's nest (Hos

7:11). Historical records confirm frantic envoy traffic during 8th-century power shifts; tribute payments drained treasuries in hope of military umbrellas. The prophets saw beneath the treaties: Israel's leaders believed foreign muscle could compensate for covenant breach. The irony is painful—seeking health from nations God Himself was steering as instruments of judgment (Hos 5:12-13). Modern parallels include smaller states hedging between superpowers or churches chasing celebrity endorsements to shield cultural relevance. Hosea's dove image also critiques impulsivity; doves startle easily, mirroring leaders who act from fear rather than deliberation. The prophet's solution is rootedness: "Return to your God; observe love and justice" (Hos 12:6). Political alliances aren't inherently evil—Joseph served Pharaoh—but must never outrank divine allegiance.

7.2.2 ▪ Military Horsepower vs. Covenant Cloud and Fire (Psalm 20:7)

Psalm 20 contrasts those who "trust in chariots and horses" with those who remember the Lord's name. Egypt's cavalry epitomized Iron-Age deterrence; hiring such regiments seemed prudent. Yet Israel's foundational narrative features exactly zero chariots—only a pillar of fire and a parted sea (Ex 14). By counting horses, kings tacitly denied Red Sea precedent. Deuteronomy 17:16 explicitly forbade accumulating war-horses, anticipating this drift. Hosea 1:7 promises God will "save by the LORD their God, not by bow or horse," underscoring miraculous deliverance over mechanized security. Contemporary equivalents involve missile shields, cyber arsenals, or private militias—technologies God may permit but never as substitutes for trust. When national budgets fatten defense while starving the poor, cracked-cistern logic resurfaces. Scripture does not advocate pacifist naïveté; rather, it insists ultimate safety flows from covenant faithfulness. History vindicates the principle: Gideon's downsized army, Jehoshaphat's choir corps, and Hezekiah's angelic defense illustrate victories disproportionate to hardware. Therefore, communities should pray more resources than they stockpile and measure security by obedience metrics rather than arsenal tonnage.

7.2.3 ▪ Contemporary Parallels—Nationalism, Nuclear Deterrence, and Lobby Power

Nationalism baptizes ethnicity or ideology, proclaiming salvation through geopolitical supremacy. Nuclear deterrence exemplifies mutually assured destruction logic—peace by threat of annihilation—an ultimate cracked cistern if ever there was one. Lobby power, whether corporate or religious, pursues policy leverage believing legislative wins secure kingdom outcomes. Hosea would call this "planting wickedness and reaping injustice" (Hos 10:13). The church's recent flirtations with partisan power reveal temptation to trade prophetic voice for seat at king's table, echoing Israel's treaty seductions. When faith communities tie eschatology to national destiny, they risk idolatry masked as patriotism. Christians can honor nation while resisting Babylon's boasts (Jer 29:7; Rev 18). Engagement becomes stewardship when informed by neighbor-love and tempered by confession of shared human frailty. The cross, not the flagpole, defines victory; resurrection, not reelection, anchors hope.

7.2.4 ▪ Prophetic Posture—Praying for Leaders without Deifying Them

Paul urges Timothy that intercession for kings enables peaceful gospel witness (1 Tim 2:1-2), demonstrating political prayer as missional strategy, not power grab. Prophetic posture blends respect—"Honor the emperor" (1 Pet 2:17)—with willingness to rebuke, as Nathan did David. Practical outworking: churches host nonpartisan prayer vigils after elections, naming officials from all parties, requesting wisdom and justice. Sermons critique policies through biblical lens rather than endorsing platforms wholesale. Congregants are taught to write respectful letters urging righteous laws, while guarding hearts from Messiah projections onto candidates. Liturgies include confessions for national sins—racism, greed—preventing triumphalism. When leaders err, prophets lament and advocate, but never rejoice over downfall; Ezekiel 33:11 notes God takes no pleasure in catastrophe. This balanced posture keeps trust anchored in the King of kings while seeking shalom through earthly governance.

7.3. Economic Strongholds—Silver, Shekels, and Stock Markets

7.3.1 ▪ Hosea 12:7-8—Dishonest Scales and Boasts of Wealth

Hosea exposes merchants who manipulate ephah and shekel sizes, then brag, "In all my labors they cannot find in me iniquity" (Hos 12:7-8). The cracked cistern here is wealth acquired by cunning, promising immunity from judgment. Archaeology unearthed weight sets calibrated to cheat buyers—literally skewed economics. The self-deception—believing divine audit lacks sophistication—mirrors modern tax evasion or exploitative pricing algorithms. Wealth itself is neutral; Abraham was rich. Sin emerges when profit eclipses covenant ethics. Dishonest scales also symbolize distorted self-assessment: we overweigh virtues, underweigh faults. Repentance involves transparent accounting, fair wages (Jas 5:4), and restitution à la Zacchaeus. Kingdom economics values integrity over margin; businesses become witness sites when invoices reflect truth.

7.3.2 ▪ Sabbath Economics—Trust Expressed through Rhythmic Restraint

Sabbath year land rests (Lev 25) and debt-release cycles disrupt accumulation idolatry. Choosing not to plant in seventh year or canceling loans every fiftieth tested reliance on Yahweh, not spreadsheets. Modern Sabbath economics includes closing shops one day weekly, capping CEO pay ratios, and resisting 24-hour trading that never sleeps. Personal application: declining side hustle to preserve family Sabbath, trusting God to multiply six-day yield. Churches practice Sabbath economics by refusing prosperity gospel fundraisers that monetize faith. Such restraint testifies that provision rides on covenant faithfulness, not frantic hustle (Mt 6:33).

7.3.3 ▪ Consumer Culture's Broken Bucket—Debt, Advertising, and Discontent

Advertising spends billions to convince hearts they leak happiness unless refilled with upgrades. Credit cards widen cistern cracks—delivering goods without prior rainfall, then charging interest for

177

evaporated satisfaction. Average household debt statistics echo Hosea's lament of sowing wind and reaping whirlwind (Hos 8:7). Spiritual disciplines like gratitude journaling and contentment fasting (skipping non-essential purchases) plug leaks. Teaching children budgeting and generosity inoculates next generation. Simplicity becomes prophetic protest: wearing clothes till threadbare, sharing tools via neighborhood libraries, enjoying free park concerts. Consumer culture also commodifies spirituality—pay-to-pray apps promising mindfulness packages—further proof of marketing's reach. Recognizing manipulative algorithms allows believers to opt out and reclaim soul bandwidth.

7.3.4 ▪ Generosity and Jubilee—Cracking Mammon's Spell

The surest way to break cistern dependence on money is radical generosity. Jesus prescribes treasure transfer to heaven via alms (Lk 12:33). Jubilee vision—land resets, slaves freed—inspires modern debt-forgiveness initiatives, micro-loan programs, and fair-trade cooperatives. Tithing the first fruits, not leftovers, declares God senior partner in finances (Prov 3:9-10). Spontaneous giving exercises detach fingers from wallets; carrying "blessing cash" to hand out discreetly cultivates readiness. Corporate bodies fund benevolence grants without bureaucratic red tape, mirroring Acts 4:34. Celebrating generosity testimonies shifts culture from scarcity to abundance mindset. Over time, Mammon's enchantment fades; money becomes seed rather than security, irrigating fields of righteousness and joy.

7.4. Religious Engineering—When Worship Becomes a Human Product

7.4.1 ▪ Hosea 8:4-6—Calves of Samaria and Designer Deities

Hosea zeroes in on Samaria's golden calf, a glittering mash-up of Exodus nostalgia and Canaanite iconography. By announcing, "This calf of yours was made by a craftsman" (Hos 8:6), he exposes the absurdity of worshiping a god you can pick up and relocate when the temple floods. Israel had taken Yahweh's liberation narrative, melted it down, and recast it into a manageable, marketable idol. Today, the calf might be a carefully branded worship aesthetic: the

178

perfect logo, LED wall, and merch line that subconsciously whispers, *Our hands made this, so our hands control this.* The danger is subtle—Exodus's calf was called "Yahweh" (Ex 32:5); modern equivalents still carry Christian labels. The deeper sin is not metalwork but power inversion: instead of a Creator shaping people, people shape a creator that validates their preferences. Hosea's language of "throwing silver and gold into molds" parallels church budgets that funnel disproportionate funds into stage tech while mission partners scrape by. The antidote begins with naming the calf: candid leadership audits by outside voices who have nothing to lose by telling the truth. Then comes theological re-education— preaching attributes of God that cannot be shrink-wrapped: His aseity, transcendence, and jealous love. Finally, physical acts— stripping back production for a season, celebrating communion with simple bread—inscribe dependency into muscle memory. Only when the congregation sees the power of the Spirit fall in moments of raw prayer will the calf's luster fade. Hosea promises the calf "will be carried off to Assyria," meaning idols eventually enslave those who built them; better to surrender them now before they betray you later.

7.4.2 ▪ Syncretistic Liturgies—Mixing Baal Techniques with Yahweh Vocabulary

Syncretism did not replace Yahweh; it simply grafted Baal's fertility rites onto His altar. Israel kept the covenant calendar but infused it with sacred sex at the high places, hedging spiritual bets against drought (Hos 2:13). The modern form is doctrinal salad: a Sunday set list that includes psalms next to lyrics from secular self-affirmation anthems, sermons peppered with self-help psychology but allergic to repentance. We drink green juice and read Augustine; we smudge ash crosses and buy crystals "for ambiance." The Old Testament knows this slide: Solomon built Yahweh's temple—then shrines to Chemosh for political convenience (1 Ki 11:4-8). Syncretism thrives on the plausible argument that *all truth is God's truth*, forgetting that covenant loyalty is as exclusive as marital vows. Hosea's cure is courtship language—God will "allure" Israel into the wilderness (Hos 2:14) where extraneous voices are muted. Practically, churches must audit liturgy: does every element—call to worship, confession, songs, benediction—flow from gospel narrative? Catechesis reclaims borders by teaching why the Creed

179

forbids rival stories. Testimony nights spotlight deliverance from New Age or consumerist bondage, exposing counterfeit spiritualities. Finally, leaders model single-heart devotion by refusing to spiritualize business metrics or baptize national myths. When Yahweh vocabulary aligns with Yahweh methods—humble servanthood, sacramental depth—the Spirit has room to breathe again.

7.4.3 ▪ Celebrity Pastors, Algorithm Playlists, and the Spectacle Church

In Hosea's day, priests "rejoiced in the wickedness of the people" because more sin meant more sacrifices and bigger barbecue portions (Hos 4:7-8). Swap "priests" for "platform personalities," and the text reads like a news headline. Social media algorithms reward controversy and charisma, incentivizing spiritual influencers to provoke clicks rather than shepherd souls. Congregants grow addicted to spectacle: drone-camera baptisms, sermon one-liners engineered for Instagram, worship leaders who double as fashion icons. Like cracked cisterns, spectacle requires constant refilling— bigger stage props each Easter to top last year's confetti cannons. Meanwhile, discipleship metrics lag: biblical literacy declines, prayer closets gather dust. Scripture warns that glory stolen from God boomerangs into disgrace (Isa 42:8; Acts 12:21-23). Slow practices counteract dopamine liturgy: extended silence, un-mic'd congregational singing, lectio divina sermons that invite dialogue. Churches can detox celebrity culture by rotating teaching teams, platforming lay testimonies, and submitting preachers to communal discernment. Algorithm playlists get balanced by psalm-chanting and global hymns, widening imaginations beyond current charts. Ultimately, the spectacle church must decide whether to entertain goats or feed sheep; Hosea's sobering image of priests dining on sin should jolt leaders back to shepherd staff, not selfie stick.

7.4.4 ▪ Re-Centering on Word, Table, and Spirit—Means of Grace over Methods of Hype

Hosea's closing vision of a healed Israel features agricultural abundance that only Yahweh can supply (Hos 14:5-7). Likewise, sustainable spiritual life flows from ordinary means of grace:

Scripture preached, sacraments received, prayers lifted. Word: expositional preaching anchors minds, resisting topical fads. Table: weekly communion rehearses dependence—hands open, receiving, not performing (1 Cor 11:26). Spirit: intentional space for intercessory ministry welcomes charisms without pyrotechnics. Together these three form a fountainhead that never cracks because God Himself maintains pressure. Churches can schedule quarterly "Simplicity Sundays," stripping extras to spotlight Word-Table-Spirit synergy. Families replicate rhythm at home: reading the weekly lectionary, sharing bread, and praying for neighborhood needs. Youth ministries teach lectio and examen before guitar riffs, training taste buds early. The metric shifts from attendance spikes to fruit of the Spirit (Gal 5:22-23). As congregations drink deeply from this triune source, programs become channels rather than cisterns, and hype fades in the glow of holy habit.

7.5. Self-Reliance and Psychological Coping—Mindset Cisterns

7.5.1 ▪ Positive Thinking vs. Prophetic Truth—Jerusalem's "Peace, Peace" Illusion

Jeremiah mocked court prophets who chirped "Shalom, shalom" when there was no shalom (Jer 6:14); Hosea's contemporaries likely heard similar pep talks. Modern optimism movements, from Napoleon Hill to "manifesting" influencers, preach that attitude manifests reality. Scripture values hope but grounds it in covenant promise, not neural affirmations. Positive thinking can anesthetize conviction: why repent if I can repetition-chant success? It also collapses under tragedy; Job's friends tried a primitive version, insisting righteous living guarantees blessing—God rebuked them (Job 42:7). Prophetic truth, by contrast, names wounds so they can heal. Churches must resist saccharine theology by preaching lament psalms and Revelation's martyrs beneath the altar. Personal application: journaling both gratitudes *and* griefs, letting God's voice, not willpower, declare worth. Healthy optimism emerges post-confession, like dawn after night watch (Ps 130:6).

7.5.2 ▪ *Anxiety Management without Prayer—Secular Mindfulness Limitations (Phil 4:6-7)*

Mindfulness apps promise calm through breath awareness, yet they cannot answer the anxious question, "What if the worst happens?" Paul offers a thicker peace: prayer, supplication, thanksgiving, and petitions anchored in Christ guard hearts and minds (Phil 4:6-7). Secular mindfulness provides technique without relational anchor; Christian prayer yokes creature to Creator. Studies show faith-infused meditation lowers stress more than generic breathing exercises. Practical synthesis: begin meditation by inhaling "Lord Jesus Christ" and exhaling "have mercy on me." When intrusive thoughts arise, mindfulness says, "Notice, release"; Christian prayer says, "Cast your cares on Him" (1 Pet 5:7). Churches teach "breath prayers," integrating body regulation with theological trust. Psychological therapies remain gifts, but they flourish when plugged into prayer current.

7.5.3 ▪ *Identity DIY—Enneagram, Fitness Apps, and Image Crafting*

Self-help industries sell identity kits: personality tests, bio-hacking routines, curated social feeds. While tools can aid self-awareness, they morph into cisterns when they outshine baptismal naming. Hosea 1 records God renaming Lo-Ammi ("Not my people") into "Children of the living God," proving identity is bestowed, not built. Enneagram insights become idols when wings excuse sin or justify withdrawal. Fitness apps motivate stewardship, yet selfie culture skews body image into worth scoreboard. Image-crafting extends online: LinkedIn profiles stack accolades, harvesting likes for validation. Christian counter-practice: weekly Eucharist places all believers—type 7 or type 4, CrossFit or couch-fit—on equal footing at grace table. Daily declaration "I am hidden with Christ in God" (Col 3:3) undermines merit metrics. Mentors remind protégés that callings evolve; identity rooted in Christ remains when career pivot erases brand.

7.5.4 • *Vulnerable Dependence—Confession, Counsel, and Holy Spirit Help*

Self-reliance addicts fear being a burden, but Scripture depicts saints leaning: Moses on Aaron and Hur, Paul on Barnabas, Jesus on angels in Gethsemane. Confession to one another (Jas 5:16) punctures lone-wolf mythology. Professional counseling integrates Hebrews 4:16—approaching throne of grace through therapist's questions. Dependence on Spirit appears as breath prayer before meetings, listening prayer for guidance, tongues in private devotion building inner man (1 Cor 14:4). Vulnerability fosters community—small groups practicing "high-low-hear-obey" check-ins cultivate honesty. Physical symbols reinforce reliance: kneeling in prayer, open-hand posture. When believers drop stoic façades, Spirit power fills the vacuum (2 Cor 12:9). Over time, dependence becomes joyful default, a living spring that renders cracked cistern strategies unnecessary.

7.6. Consequences of Broken Cisterns—Social, Moral, and Spiritual Fallout

7.6.1 • *Hosea 10:13-15—Harvest of Violence and Political Collapse*

Hosea warns that sowing wickedness yields a "harvest of violence," climaxing in Beth-arbel's horrific war memory (Hos 10:14). Trust in military fortresses backfired when Assyria crushed them, illustrating how cracked-cistern alliances invite destruction they sought to prevent. Societies today witness similar feedback loops: arms races escalate tensions, cyber-espionage provokes retaliation, and violent rhetoric spawns street violence. Political collapse often follows moral rot; when leaders prize polling over truth, institutions erode. Corruption scandals mirror Hosea's statement, "You have eaten the fruit of lies" (Hos 10:13). Nations fracture along tribal lines, echoing Israel's civil strife pre-exile. Therefore, moral renewal is national security; prayer for revival doubles as policy for peace.

7.6.2 • *Fragmented Families and Exploited Poor—Social Repercussions*

Broken cistern economics widens wealth gaps; Israel's elite "add house to house" (Isa 5:8) while widows starve. Hosea notes merchants love to oppress (Hos 12:7-8); modern parallels include predatory loans and gig-economy instability. Family fragmentation surfaces as parents chase career cisterns, leaving children emotionally dehydrated. Divorce rates correlate with financial stress and identity idol failure. Church food pantries fill gap but cannot substitute systemic repentance. Restorative practices—job-training partnerships, financial literacy courses—translate living water into social policy. Adoption and foster care ministries counter orphanhood produced by drug epidemics—another cracked cistern of escape.

7.6.3 • *Environmental Depletion—Land "Mourns" under Idolatrous Management (Hos 4:3)*

Hosea links idolatry to ecological catastrophe: beasts, birds, and fish vanish (Hos 4:3). Modern data confirm: consumption idolatry fuels deforestation, species loss, and climate disruptions. Broken cistern lifestyles—single-use plastics, fast fashion—pollute oceans. Environmental grief can spiral into nihilism unless rooted in biblical hope of new creation. Churches planting community gardens enact micro-Jubilee, healing land and relationships. Preaching integrates creation care into discipleship, dismantling dualistic "souls only" gospel. Sabbath rest for land—crop rotation, reduced chemical inputs—embodies trust. Indigenous theologians offer wisdom on stewarding ecosystems as worship, broadening western perspectives.

7.6.4 • *Personal Burnout and Cynicism—The Soul's Slow Leak*

Cracked cistern striving leaves individuals exhausted; Elijah's post-Carmel collapse showcases prophetic burnout (1 Ki 19:4). Symptoms include compassion fatigue, numb worship, and sarcasm masking disappointment. Social psychologists label it "decision fatigue," pastors call it "soul drought." Technology amplifies leak rate: constant notifications prevent deep replenishment. Without

184

intervention, cynicism metastasizes—leaders fall, congregants deconstruct, hope evaporates. Remedy starts with honest lament, then sabbath rhythms, counseling, and reconnection to living water promises. Re-reading Gospel stories where Jesus restores weary disciples—breakfast on beach (John 21)—rekindles affection. Community sabbaticals grant burnt-out servers permission to sit, receiving instead of pouring. Over time, souls rehydrate; ministry flows again, not from cracked cistern hustle but from fountain overflow (John 7:38).

7.7. Digging Again the Ancient Wells—Practices of Re-Trusting God

7.7.1 ▪ Covenant Remembrance—Story, Symbol, and Testimony Nights

Israel's faithfulness flourished whenever the people paused to remember—stone heaps at the Jordan (Jos 4:6-7), handwritten law for new kings (Dt 17:18-19), Passover reenactments for restless generations (Ex 12:24-27). Remembrance is no nostalgic luxury; it is a survival discipline that seals cracks in leaky cisterns by rehearsing the reliability of the spring. Modern churches can host quarterly "Ebenezer Evenings" where members recount answered prayers, prodigal returns, or provision during unemployment, echoing Psalm 107:2's call to "tell of his deeds." Visual aids intensify memory: jars of dried River Jordan water, ripped credit-card shards mounted in frames after debt-freedom, or quilts stitched from baptismal towels. Children join the circle, absorbing family lore that will outmuscle future doubt (Joel 1:3). Musicians intersperse testimonies with antiphonal songs ("His Steadfast Love Endures Forever," Ps 136), engraving narrative onto melody pathways of the brain. Personal journals supplement corporate gatherings; writing three lines daily—"I saw God when…"—anchors the soul against amnesia currents. Households display a "grace timeline" along hallway walls, sticky-noting milestones of mercy so that trips to brush teeth become catechesis. Every communion service already carries remembrance DNA—"Do this in remembrance of me" (1 Co 11:24)—but churches can deepen the moment by projecting historical photos of congregational baptisms while the cup passes, linking past grace to present sip. When crises strike, these memorial banks release stored courage, reminding hearts that the One who split seas can surely supply rent. Covenant remembrance therefore functions like well-digging: each story excavates sediment of forgetfulness and taps aquifers of fresh trust.

7.7.2 ▪ Intercessory Dependence—From Lobbying Heaven to Leaning on Heaven

Ancient kings dispatched envoys to lobby Egypt; prophets dispatched tears to Yahweh (Hos 12:4; Ex 32:11-14). Intercession is not twisting God's reluctant arm but leaning wholly on His willing character, replacing cracked political cisterns with pipeline to the throne. Practically, believers adopt Daniel's three-times-a-day kneeling rhythm (Dn 6:10), structuring calendars around dependence rather than deadlines. City-wide prayer walks trace embassy routes for the kingdom, claiming neighborhoods with Psalm 24:1 declarations that the earth already belongs to the Lord. "Pray-and-fast Mondays" replace power lunches; skipped meals become petitions that God feed refugees, change zoning laws, or thaw icy marriages. Intercessory teams email elected officials a polite notice: "We prayed for you by name this morning—may justice roll down" (1 Ti 2:1-2; Am 5:24). Breath-prayers ("Lord, have mercy") puncture rumination loops, turning anxiety into supply line (Php 4:6-7). Congregations install 24-7 prayer rooms; each hour logged confesses that outcomes hinge not on marketing budgets but on heaven's rainfall (Zec 10:1). Digital platforms host real-time requests; emojis of folded hands flash across continents within minutes, globalizing dependence. When answers arrive—tumor markers drop, visas clear—teams celebrate with thanksgiving feasts, preventing intercession fatigue. Over years, muscle memory grows: crisis reflex becomes "pray" before "plan," transforming lobbying posture into abiding posture.

7.7.3 ▪ Simplicity, Sabbath, and Slow Living—Creating Margin for Divine Provision

Cistern culture screams scarcity, urging 24/7 grind to keep cracks from showing. Simplicity strikes the opposite note, proclaiming sufficiency by trimming non-essentials. Families audit possessions: if an item hasn't served mission or joy in a year, it's donated—

echoing Jesus' "life does not consist in abundance of possessions" (Lk 12:15). Bank statements undergo Sabbath: automated spending fasts on the seventh day mirror land rest (Lev 25:4) and reveal impulse patterns. Digital slow-downs disable push notifications after 8 p.m., gifting hearts a dusk to dawn manna zone free of algorithmic anxiety. Meal prep shifts from fast-food anxiety to simmer-all-day soups, teaching patience through aroma theology. Walking or biking within two-mile errands shrinks carbon footprints and magnifies neighborhood prayer opportunities. Garden plots—even windowsill herbs—remind disciples that genuine growth cannot be microwaved. Annual silent retreats grant minds a holy fallow field, so creative fruit can sprout later. Margin carved by simplicity becomes reservoir for generosity; unused vacation days convert into mission-trip chaperoning, echoing Isaiah 58:10's promise that those who satisfy the afflicted will be "like a watered garden." Slow living is not laziness but strategic deceleration that keeps pace with a Savior who often "walked" and rarely ran.

7.7.4 ▪ *Communal Accountability—Guardrails against New Cistern Construction*

Left to ourselves, we dig in circles; community provides the GPS that says, "Stop—rock ahead." Regular financial transparency— friends reviewing budgets—catches early seepage into materialism (Prov 15:22). Church boards install policy that no ministry launch occurs without prayer retreat, preventing hype-driven holes. Small groups practice quarterly idol audits, asking, "What's tempting me to trust it more than God this season?"—marriage, keto diet, crypto gains—nothing off limits. Mentors have authority to call time-out on overwork, instructing protégés to book Sabbath retreat before burnout headlines break. When members drift toward partisan obsession, peers gently redirect focus to Philippians 3:20 citizenship. Congregational covenants forbid pastor-celebrity branding; leadership rotations keep one voice from monopolizing hope supply. Annual teaching calendars guarantee lament, justice, and eschatology sermons, so doctrinal balance curbs lopsided loyalties. If someone insists on digging a cistern—say, multi-campus empire without rooted discipleship—the community references Hosea 8:7 ("they sow the wind") and withholds shovel funding. Healthy accountability doesn't shame; it shepherds, installing guardrails that free disciples to run without cliff-edge dread. Thus, wells are dug collectively, buckets shared, and no one wanders thirsty unnoticed.

7.8. Christ the Fountain—Living Water and Eschatological Overflow

7.8.1 • John 4:13-14—Jesus vs. Jacob's Well, Ultimate Source Revealed

At Sychar, a Samaritan woman reaches for ancestral cistern water while lugging relational heartbreak under noon sun. Jesus redirects her thirst: Jacob's well offers daily labor; His gift "will become in you a spring…welling up to eternal life." He is not another container but a subterranean artesian surge that obliterates bucket routines. The dialogue exposes layers: cultural bigotry (Jew vs. Samaritan), moral shame (five husbands), and theological debate (Mount Gerizim vs. Jerusalem). Christ answers each by presenting Himself, not a program. Her abandoned jar (Jn 4:28) symbolizes dropped cistern labor once she tastes the spring. Believers reenact the scene every time they relinquish coping addictions for Spirit consolation. Catechesis frames evangelism as thirst-naming, helping friends identify saltwater strategies—porn, prestige, politics—and offering living water testimony. The well becomes mission HQ; her village believes through overflow, proving springs instinctively irrigate others. Thus, John 4 inaugurates a new hydrology: covenant intimacy inside the human heart, unstoppable by drought or social fences.

7.8.2 • John 7:37-39—Spirit as Rivers from the Heart, Replacing Stale Reservoirs

During Feast of Tabernacles water-drawing ritual, Jesus shouts an audacious upgrade: "Whoever believes in Me…streams of living water will flow from within him." John clarifies—He spoke of the Spirit, not yet given because Jesus was not yet glorified. Pentecost fulfills the promise: cracked cisterns shatter under Spirit pressure and disciples gush multilingual proclamation (Acts 2:4-11). Rivers plural, not trickles, imply diversity of gifting—prophecy, mercy, administration—all sourced from one aquifer (1 Co 12:4-7). Living water is both satisfaction and overflow: the Spirit quenches thirst *and* compels mission. The verb "flow" suggests continual movement; stagnant believers reveal blockage, prompting confession and fresh surrender. Practices like praying in tongues, Spirit-listening silence, and spontaneous worship keep channels unclogged. When congregations corporately yield, worship services feel like Ezekiel's river rising from ankles to swimming depths (Ezk 47:3-5). Social impact follows: wherever river flows, trees heal nations—addiction recovery, racial reconciliation, ecological renewal. Thus, Spirit baptism is not charismatic option but cistern-shattering necessity for new covenant life.

7.8.3 ▪ Revelation 22:1-2—Crystal River through the City, Cisterns Forever Obsolete

John's finale unveils eschatological hydrology: a crystal river from God's throne cascading through New Jerusalem. No reservoirs, dams, or water taxes—direct supply forever. The throne-source means life will always be theocentric; worship and sustenance are one stream. Trees lining banks match Eden but upgrade: twelve crops monthly, perpetual harvest abolishing scarcity cycles. Leaves heal nations, erasing war cisterns built on resource fear. Throne proximity suggests governance fused with grace; politics redeemed, lobbyists redundant. Light from Lamb negates need for firepower or nuclear deterrence; safety flows from glory, not walls (Rev 21:25). Urban planners glimpse future city design and start incorporating park rivers, renewable energy, and pedestrian culture as prophetic foreshadows. Every sip of clean water today becomes sacramental preview of crystal torrents ahead. Reading Revelation cultivates ecological hope: creation's destiny is not discard but drink. Thus, eschatology legitimizes current justice work; building wells in Malawi echoes eternal river pledge.

7.8.4 ▪ Missional Invitation—"Come, All Who Thirst" (Isa 55:1) as Global Gospel Call

The Bible closes with an altar call: "The Spirit and the Bride say, 'Come!'" (Rev 22:17). Mission is therefore a hydration campaign, not just sin management. Isaiah 55 frames gospel as marketplace offer—water, milk, wine—priced at zero cost because Messiah paid full tab (v. 1-3). Churches craft outreach around thirst language:

"Feeling burnt out? Drink deeply." Testimony videos open with emptiness stories, climaxing in fountain encounter. Short-term teams dig literal wells, preaching living water at dedication, integrating deed and Word. Hospital chaplains read John 7 with terminal patients, offering inner springs beyond failing organs. Artists design public fountain installations engraved with Isaiah 55, inviting passersby to fill bottles and ponder soul thirst. Digital evangelism sets up chat rooms titled "Ask for a Drink," where seekers anonymously voice ache. Muslims during Ramadan hear Jesus' invitation to living water at dusk gatherings; Hindus at Ganges festivals receive New Testament water motif tracts. The Bride's role is amplifying Spirit's cry; silence here is mission malpractice. Each new believer adds voice, swelling the global "Come!" chorus until every cracked cistern lies abandoned under weight of glory streaming from Christ the Fountain.

Conclusion Every broken cistern eventually tells the truth. Political saviors disappoint, markets convulse, curated images blur, and the heart awakens to its dehydration. Hosea did not expose idolatry to shame Israel but to shepherd her toward living water. That water has now broken through the rock in the pierced side of Christ, flows by the Spirit into the cracked places of human history, and will one day rush clear and deep through the streets of the New Jerusalem. Until that consummation, disciples carry two simple tools: a hammer to smash fresh-dug cisterns the moment we spot them, and a bucket of gospel hope to share with fellow wanderers. The invitation remains open—*"Come, everyone who thirsts."* Trading human power for divine presence may feel risky, yet only those who set down empty buckets discover the fountain that can never be exhausted and the life that finally, joyfully, never runs dry.

Chapter 8. The Roar of the Lion— Discerning God's Prophetic Voice

When a lion roars in the wild, every creature within range reorients—predators pause, antelope freeze, and birds lift in startled flight. Hosea harnesses that visceral image to describe the moment God breaks into human history with prophetic speech: it is unsettling, unignorable, and ultimately protective, summoning wandering children back to safety even as it rattles the cages of false security. In our age of nonstop notifications and competing pundits, the divine roar can feel muffled or confused with ambient noise. Yet Scripture insists God still speaks, not as a domesticated housecat purring affirmations, but as the Lion of Judah whose voice splits cedars, heals nations, and guides saints. This chapter invites you into the art and discipline of recognizing that authentic roar—tracing its biblical profile, exposing counterfeit growls, and cultivating the posture that turns fragile ears into tuned instruments of holy discernment.

8.1. Biblical Foundations—The Lion Motif and Prophetic Speech

8.1.1 ▪ Hosea's Lion Imagery—Warning, Judgment, and Return (Hosea 5:14; 11:10)

Hosea deploys leonine language at decisive junctures of his book to jolt complacent hearers awake. In 5:14 God says, "I will be like a lion to Ephraim... I will carry them off," conjuring the terrifying moment a predator pounces, shredding illusions of security in political alliances. The roar here is not random violence but covenant litigation—Yahweh enforcing clauses Israel signed at Sinai (Lev 26; Deut 28). Yet in 11:10 the same roar functions differently: "They shall go after the LORD; he will roar like a lion, and when he roars his children shall come trembling." The growl that once scattered now gathers, revealing judgment as restorative strategy, not vindictive finale. Both passages assume a hear-and-respond dynamic; lions hunt partly by paralysing prey with sound, and prophets expect auditory shock to spark moral recalibration. Ancient Near-Eastern readers, familiar with lion hunts of Assyrian kings, would sense political satire—Assyria thinks it's top predator, but Yahweh roars louder. Intertextually, the motif echoes Amos 3:8 ("The lion has roared—who will not fear?") sharpening Hosea's edge: refusal to fear is irrational when the ultimate Apex speaks. Modern believers can map seasons of warning—diagnosis, economic shake-up—and seasons of gathering—revival stirrings—through this twin-roar lens. The oscillation also answers pastoral tension between holiness and mercy; same mouth, different mission stage. Importantly, Hosea never lets roar eclipse voice; lions roar to communicate territory, prophets to reassert divine ownership. When disciples today hear Scripture slice conscience, they are experiencing Hosea's first roar; when forgiveness invitations flood worship, they meet the second.

8.1.2 ▪ The Lion of Judah—Messianic Fulfillment (Genesis 49:9-10; Revelation 5:5)

Jacob's deathbed oracle brands Judah a "lion's whelp," predicting royal dominance until Shiloh comes (Gen 49:9-10). The image sleeps through centuries of tribal squabbles, then awakens in David's battlefield roar over Goliath (1 Sam 17). Yet ultimate fulfillment surfaces in Revelation 5 where heaven's elder announces, "Behold, the Lion of the tribe of Judah has conquered." The surprise twist is that John looks and sees—not a lion—but a slaughtered Lamb, teaching that messianic conquest arrives via sacrificial self-giving. Hosea's lion therefore foreshadows Christ's dual nature: terrifying in holiness, tender in redemption. Apostolic preaching leverages the motif for evangelism; Peter's Pentecost sermon frames resurrection as Davidic enthronement (Acts 2:30-36), essentially echoing lion imagery. Eschatologically, the lion returns in Rev 19's rider who "strikes the nations," tying first advent meekness to final roar of consummation. For practical discipleship, lion Christology balances sugar-coated images of a friendly Jesus by re-introducing awe. Spiritual warfare texts (Eph 6) assume believers fight under Lion's banner, not as independent vigilantes. Worship songs draw on motif—"Roar" by Bethel, "Lion and the Lamb" by Leeland—encoding theology in congregational memory. In counseling, victims of injustice find comfort that their Savior is not merely pastoral but predatory toward evil. Thus, Genesis to Revelation stitches a leonine through-line, anchoring Hosea's local roar in cosmic Christology.

8.1.3 ▪ Roaring through the Prophets—Amos, Isaiah, Jeremiah, and Others

Amos opens his scroll: "The LORD roars from Zion" (Am 1:2), igniting a judgment chain-reaction on surrounding nations before homing in on Israel, demonstrating that covenant people are not exempt. Isaiah hears seraphim declare earth full of glory; moments later Yahweh roars "against the nations" (Is 42:13), coupling doxology with dread. Jeremiah 25 pictures God roaring from on high, winery imagery of treading nations—a sensory overload linking auditory and visual metaphors. In Joel 3:16, the roar shakes heavens but simultaneously promises refuge for Zion, reinforcing Hosean dialectic of terror and shelter. Micah 5 reveals Messiah shepherding in Yahweh's strength "like a lion among flocks," blending pastoral and predatory traits. The cumulative prophetic witness treats roar as both cosmic seismograph—detecting moral fault lines—and midwife cry—birthing new covenant hope. Scholarly consensus notes how roar formula marks new oracle units, functioning as divine signature. Pastors today might structure sermon series around these roar texts, tracing divine pathos across centuries. In personal study, cataloguing each roar verse with situational context becomes a diagnostic mirror: which roar addresses my current compromise? Prophetic roar is not Old-Testament relic; Hebrews 12:26 cites Haggai's "once more I will shake" indicating ongoing acoustic earthquakes whenever God advances history.

8.1.4 • Word and Spirit Together—Revelation, Inspiration, and Canon

God's roar never emerges as vague vibration; it crystallises into words that can be tested, transmitted, and treasured. Hosea 1:1 locates his speech "during the reigns of..." grounding it in history, while 2 Peter 1:21 explains prophets "spoke from God as carried along by the Holy Spirit." The dual authorship—divine breath, human vocabulary—guards against two cisterns: rationalism (Word without Spirit) and mysticism (Spirit without Word). Canon formation collects roars, forming Scripture's fixed perimeter; any contemporary prophetic claim must harmonize, not compete, with closed canon (Rev 22:18-19). Yet illumination remains—Spirit whispers inside the text, turning black-ink roars into living voice (Heb 4:12). Practical outworking: believers weigh impressions against biblical grid, and churches teach hermeneutics as spiritual discernment skill, not academic luxury. Private 'words' that contradict gospel—e.g., license to divorce without grounds—are static, not roar. Likewise, mere quoting verses without Spirit breathing becomes clanging cymbal; Jesus rebuked Satan's proof-text temptation (Mt 4:6-7). Pentecost marries Word and Spirit: Peter explains tongues via Joel; Spirit phenomena drive hearers back to written prophecy. Thus, roaring God equips church with dual ears—Scripture and Spirit—so guidance remains both anchored and animated.

8.2. Anatomy of a Prophetic Word—From Prompt to Proclamation

8.2.1 ▪ Inner Witness vs. Audible Voice—Hebrew nābā *and NT* rhēma

The Hebrew verb *nābā* means "to bubble up," suggesting spontaneous internal pressure rather than detached dictation. Prophets often preface messages, "The word of the LORD came to me," ambiguous about sensory modality. Samuel mistakes God's call for Eli's voice—a faint audible quality (1 Sam 3). In the New Testament, *rhēma* denotes a "spoken word" freshly applied—Peter's rooftop vision and Spirit command (Acts 10:19). Paul describes inward compulsion: "The love of Christ constrains us" (2 Cor 5:14). Contemporary believers testify of inner nudges—scripture illuminated, sudden burden to pray, or empathetic pain mirroring another's need. Audible occurrences are rare but not excluded; missionary anecdotes include hearing a name to call that prevents suicide. The key is not volume but veracity. Training workshops help distinguish Spirit witness from adrenal rush—pausing, breathing, asking "Does this align with Christ's character?" Journaling impressions with date/time prevents hindsight editing. As intimacy grows, inner whisper can guide mundane choices—route to work changed, leading to providential encounter. Hebrews 5:14 says mature have "senses trained," implying practice refines receptivity.

8.2.2 ▪ Images, Impressions, and Dreams—Diverse Delivery Systems

Prophecy is multimedia. God shows Jeremiah an almond rod pun on *shaqed/shoqed* (Jer 1:11-12) and Ezekiel a valley of bones (Ezk 37). Dreams saved infant Jesus via Joseph (Mt 2:13). Visual impressions today might appear during worship—flash of chains breaking over a person—prompting prayer ministry. Symbol literacy aids interpretation; water often signals Holy Spirit (Jn 7:38), but context matters. Not every pizza-dream is prophetic; Daniel fasted and sought meaning (Dan 10:2-3). Recording dreams upon waking preserves details before daylight erodes narrative. Colors, numbers, and emotions embedded in image provide prayer prompts. Group

195

discernment sessions allow multiple interpreters to triangulate meaning, reducing ego bias. Ultimately, variety reveals God's creativity; He tailors channels to receivers' wiring—artists get pictures, analysts receive verses.

8.2.3 ▪ Testing the Origin—Four-Way Filter: Scripture, Character, Fruit, Community

Paul commands "Do not despise prophecies, but test everything" (1 Th 5:20-21). The first sieve is Scriptural congruence: a word endorsing revenge flunks instantly (Rom 12:19). Second is deliverer's character; Balaam spoke truth yet loved wages (Num 22; 2 Pet 2:15)—warns that accurate data doesn't equal divine source. Third filter examines fruit: does word produce repentance, joy, justice, or fear, control, division? Jesus said tree known by fruit (Mt 7:16). Fourth is community evaluation; Corinthians "weigh" prophetic utterances (1 Cor 14:29). Practically, teams appoint note-takers and debrief after services. In private contexts, sharing tentative language—"I sense..."—invites feedback, not coercion. Rejected words are shredded, not nursed; humility accepts fallibility. Positive test results often come with confirmations—scripture read that morning, stranger's affirmation—bolstering faith.

8.2.4 ▪ From Private Weight to Public Release—Timing, Tone, and Venue

Habakkuk sat on rampart to hear correction on how to deliver vision (Hab 2:1-2); timing matters. Sometimes immediate declaration is obedience—as Agabus warned famine (Acts 11:28). Other times, Mary "pondered these things in her heart" (Lk 2:19) until season ripened. Factors influencing release: leadership covering, emotional composure, and recipient openness. Tone transforms impact; Nathan's parable softened David before pronouncing "You are the man" (2 Sam 12:7). Volume doesn't equal authority; whisper can carry roar weight if Spirit backs. Venue choice—personal coffee, small-group circle, or congregational mic—depends on content sensitivity. Recording words avoids memory drift and allows accountability follow-up. Post-release, intercessory backing sustains seeds until fulfillment. Failure to consider timing can wound;

Joseph's premature dreams alienated brothers (Gen 37). Thus, stewardship extends beyond hearing to strategic sowing.

8.3. Counterfeits and Distortions—When Roars Become Growls

8.3.1 ▪ False Prophets in Hosea's Day—Court Pleasers and Baal Echoes (Hosea 9:7-9)

Hosea labels fraudulent seers "mad" and "snared," diagnosing moral rot behind their ecstatic claims (Hos 9:7-9). These prophets thrived on royal stipends, crafting messages that soothed national ego, much like Ahab's four-hundred yes-men (1 Ki 22). Their rhetoric borrowed Yahweh's name yet smuggled Baal's promise of guaranteed fertility, producing religious syncretism. They attacked genuine prophets—"a trap for a watchman"—mirroring modern smear campaigns against truth-tellers. Sociologically, false prophets exploit crisis by offering simple slogans; economically, they benefit from sacrificial demand—more offerings mean more priestly portions (Hos 4:8). Discerning listeners look for repentance call; if absent, lion growl likely counterfeit.

8.3.2 ▪ Modern Imitations—Clickbait Prophecy, Political Fortune-Telling

Today's digital landscape monetizes sensational headlines: "God told me 2026 is rapture," harvesting views and donations. Predictive specificity draws anxious audiences, but Deut 18:22 sets 100 % accuracy bar; serial date-setters fail test. Political prophecy morphs into partisan fortune-telling—proclaiming guaranteed election victories to mobilize voting blocs. When outcomes contradict proclamations, revisionist spin—"spiritual victory"—undermines credibility of genuine prophetic ministry. Mature leaders resist public pressure to inflate claims; they model Acts 21 Agabus-style humility, acknowledging partial knowledge.

8.3.3 • Manipulation and Merchandising—Simon the Sorcerer Syndrome (Acts 8:18-23)

Simon sought to purchase apostolic power, revealing heart poisoned by bitterness and greed. Modern Simons traffic in pay-per-prophecy phone lines, VIP impartation tickets, or tailored "breakthrough seeds" of $1,000. Emotional manipulation employs music swells and peer pressure to elicit offerings. Scripturally, prophets refused profit—Elisha rejected Naaman's gifts (2 Ki 5:16) and Peter rebuked Simon sharply. Accountability boards, transparent finances, and bi-vocational models counter commodification. Congregations must discern giving motives—is it gratitude or witchcraft attempt to control outcomes?

8.3.4 • Deliverance from Deception—Cultivating Berean Skepticism (Acts 17:11)

Bereans "examined Scriptures daily to see if these things were so," embodying healthy skepticism. Training believers in Bible literacy—context, genre, original audience—fortifies against proof-text traps. Encouraging questions during prophecy sessions affirms inquiry as faith, not doubt. Corporate liturgies include confession of collective gullibility, asking God to "search and know" (Ps 139:23). Fasting seasons sharpen discernment; Daniel's vegetable fast preceded apocalyptic visions (Dan 10). Teaching spiritual gift of distinguishing spirits (1 Cor 12:10) legitimizes critical voices often sidelined. In cases of deception fallout, pastoral teams offer gentle restoration—victims need safe space to process betrayal without abandoning charismatic openness. Ultimately, humility and truth-love synergy form antidote: ears attuned to Lion learn to detect counterfeit growls by prolonged exposure to authentic roar.

8.4. Personal Posture—Preparing to Hear the Lion

8.4.1 • Reverent Fear and Humble Expectation—Isa 66:2 Balance

Scripture insists that the person God esteems is "the one who is humble and contrite in spirit and trembles at My word" (Isa 66:2), a verse that yokes two attitudes modern disciples often separate. Reverence without expectancy devolves into paralyzing dread, while expectancy without reverence mutates into casual presumption. Healthy fear begins with a steady gaze on God's holiness—meditating on Sinai's thunder (Ex 19:16-19), Uzzah's fatal touch (2 Sam 6:6-7), and Ananias and Sapphira's collapsed charade (Acts 5:1-11). These narratives inoculate hearts against trivializing divine speech. Yet the same Bible commands bold approach to the throne of grace (Heb 4:16), teaching that the Lion who roars is also the Lamb who was slain. Humility flows from remembering creatureliness; journaling daily gratitudes reminds us every breath is borrowed oxygen. Expectation grows by rehearsing answered prayers, effectively building a testimony reservoir. In prayer meetings, speaking phrases like "We wait for Your direction" before sharing impressions models tremble-and-trust equilibrium. Physically, some kneel to underscore lowliness, then lift hands to signal readiness, turning posture into pedagogy for the soul. Confessing known sin before listening sessions prevents static; James links righteousness and effective prayer (Jas 5:16). Quoting Psalm 25:14—"The LORD confides in those who fear Him"—anchors the conviction that awe invites disclosure. When believers maintain this tension, prophetic impressions arrive without the poison of entitlement or the paralysis of unworthiness, and the community learns to expect God's roar as merciful revelation rather than random lightning.

8.4.2 • Listening Practices—Silence, Journaling, Lectio, and Examen

The roar of the Lion must be distinguished from the buzz of digital beehives, and ancient disciplines provide noise-canceling headphones for the soul. Intentional silence—five unbroken minutes at the start of prayer—allows cortisol levels to drop, clearing neural space for divine whisper (1 Ki 19:12). Many set a timer to avoid clock-watch anxiety. Journaling converts ephemeral impressions into tangible text; Habakkuk was told, "Write the vision" (Hab 2:2), and the same wisdom curbs forgetfulness and exaggeration. A two-column method works well: left side records raw data (image, phrase, emotion), right side maps possible meanings and scriptures. Lectio divina turns Bible reading from information intake to conversational space: read, ruminate, respond, rest. When a verse "shimmers," the listener pauses, asking, "Lord, is this Your emphasis today?" Ignatian *examen* each evening reviews the day for

199

consolation (where God felt near) and desolation (where He seemed absent), sharpening radar for future guidance. Corporate listening circles apply Acts 15's model—participants report perceived leading, then collectively discern "it seemed good to the Holy Spirit and to us." Technology can assist rather than distract; noise-blocking playlists of instrumental worship create acoustic privacy on public transit. Setting phone wallpapers to a monthly theme verse triggers micro-lectio every unlock. Over time, these micro-rhythms stitch a life in which God's voice need not shout; the heart, already quieted, can detect the subtlest lion growl amid cultural clamor.

8.4.3 ▪ *Purity of Heart—Repentance, Forgiveness, and Idol Cleansing*

Jesus promised that "the pure in heart...shall see God" (Mt 5:8), implying impurity clouds prophetic perception like algae film over cistern water. Purity begins with ruthless repentance—naming sin at forensic detail (lies, envy, hidden clicks) rather than vague "shortcomings." 1 John 1:9 guarantees cleansing, but confession also dismantles self-deception, a major static source. Forgiveness of others is equally non-negotiable; lingering bitterness acts as spiritual tinnitus. During listening prayer, the Holy Spirit may spotlight a name; immediate choice to release debt clears bandwidth (Mk 11:25). Idol cleansing addresses attachments—not just obvious vices but subtle securities such as ministry success or political ideology. Ezekiel 14 warns that idols in the heart color what prophets hear, leading to self-confirming messages. Periodic fasts reveal hidden dependencies: skipped caffeine exposes irritability, prompting repentance. Purity also involves media diet; Psalm 101:3 resolves, "I will set before my eyes no vile thing," guarding imagination from corrosive images. Environmental audits— removing occult objects, offensive playlists—echo Acts 19:19 bonfires, signaling full allegiance. Positive pursuit follows subtraction: filling mind with Philippians 4:8 virtues re-pattern synapses. Communities can schedule "cleansing retreats," combining teaching on holiness with communion, foot washing, and vow renewal, ensuring prophetic culture springs from holy soil.

God formed humans from dust; therefore, bodily rhythms impact spiritual receptivity. Fasting mixes hunger pangs with heightened spiritual alertness, as Daniel experienced before receiving apocalyptic insight (Dan 10:2-14). Whether a single meal or a three-day water fast, the discipline reminds the stomach who the real Bread is (Jn 6:35). Sabbath rest, by contrast, declares trust that revelation cannot be earned through nonstop striving; God spoke to sleeping Joseph in dreams (Mt 1–2). Practicing a 24-hour technology sabbath unclutters mental space, making room for unhurried meditation. Attentive rest includes adequate sleep—Elijah needed a nap and food before hearing God's whisper (1 Ki 19:5-12). Gentle exercise—walking, stretching—oxygenates the brain, promoting creative listening. Some believers adopt "body postures of openness," sitting upright, palms up, symbolizing receptivity. Breath prayers synchronize inhale with "Speak, Lord" and exhale with "Your servant listens," anchoring attention. Seasonal practices help: Advent fasting from noise to heighten Christmas proclamations; Lent deserts mirroring Hosea's wilderness (Hos 2:14) to amplify resurrection roar. Embodied readiness signals to the Lion that the prey—our will—stands still, ears perked, prepared to heed the approaching voice.

8.5. Communal Discernment—The Prophetic in the Local Church

8.5.1 ▪ New-Testament Paradigm—"Let Two or Three Speak...Judge" (1 Cor 14:29)

Paul's instructions to Corinth create the skeletal framework for congregational prophecy: plurality of voices, sequential sharing, and immediate evaluation. The permissive "two or three" guards against monopolies; even seasoned prophets take turns, embodying mutual submission (Eph 5:21). Judgment happens in real time—listeners assess content, congruence with Scripture, and inward witness. Practical models include a "prophetic mic" during worship with moderators who know the speakers' character. Words are recorded by scribes for accountability and future testimony. Teaching on 1 Cor 14 precedes practice, so members know difference between revelation and exhortation. Time limits (e.g., two minutes) prevent rambling. When words contain directive elements ("move cities," "marry"), leaders remind recipients to seek confirmation through counsel and circumstance, deterring impulsive life changes. A culture of encouragement dominates; corrective words come seasoned with tears, following Matthew 18's private-first principle. Over months, shy saints gain confidence, while dominant voices learn brevity, producing a balanced, many-faceted roar within worship.

8.5.2 ▪ Eldership Oversight—Guardrails without Quenching (1 Th 5:19-22)

Paul's rapid-fire imperatives—"Do not quench the Spirit…test everything; hold fast what is good"—task elders with dual responsibility: fan flames and douse wildfires. Oversight begins with doctrinal baseline; elders steeped in Scripture spot heretical drift instantly. They vet guest speakers, review prophetic track records, and ensure financial transparency to block merchandising. Yet they also create space—prophetic weekends, prayer rooms—so gifts emerge. Monthly debriefs ask, "Did we over-police or under-shepherd?" When errors occur, elders correct privately, publicly if necessary (Gal 2:14), modeling restorative, not punitive, governance. Written guidelines—tone, length, submission process—provide clarity. Elders intercede for prophetic teams, knowing spiritual warfare intensifies around revelation (Rev 12:17). Healthy oversight transforms fear into confidence; members know safety nets exist, so they climb the high-wire of faith.

8.5.3 ▪ Prophetic Teams and Prayer Rooms—Safe Laboratories for Growth

A biology lab equips students before field research; prophetic teams serve similar apprenticeship. Teams meet weekly to practice listening for strangers, share images, then receive coaching. Mistakes become learning material, not reasons for exile. Prayer rooms, inspired by Acts 13:1-3 Antioch model, host rotating worship-intercession sets, cultivating sensitivity. Written request cards guide focus: healing, guidance, justice. Teams test impressions by silent consensus—if three members sense "peace," the group

202

prays accordingly. Documentation tracks outcomes, building faith and data for refinement. Periodic workshops teach dream interpretation, cultural humility, and trauma-informed ministry. Mentors emphasize confidentiality; words shared in rooms stay there unless permission given. International students join via Zoom, globalizing perspective. Over time, these labs produce calibrated voices ready for congregational platforms and mission fields.

8.5.4 ▪ Integrating Word with Worship, Teaching, and Mission

Prophecy is most potent when woven, not stapled, into church fabric. Worship leaders craft set lists that echo prophetic themes released earlier, fostering response rather than whiplash. Teachers reference recent words in sermons, connecting fresh rhema to timeless logos. Mission departments solicit prophetic insight before launching outreach, mirroring Paul's Macedonian call (Acts 16:9-10). Prophetic art installations—paintings birthed in prayer—decorate lobbies, extending impact beyond audible moment. Testimony videos of fulfilled words play during offering, linking revelation to stewardship. Small-group curriculum includes discussion questions: "How did Sunday's prophetic word shape your week?" Thus, prophecy is not event but ecosystem, saturating education, worship, and service.

8.6. Prophetic Ethics—Stewarding Revelation with Integrity

8.6.1 ▪ Servant Identity vs. Celebrity Branding—John 3:30 Humility

John the Baptist's creed—"He must increase, I must decrease"—rebukes modern temptation to treat revelation as career ladder. Prophetic servants remember they are mail carriers, not authors; applause belongs to Sender. Practical safeguards: prophets travel with accountability partners, decline personal merchandising booths, and redirect social-media followers to local church resources. They submit itineraries to home-church elders, avoiding rogue independence. Platform invitations are weighed for kingdom fruit, not honorariums. Language choices—"we sense" over "God told me"—reflect humility. After ministry, prophets join clean-up crew, signaling servanthood. Regular meditation on Isaiah 42:8

("My glory I will not give to another") shields heart. When compliments come, quick deflection to Christ models John's posture. Should fame rise, sabbatical hiatuses recalibrate motivations, ensuring roar remains untarnished by ego echo.

8.6.2 ▪ Accountability Structures—Peer Review, Record-Keeping, Follow-Up

Acts 15 demonstrates apostolic letters vetted by council; prophetic communities mirror with peer boards reviewing controversial words before public release. Digital archives store transcripts, dates, and outcomes, deterring revisionism. Annual audits assess accuracy rate; chronic misses prompt retraining or suspension. Follow-up teams contact recipients months later, asking, "Did this resonate? Any fruit?" Feedback loops refine clarity and provide pastoral care for confusing words. Financial accountability matters: offerings collected at events flow through church treasuries, not personal accounts. Sexual-conduct policies prevent counseling sessions from becoming grooming arenas. These structures free prophets from isolation, cultivating trust with congregations wary from past abuses.

8.6.3 ▪ Compassionate Delivery—Truth in Tears, Not in Triumph

Jeremiah's nickname, the weeping prophet, reveals emotional posture God favors. Even hard words—"plucked up and torn down"—were uttered with quivering lip (Jer 9:1). New-covenant equivalents share corrective words privately first, with gentle tone (Gal 6:1). They avoid shaming language, remembering Jesus refused to break bruised reeds (Isa 42:3). Prophetic correctives provide redemptive pathway: identify sin, invite repentance, proclaim mercy. Body language matters: eye contact, softened facial muscles, occasional pause for listener processing. Metaphors cushion impact; Nathan's lamb story disarmed David (2 Sam 12). Compassion includes timing sensitivity—delaying word at a funeral, releasing hope instead. Prophets pray afterward, not drop bombs. Such tenderness convinces audience roar aims to save, not devour.

Deuteronomy 18 sets severe standards; yet 1 Cor 13:9 admits partial prophecy. When words fail, integrity requires public acknowledgment—"I spoke presumptuously." Leadership may impose temporary silence for reflection. Teams dissect miss: Was interpretation flawed? Did timing slip? Did conditional clause go unheeded? Repentance restores credibility; Jonah owned anger when Nineveh's destruction delayed, albeit grudgingly. Clarification letters articulate lessons, turning stumble into teaching. Some words morph—Joseph's dream fulfilled differently than youthful assumption—so humility keeps interpretation open. In all, failure becomes forge; prophets emerge warier of hype, keener on love, aligned with Paul's reminder that without love, even accurate mysteries are nothing (1 Cor 13:2).

8.7. Prophetic Impact—Roar Results in Scripture and History

8.7.1 ▪ National Turning Points—Nineveh's Repentance, Reformations, Revivals

When Jonah finally shook the dust of rebellion from his sandals and strode into Assyria's capital, his eight-word sermon—"Yet forty days, and Nineveh shall be overthrown" (Jon 3:4)—roared louder than any political decree. From king to cattle, the entire city donned sackcloth, demonstrating that a genuine prophetic voice can alter the moral trajectory of an empire overnight (Jon 3:5-10). Centuries later, a single Augustinian monk nailing ninety-five theses to Wittenberg's door unleashed the Protestant Reformation—another lion-roar moment that reshaped constitutions, economies, and education systems across Europe. The 18th-century Great Awakening, catalyzed by Whitefield's open-air preaching and Wesley's circuit rides, revived moribund churches, birthed abolition movements, and even laid social foundations for the American Revolution. Each of these turnarounds shares common anatomy: a courageous messenger, a confronting word, a critical window of national vulnerability, and an ensuing cascade of systemic change. Prophetic roar exposes both personal sin and structural injustice; Nineveh fasted from violence (Jon 3:8), Luther denounced indulgence economies, and Wesley campaigned against brutal industrial practices. Historians note measurable fruit—crime rates plummet, philanthropy spikes, and legislation shifts—whenever authentic repentance sweeps a populace. Contemporary nations remain candidates; Scripture says God "changes times and seasons; He removes kings and sets up kings" (Dan 2:21). Therefore, prayer for national awakening is not nostalgic romanticism but biblical realism rooted in the Lion's historical track record.

8.7.2 ▪ Social Justice Catalysts—Wilberforce, MLK, and Modern Voices

William Wilberforce heard John Newton's prophetic plea to choke the slave trade, and that roar echoed through thirty-three parliamentary defeats until Britain finally abolished the traffic of human beings in 1807. Martin Luther King Jr., steeped in Amos's cry for justice to roll like waters (Am 5:24), galvanized civil-rights reform through sermons that blended biblical thunder with non-violent strategy. Both men illustrate how prophetic conviction converts private anguish into public policy: letters written in prison cells and late-night legislative drafts trace their genealogy to hours spent wrestling with God's burden. Their ministries also reveal prophetic cost—Wilberforce endured ridicule from plantation lobbies; King faced bombs and bullets. Yet the roar's ripple has proved durable: modern anti-trafficking networks, Creation-Care advocacy, and mass-incarceration reforms cite these forebears as precedent. Scripture reinforces such activism: Isaiah ties true fasting to loosing injustice chains (Isa 58:6), and Jesus inaugurates ministry by declaring liberty to captives (Lk 4:18-19). Prophetic justice never separates proclamation from action; words ignite hearts, but policies dismantle yokes. Local churches joining neighborhood coalitions, drafting fair-housing petitions, or tutoring underserved youth participate in that same lion-lineage, proving that the roar's decibels are measured not only in decibels but in delivered captives.

8.7.3 · *Personal Destiny—Timothy's War with Prophecies (1 Tim 1:18)*

Paul reminds his young protégé Timothy to "wage the good warfare" by the prophecies previously spoken over him, treating those words like strategic maps in hostile territory. Personal prophetic words often arrive as whispers during youth camps, dreams in dark nights, or quiet impressions beneath worship choruses, yet they can steer vocational trajectories more decisively than scholarship grants or job offers. Joseph held onto adolescent dreams through pit, prison, and foreign promotion, demonstrating patience is the military discipline of destiny (Gen 37–41). David's anointing at Bethlehem fields fortified him against Saul's spears; each cave became rehearsal space for psalms fueled by remembered oil (1 Sam 16; 1 Sam 24). For believers today, journals of vetted prophetic words operate like scrolls in a quiver—pulled out when doubt snarls. They impose holy constraints, steering choices away from lucrative detours that contradict calling, and they provide comfort when outcomes lag behind promise ("the word of the LORD tested Joseph," Ps 105:19). Paul's counsel also implies warfare: competing voices—fear, comparison, cultural scripts—attempt to sabotage destiny. By declaring prophetic promises aloud in prayer, disciples swing those words like swords (Eph 6:17). Fulfillment rarely unfolds linearly; delays refine character so the dreamer can sustain weight of the dream. Ultimately, personal destiny is not narcissistic spotlight but kingdom assignment; Timothy's call anchored budding congregations in Ephesus, and modern Timothys will shepherd arenas only God currently sees.

8.7.4 · *Global Mission—Macedonian Call to Ends-of-Earth Commission*

Acts 16 records Paul's nocturnal vision of a Macedonian man pleading for help, a single prophetic scene that rerouted the gospel westward, seeded European Christianity, and altered world history. That pivot underscores mission's dependence on real-time divine intel, not merely demographics or travel feasibility. Later, the Spirit forbade Paul to enter Bithynia (Acts 16:6-7), showing that closed doors can be as prophetic as open ones. Modern equivalents include missionaries redirected by dreams to unreached tribes, prayerwalkers hearing a phrase in unknown tongue then discovering it matches a local dialect, or humanitarian teams canceling flights moments before coups. Strategic mission agencies now pair data analysts with intercessory councils, mirroring Antioch's fast-and-listen culture (Acts 13:2-3). Prophetic guidance also fuels contextualization; Hudson Taylor shaved his head in China because inward conviction demanded outward identification, and thousands followed suit. Funding miracles often follow roar-shaped vision— George Müller's orphanages testify that prophetic compassion can attract resources without marketing. Scripture promises the endgame: every tribe before the throne (Rev 7:9); prophecy supplies micro-directions so macro-promise is met on schedule. Thus, global mission remains an acoustic enterprise—ears pressed to the Lion's mouth, feet ready to sprint wherever the next roar reverberates.

8.8. Eschatological Roar—Final Trumpet and the Voice Like Many Waters

8.8.1 ▪ End-Time Warnings—Birth Pains, Apostasy, and Hope (Matthew 24)

Jesus' Olivet Discourse functions as a seismic early-warning system: wars, earthquakes, and love grown cold are tremors signaling the earth's labor toward new creation (Mt 24:6-12). These "birth pains" are not random tragedies but contractions announcing forthcoming glory. Prophetic voices amplify the pattern—calling churches to resilient faith rather than panic stockpiling. Apostasy, another foretold sign, demands internal discernment; false messiahs and diluted gospels will proliferate, so lion-ears must sift pulpits and podcasts (Mt 24:24). Yet end-time roar carries hope: "This gospel of the kingdom will be proclaimed... and then the end will come" (Mt 24:14). Warnings therefore fuel mission, not bunker mentality. Believers heed Jesus' fig-tree analogy—reading cultural seasons and adjusting lamps like wise virgins (Mt 24:32; 25:1-13). The ultimate trumpet in 1 Thessalonians 4:16 will be the loudest roar, drowning every counterfeit. Until then, eschatological sobriety anchors ethics—stewards manage talents, servants feed household, evidencing readiness (Mt 24:45-47).

8.8.2 ▪ Bride Prepared by Prophetic Refinement—Ephesians 5:26-27

Paul envisions Christ cleansing His bride "by the washing of water with the word," presenting her radiant and wrinkle-free (Eph 5:26-27). Prophetic ministry supplies that washing action, scrubbing cultural grime from ecclesial garments. When Nathan confronted David, the king emerged cleaner, though bruised (2 Sam 12); so too congregations confronted by present-day Nathans exit idolatry cycles. John's letters to Asia's churches demonstrate lion-love: commendation paired with correction (Rev 2–3). Each message ends with, "He who has an ear, let him hear," tying bridal purity to auditory obedience. Corporate repentance services—tears, restitution, covenant renewal—operate as fitting-rooms where blemishes are steamed out. Prophecy also ignites first-love passion; Ephesus lost love, and prophetic warning sought rekindling (Rev 2:4-5). Holiness teaching without prophetic fire calcifies into moralism; prophetic roar without holiness framing devolves into emotional spectacle. Balanced, they season the bride for a wedding where linens are "the righteous deeds of the saints" (Rev 19:8).

8.8.3 ▪ The Lion-Lamb Convergence—Justice and Mercy Kiss at Consummation

Revelation 5 reveals a paradox: the conquering Lion is simultaneously a slaughtered Lamb. Eschatology thus harmonizes retributive justice with redemptive mercy. Final judgment is a roar that silences oppression—Babylon falls (Rev 18), beast and false prophet cast into fire (Rev 19:20). Yet the same agenda enthrones martyrs, welcomes nations, and wipes tears (Rev 21:4). Prophetic preaching must mirror this convergence, refusing caricatures of doom-only or love-only. Communion becomes eschatological appetizer: proclaiming death until He comes (1 Cor 11:26), participants taste Lamb's mercy while anticipating Lion's return. Social ethics draw courage—activists fight trafficking knowing Lion will finish the job; evangelists plead with rebels that mercy still bleeds. Worship songs alternate minor-key lament for current injustice and major-key triumph for guaranteed victory. At the cross, justice kissed mercy (Ps 85:10); at consummation, the kiss reverberates universe-wide, validating every roar that ever summoned repentance.

8.8.4 ▪ Living in the "Already Roaring, Not Yet Consumed" Tension

Hebrews 12:26-29 says God's voice once shook earth and will shake heavens, then adds, "Our God is a consuming fire." Yet, paradoxically, believers already receive an unshakeable kingdom. The present era is thus acoustic overlap: roars rumble, but final incineration awaits. Christians inhabit tension by practicing "proleptic living"—behaviors that belong to future age enacted now. Gratitude and reverent worship (Heb 12:28) preview eternal liturgy. Financial generosity anticipates currency-less city where gold paves streets. Peacemaking foreshadows weapons-to-ploughshares world (Isa 2:4). Prophetic communities become early-warning sirens and early-arrival previews simultaneously. Spiritual gifts are "powers of the age to come" (Heb 6:5); each healing whispers end of sickness, each deliverance forecasts devil's doom. Suffering, too, fits schema; groans are birth pangs, not death rattles (Rom 8:22-23). Living between roars demands resilience: helmet of salvation guards hope, while shoes of gospel readiness sprint toward every thirsty soul (Eph 6:15-17). Ultimately, disciples who master this tension neither hibernate in nostalgia nor hyperventilate in alarm; they simply keep ears tuned, hands busy, hearts pure, awaiting the moment when the Lion's final roar melts shadows into everlasting day.

Conclusion A true lion never roars without purpose; the sound is both a warning to rivals and a rallying cry to the pride. So it is with God's prophetic voice. It confronts idols, yes, but equally it gathers sons and daughters into covenant confidence, assuring them that the wilderness is patrolled by a faithful King. Having explored the ways that roar reverberates—from the pages of Scripture to the corridors of church life and the frontiers of mission—we stand at a crossroads familiar to Hosea's audience: will we keep chasing the echo of our own ambitions, or will we humble ourselves, still every lesser sound, and follow the unmistakable timbre of heaven's call? The choice will shape not only our personal trajectories but also the witness of communities hungry for authenticity. May we be found among those who, when the Lion speaks, answer without hesitation, "Speak, Lord, for Your servants are listening."

210

211

Chapter 9. Healing Backsliding— Receiving Restoration in Christ

Every believer knows the uneasy sensation of spiritual drift—the slow loosening of prayer's grip, the quiet return of old cravings, the subtle cynicism that replaces early wonder. Hosea names that drift *backsliding*, a heart-swerve that seduces covenant people into barren fields of self-reliance. Yet the prophet also delivers one of Scripture's most breathtaking promises: "I will heal their backsliding; I will love them freely" (Hos 14:4). The scene is not an angry judge banging a gavel but a relentless physician pursuing patients who keep cancelling appointments. This chapter traces that healing journey. We will examine the spiritual pathology that leads to relapse and, far more importantly, the divine remedies that restore vitality in Christ. Along the way you'll encounter honest portraits of failure, practical rehab rhythms, and the surprising truth that your scars can become road signs for others still wandering.\

9.1. Understanding Backsliding—Symptoms, Stages, and Root Causes

9.1.1 ▪ *Vocabulary of Drift—Hosea's Terms (*meshuvah, *"turning away")*

Hosea repeats the Hebrew noun *meshuvah* six times, painting a portrait of covenant disloyalty as a slow, almost imperceptible pivot rather than a sudden leap (Hos 4:16; 11:7; 14:4). The word pictures a door that once faced Yahweh gradually swinging toward substitute lovers until the house's interior receives a different light. In English, we call that "backsliding," but in Hosea's mind it is more like gravitational drift—an unattended boat pulled from anchor by subtle currents. The term also suggests circular motion; Israel keeps "turning back" to idols, exhausting grace with repetitive loops (Hos 11:7). Linguists note the root *shuv* normally means *return*—ironically, the same verb for repentance—so backsliding is repentance in reverse. Other prophetic synonyms amplify nuance: Isaiah speaks of "rebellion" (*pasha'*, Isa 30:1), Jeremiah of "stubbornness" (*sarar*, Jer 3:17), each highlighting different facets of the same decay. Recognizing Hosea's vocabulary matters because diagnosis shapes treatment; if we call drift "normal," we will medicate with excuses instead of repentance. When sermons translate *meshuvah* merely as "sins" they flatten process into event, robbing listeners of the early-warning lexicon Hosea intends. The apostle James echoes the idea using maritime imagery—"each person is dragged away by his own desire" (Jas 1:14)—linking Old-Testament drift to New-Testament psychology. Modern disciples might rename *meshuvah* as disengagement: skipping small group, muting conviction podcasts, or scrolling during communion. By restoring Hosea's term to our vocabulary, we gain a radar screen for tiny course deviations before they calcify into apostasy.

9.1.2 ▪ *Cold Hearts, Compromised Habits, and Cynical Talk—Early Warning Signs*

Backsliding rarely begins with scandal; it usually commences with cooling affections. Jesus warns Ephesus that loss of "first love" precedes lampstand removal (Rev 2:4-5). A cold heart shows up as

213

prayer boredom—conversations shrink to grocery-list petitions—or worship disengagement, where lips move but inner applause withers. Compromised habits soon follow: bedtime scrolls replace Scripture meditation, generosity pauses "until the next raise," and Sabbath surrenders to side-hustle economics. Over time cynicism manifests in speech; jokes about "radical believers" cloak self-defense (Luke 6:45). Hosea's contemporaries boasted, "No one can find in me iniquity" (Hos 12:8), a sarcastic self-acquittal that mirrors modern virtue-signaling. Emotional indicators also surface: irritability during conviction, envy of boundary-keeping friends, and nostalgia for pre-conversion thrills. Relationally, drifting Christians dodge accountable friendships, gravitate toward permissive company, and critique church leadership to justify distance. Sleep patterns shift—either insomnia due to unresolved guilt or oversleep to escape nagging conscience. Even the body testifies; Proverbs links bones wasting to hidden sin (Prov 17:22). Catching these indicators early allows believers to confess before scaffolding of sin cements. Like dashboard warning lights, they are mercies—announcing misalignment while repair is minor.

9.1.3 ▪ Underlying Idols—Fear, Pain-Avoidance, and Performance Addiction

Surface behaviors stem from subterranean idols. Fear idol says, "God might not protect me, so I must hedge with compromise," producing Egypt-alliances Israel pursued (Hos 7:11). Pain-avoidance idol whispers that numbing is safer than healing; thus Gomer runs to lovers who "pay" her in comfort commodities (Hos 2:5). Performance addiction applauds effort over intimacy, echoing Peter's boast before denial (Matt 26:33). These idols often intertwine: fear fuels performance, performance masks pain, pain breeds more fear. Hosea unmasks them by naming Baal—god of storms—behind agricultural anxieties; worshipers placated markets rather than trusting Provider (Hos 2:8). In counseling rooms, equivalent idols appear as workaholism, pornography, or substance use—functional saviors. Tim Keller labels them "counterfeit gods," answering legitimate needs with illegitimate sources. Diagnostic questions expose allegiance: What do I daydream about? What would devastate me if lost? What am I defensive about? Until idols are dethroned, behavior-mod programs merely reshuffle symptoms.

The gospel's answer is deeper affection; Hosea's God promises to "allure" Israel, addressing desire not just duty (Hos 2:14).

9.1.4 • Case Studies—Gomer, Demas (2 Tim 4:10), and Modern De-Conversions

Gomer personifies chronic relapse—rescued, then selling herself again—illustrating addiction cycle: rescue, honeymoon, boredom, triggers, relapse (Hos 3:1-3). New-Testament disciple Demas exemplifies gradual desertion; once Paul's coworker, he later "loved this present world" and fled to Thessalonica (2 Tim 4:10). Church history adds de-conversion memoirs, from enlightenment skeptics to current ex-evangelicals documenting deconstruction online. Patterns emerge: unmet expectations, unresolved suffering, intellectual doubts left unprocessed, or relational wounds inflicted by believers. Social media accelerates exit narratives; applause from like-minded exiles rewards public renunciation. Yet many return: Augustine wandered through Manichaeism before finding rest in Christ; modern prodigals testify at Celebrate Recovery. Analyzing stories reveals pain points congregations can address—safe doubt forums, trauma-informed pastoral care, and robust apologetics. Hosea gives hope that even repeat offenders can be redeemed; God's final word is not Gomer's infidelity but marital renewal (Hos 14:4).

9.2. Divine Initiative—The Physician Who Pursues the Patient

9.2.1 • "I Will Heal"—God's Self-Imposed Mission Statement (Hosea 14:4)

The Hebrew grammar places Yahweh as both subject and actor: *'erpa'* ("I Myself will heal"), stressing unilateral grace. Israel contributes only sickness; Yahweh supplies diagnosis, treatment, and payment. This echoes Exodus 15:26—"I am the LORD who heals you"—and anticipates Christ's claim, "It is not the healthy who need a doctor" (Mk 2:17). The verb "heal" (*rapha'*) covers physical, relational, and spiritual repair, so salvation is holistic. God's mission statement counters shame scripts: He doesn't merely tolerate backsliders; He strategizes their cure. Contrast pagan deities

215

that demanded self-mutilation; Yahweh bears cost Himself. The pronoun "freely" amplifies motive—no transactional strings. Such initiative dismantles bargaining prayers ("If You restore me, I'll serve"). It invites surrender rooted in gratitude. Pastoral application: preach God's *I will* louder than congregants' *I promise.* Counseling begins by showcasing divine pursuit, not penitent perfection plans.

9.2.2 ▪ Love Before Law—Covenant Compassion Preceding Human Response

Israel's Exodus preceded Sinai; liberation birthed obedience, not vice versa (Ex 20:2). Hosea mirrors order: God pledges healing, then calls to "return" (Hos 14:1-4). Paul repeats pattern: while we were sinners, Christ died (Rom 5:8). Love before law reorients motive— obedience becomes gratitude expression, not entrance fee. When backsliders hear this, defenses drop; they stop hiding like Adam behind fig leaves. Pastoral frameworks that front-load rules risk reinforcing shame loops. Instead, leaders articulate covenant history—God's steadfast love (*hesed*) spanning betrayal episodes. Spiritual disciplines then become medicine packets handed by caring Physician, not probation tasks.

9.2.3 ▪ Incarnation as House Call—Jesus Among the Sick, Lost, and Failed (Mark 2:17)

Doctors typically wait in clinics; Christ dons flesh and knocks on leper colonies. He dines with tax collectors (Lk 5:29-32), converses with adulterous Samaritans (Jn 4), and reinstates deniers over charcoal fires (Jn 21). Incarnation translates Hosea's pursuit into geographical proximity. Every healing miracle embodies Hosea 14:4 in real time—paralytics walk, thus symbolizing spiritual mobility restored. The cross is ultimate house call: Physician absorbs infection to grant immunity (1 Pet 2:24). Understanding this reframes communion as clinic visit—bread and cup deliver ongoing grace infusion. Incarnational pursuit also informs mission: believers step into relapse spaces—bars, chat rooms—not as judges but medics.

Jesus promised the Spirit would "convict the world concerning sin, righteousness, and judgment," functioning as internal surgeon. Conviction differs from condemnation; the latter paralyzes, the former pinpoints for removal. Hebrews 4:12 likens the Word to a scalpel dividing bone and marrow, precise rather than bludgeoning. Practical experience: a verse unexpectedly pierces, a sermon line lingers uncomfortably, or a friend's gentle question exposes hidden motives. Resistance feels like anesthesia wearing off; yielding leads to peace incision sites (Phil 4:7). Churches pray for Spirit searchlights pre-sermon; worship sets include time for listening, not only singing. Conviction confirms sonship (Heb 12:6), proving patient file is still on Physician's desk.

9.3. Repentance Pathway—Turning, Confessing, Returning

9.3.1 ▪ Take Words with You—Hosea 14:2 and the Gift of Honest Liturgy

Hosea instructs, "Take words and return to the LORD," implying repentance is verbal, not vague remorse. Words function like antibiotics prescription—specific dosage targeting infection. Ancient Israelites recited formula: "Forgive all our iniquity; accept what is good" (Hos 14:2). Christians inherit Psalm 51, the Lord's Prayer, and historic confessions (e.g., Book of Common Prayer) as soul scripts when emotions fog. Writing prayers in journals externalizes chaos; spoken aloud enlists body's participation. Honest liturgy names sin without euphemism—"lust," not "needs." It also names God's character—"compassionate and gracious" (Ex 34:6)—balancing confession with assurance. Families can practice "blessing/forgive" rounds at dinner, training children in micro-repentance vocabulary. Churches that neglect prepared words risk silence of shame; providing liturgical rails helps derailed saints regain track.

9.3.2 ▪ Naming the False Lovers—Specific, Root-Level Confession

Gomer had actual lovers; modern backsliders nurse digital affairs, hidden bottle stashes, or pride applause. Naming these idols aloud disarms their secrecy power (Eph 5:11-13). Root-level confession goes beneath behavior: not just "I over-ate" but "I sought comfort apart from God." Tools like the "seven deadly sins" grid or Enneagram shadow side help drill down. Counselors employ genograms to uncover generational patterns fueling relapse. Confession includes restitution plans—Zacchaeus style (Lk 19:8)—clarifying sincerity. Public admission may be necessary when sin harmed community; 2 Cor 2:6-8 shows how church later reaffirms repentant offender.

9.3.3 ▪ Receiving Pardon—Justification, Adoption, and the End of Self-Pay

After confession, many linger in self-punishment, but gospel logic demands immediate reception of pardon. Justification declares right standing (Rom 5:1); adoption confers family seat (Gal 4:5-7). Hosea portrays God saying, "My anger has turned away" (Hos 14:4), indicating propitiation accomplished. Sacrificial system pointed to Christ's once-for-all payment (Heb 10:14). Practically, believers can enact reception by visualizing handing sin to Jesus and taking His righteousness robe (Isa 61:10). Singing grace-saturated hymns ("It Is Well," "Before the Throne") helps emotions catch up with verdict. Pardon also ends penance vows—no extra volunteer hours to earn forgiveness. This freedom births joy, the energy for new obedience.

9.3.4 ▪ Renewed Allegiance—Fresh Surrender of Time, Talent, Treasure

Repentance culminates in allegiance, not mere apology; Israelites vowed, "We will no longer say to the work of our hands, 'You are our gods'" (Hos 14:3). New allegiance reallocates resources: credit-card statements start reflecting kingdom first-fruits, calendars include Sabbath and service slots, talents once used for self-brand now lift the poor. Rule-of-life documents make vows concrete—daily prayer, weekly community, monthly generosity targets. Romans 12:1 calls this offering "reasonable worship." Obedience tests allegiance; forgiving an abuser or returning stolen funds proves lordship transfer. Baptism renewals or communion participation with open hands symbolize pledge. Ongoing discipleship groups provide accountability for stewardship choices. Ultimately, renewed allegiance transforms backslider into builder; the once-wayward now erects altars of praise where former idols stood, embodying Hosea's vision of vineyards replacing thorn bushes (Hos 2:15).

9.4. Means of Grace—Scripture, Prayer, and Sacrament as Healing Channels

9.4.1 • Medicinal Word—Promises, Warnings, and Identity Declarations

Scripture is a pharmacy with many prescriptions, and the Spirit is the chief pharmacist who selects the right pill at the right time. There are analgesic passages that soothe acute shame ("There is therefore now no condemnation," Rom 8:1), anti-inflammatory warnings that shrink swelling pride (Prov 16:18), and immunity-boosting identity texts that build long-term resistance against relapse (1 Pet 2:9-10). Jesus modeled daily dosage; He countered wilderness temptations with three targeted "It is written" statements (Matt 4:4-10), showing that memories of truth can starve seductive lies. Backsliders often binge-read in crisis and then starve afterward; wiser patients adopt a steady drip—perhaps a chapter of Gospel in the morning for affection, a Psalm at lunch for honest lament, an Epistle paragraph at night for worldview recalibration. Lectio divina slows chewing so nutrients absorb; reading aloud engages ears, doubling intake paths. Marginal notes that connect verses to personal failures create case histories for future reference. Memorization stores portable antidotes; during commute traffic, reciting Romans 6:14 ("Sin shall not be master") re-anchors identity. Group Bible studies add communal safety—others notice when interpretation veers toward self-justification. Finally, prophetic reading expects God to highlight a particular phrase—Hosea's "I will love them freely" may suddenly glow, turning black ink into living voice. Every healing story in church history—Augustine, Luther, Wesley—features a decisive encounter with Scripture, underscoring its primary role in spiritual rehab.

Ignatius of Loyola's five-step *examen* operates like an end-of-day vitals check: (1) invite God's light, (2) review with gratitude, (3) examine emotions, (4) confess shortcomings, (5) ask grace for tomorrow. Practiced nightly, it converts 24-hour segments into miniature repentance cycles, preventing small compromises from calcifying into chronic disease. Hosea's call "Return every day" (paraphrased from Hos 12:6) foreshadows this rhythm. Begin with two deep breaths to signal shift from activity to awareness; then replay the day like film reels, pausing at scenes where joy spiked— these are consolations revealing where God's river bubbled (Ps 46:4). Next note moments of agitation, envy, lust—desolations hinting at cracked cistern leakage. Name each without excuse, receive mercy (1 Jn 1:9), and visualize Jesus washing feet—your feet—in that scene (Jn 13:14). Finish by previewing tomorrow's calendar, asking Spirit to occupy time-slots before anxiety does. Over weeks, patterns emerge: desolations cluster around late-night phone use, consolations bloom after afternoon walks; you adjust environment accordingly. Couples or roommates can share abbreviated examens, deepening intimacy and providing early warning if either begins drifting. Writing one-sentence nightly summaries crafts a longitudinal chart of God's faithfulness—ideal material for testimony nights.

9.4.3 ▪ Baptism Remembered—The Once-for-All Bath and Its Daily Splash

Paul calls baptism a burial with Christ and a resurrection to new life (Rom 6:4), meaning the backslider's truest story remains under water even when behavior resurfaces in mud. Remembering baptism is not sentimental nostalgia but legal appeal: the certificate of adoption still stands. Martin Luther, battling despair, touched his forehead and declared, "I am baptized!"—a practice any believer can mimic under morning shower streams. Churches reinforce identity by locating baptismal fonts at sanctuary entrances so worshippers cross invisible resurrection thresholds each week. Anniversary celebrations—re-reading baptism vows on date of immersion— combat amnesia. Parents can tell children their baptism stories like birth narratives, embedding lineage. Visual cues help: a small bowl of water on study desk, a screen saver of baptism photo, or a scented candle lit during devotions symbolizing Spirit's descent (Matt 3:16-17). Baptism remembrance also fuels ethical decisions; when tempted to gossip, recall you wear the jersey of Christ's team—would you betray colors? Finally, communal liturgies that sprinkle the congregation while reading Titus 3:5 ("He saved us through washing of rebirth") refresh collective memory that the bathwater still cleanses.

9.4.4 ▪ Eucharist as Rehab Meal—Weekly Intake of Covenant Nourishment

Early Christians called the Table *pharmakon athanasias*—medicine of immortality—viewing bread and wine as more than reminders but Spirit-transported nutrients. For backsliders, communion breaks famine cycles; the prodigal's first healthy bite was the father's fatted calf (Lk 15:23). Weekly frequency creates nutritional consistency; skipped meals lead to relapse. Preparation is diagnostic: self-examination (1 Cor 11:28) surfaces grudges, prompting reconciliation before bread reaches lips (Matt 5:24). The shared loaf confronts individualism; you can't clutch private Jesus while ignoring body of Christ. Broken bread reminds chronic achievers that healing flows from received, not produced, grace. Wine (or juice) celebrates covenant joy, inoculating against counterfeit highs. Kneeling posture trains humility, open hands embody dependence. Post-communion silence invites Spirit to seal grace, while sending hymns commission nourished saints into missional neighborhoods. Over years, the Table becomes believers' recovery group—weekly circle where failures confess, Christ forgives, and hope tastes as real as wheat on tongue.

9.5. Communal Therapy—Accountability, Encouragement, and Boundaries

9.5.1 ▪ "Restore in a Spirit of Gentleness" (Gal 6:1)—Pastoral Protocols

Paul's directive frames restoration as delicate surgery: qualified "spiritual" people set broken bones with gentleness, aware of their own fracture risk. Churches formalize protocols: initial private meeting, written repentance plan, mentor assignment, and periodic review. Gentle tone avoids shame grenades; phrases like "We're on your team" replace "How could you?" Confidentiality protects dignity; gossip is treated as malpractice. Team approach prevents power abuse; at least two leaders attend serious conversations, mirroring Matthew 18 plurality. Scripture meditation opens sessions, grounding counsel in objective truth. SMART goals (specific, measurable, attainable, relevant, timely) move abstract repentance into actionable steps—e.g., blocking pornography sites, attending trauma therapy. Pastors track progress but celebrate incremental wins, clapping when someone reaches 30 days sobriety. When relapse occurs, protocols kick in without surprise; consequences are pre-agreed (temporary ministry pause), emphasizing safety not punishment. Over time, success stories create a culture where confession is normal healthcare, not emergency room shame.

9.5.2 ▪ Peer Groups and Covenant Friendships—Open-Heart Practices

James 5:16 links mutual confession with healing, suggesting some sickness lingers because secrets fester. Covenant groups covenant to meet weekly, share highs/lows, scripture engagement, and accountability questions ("Did anything capture your heart more than Jesus?"). Rotating facilitators flatten hierarchy and train leadership. Rules ban rescuing—listeners empathize but don't hijack story. Groups adopt "no-fix" first response: empathy before advice. Shared spiritual disciplines—fasting together before big decisions— forge solidarity. Digital group threads maintain midweek connection with prayer emojis and scripture screenshots. When a member disappears, two pursue—the lost-sheep protocol. Mixed-age groups leverage cross-generational wisdom; younger zeal inspires elders, elders' scars warn youth. Over years, friendships deepen; hospital visits, wedding toasts, and funeral stands prove covenant durability against isolation temptations.

9.5.3 ▪ Church Discipline Re-Imagined—Protective Fence, Not Punitive Wall

Discipline is family medicine, not court sentencing. Jesus' three-step process (Matt 18:15-17) prioritizes rescue: private reproof hopes to regain sibling quietly; bringing two or three adds credibility, not shame; telling church invites corporate intercession, not public stoning. Only persistent refusal triggers boundary line "treat as Gentile," which still invites evangelistic pursuit—Jesus loved Gentiles. Guidelines clarify timeframes: after X unresponsive contacts, escalate. Leaders ensure due process—allegations documented, accused heard. Restoration path spelled out before exclusion, so door remains visible. Congregations taught theology of discipline so they interpret announcements as love, not gossip fodder. Success metrics count restorations, not expulsions. Stories of reinstated members shared (with permission) fuel hope; applause signals community's joy mirroring father's feast.

9.5.4 ▪ *Celebrating Return—Public Re-Affirmation and Reintegration Liturgies*

Luke 15 climax is music, dancing, and robe gifts—archetype for church celebration. Upon completing repentance plan, returning members share testimony, then leaders read absolution scriptures— Micah 7:19, 1 Jn 1:9—over them. Congregation stands to recite Apostle's Creed, symbolizing shared faith. Anointing with oil (Jas 5:14) marks healing; gifting new Bible or service lanyard embodies restored trust. Communion served first to restored person flips shame to honor. Potluck follows, reinforcing inclusion through casseroles and laughter. Social media announcement framed as praise—not spectacle—extends joy to absent members. Follow-up buddy continues six months, ensuring support beyond confetti. Such liturgies rewrite memory; the day of worst exposure becomes anniversary of greatest grace, deterring future wanderings.

9.6. Practical Rehab Plans—Habit Re-Formation and Environment Design

9.6.1 ▪ *Replacing Triggers—From Baal Altars to Altars of Daily Worship*

Israel's relapse hotspots were high places; God ordered them demolished (2 Ki 23:13). Likewise, modern triggers—certain apps, lonely Friday nights, paycheck days—must be identified and swapped. Evening scroll becomes evening Psalm; the same couch now hosts gratitude journal. Location therapy matters: doing devotions at a sunny window associates Scripture with dopamine. Playlist replacement: worship tracks in car where talk-radio anger once reigned. Physical cues remind covenant: wedding ring prayer when tempted, cross necklace touch when anxious. Removing alcohol from house transforms stumbling block into non-issue. Accountability software emails browsing reports to mentor, neutralizing secrecy. Over months, brain rewires; triggers now prompt prayer reflex, not sin reflex.

9.6.2 ▪ *Rule of Life Templates—Rhythms for Mind, Body, Relationships, Mission*

Monastic wisdom offers scaffolding for fragile wills. A personal Rule lists daily (morning prayer, midday examen), weekly (Sabbath, small group), monthly (silence retreat), and annual (fasting week) rhythms. It covers body: 7-hour sleep goal, 30-minute walk. Relationships: date night, child one-on-one time, spiritual director monthly. Mission: volunteer hours, neighbor hospitality frequency. Rules remain grace-filled; failure triggers mercy review, not self-flagellation. Apps like "Rule of Life" send reminders and track adherence, visualizing progress. Quarterly edits accommodate life seasons—new baby, shifting job. Posting Rule on fridge invites family accountability.

9.6.3 ▪ *Digital Detox and Attention Stewardship—Guarding the Gateways*

Phones are portable Baals; disabling push notifications is modern idol-tearing. 24-hour tech sabbaths reduce dopamine dependence. Greyscale mode curbs addictive color cues. News intake capped via email digests prevents outrage inundation. Curated feeds unfollow envy-inducing influencers; follow theologians, missionaries, and nature photographers that lift eyes to Creator. Screen time replaced with book reading re-expands attention span—crucial for deep scripture meditation. Families institute charging stations outside bedrooms to protect sleep and marital intimacy. During detox month, participants record mood changes; many note decreased anxiety and increased creative ideas. Stewardship continues post-detox: intentional app re-installation only if aligns with vocation or formation goals.

9.6.4 • *Markers of Progress—Joy, Obedient Flexibility, Missional Overflow*

Jesus gauges restored Peter not by perfect record but by love and willingness to feed sheep (Jn 21:15-17). Progress indicators therefore include resurrection joy—singing returns in shower. Obedient flexibility shows when God redirects schedule and heart says "yes" without bargaining. Generosity marks freedom: tithing becomes cheerful, spontaneous giving erupts. Missional overflow appears as eagerness to share testimony, tutor youth, or join prayer walks. Emotional resilience grows—temptation triggers prompt immediate truth-recall, not spiral. Relapse intervals lengthen; if falls occur, recovery is rapid, guilt shorter. Community feedback confirms change—spouse notices patience, boss sees integrity. Celebrate milestones: 90-day chip, first holiday season sober, one-year porn-free. Ultimately, fruit of the Spirit—love, joy, peace, self-control—serves as medical chart confirming Physician's ongoing success (Gal 5:22-23).

9.7. Living in Ongoing Grace—Assurance, Resilience, and Holy Confidence

9.7.1 • *"Roots Like Lebanon, Shoots Like Olive" (Hosea 14:5-7)— Signs of Vitality*

Hosea caps his prophecy with a botanical triad—dew-kissed lily, firmly rooted cedar, and fragrant olive grove—offering a diagnostic checklist for restored believers. First, roots like Lebanon's cedars speak of hidden depth: the once-wavering saint now draws life from aquifers of Scripture memorization and contemplative prayer, unseen yet undeniable (Ps 1:2-3). Second, shoots like an olive refer to visible new growth—fresh ministry initiatives, reconciled relationships, spontaneous worship—that prove inward renewal has outward expression (Jn 15:8). Third, fragrance wafting like Lebanon's cedars hints at reputation; even skeptics notice calmer tone on social media, gentler reactions in traffic, and steadier joy under pressure (2 Cor 2:14-15). The passage also mentions shade, signifying hospitality: healed people provide refuge for newbies in faith, just as sizeable cedars host nesting birds (Mt 13:32). Moreover, grain flourishing and vines blossoming denote productivity without burnout—projects now flow from grace energy, not adrenaline (Eph 2:10). Regular check-ups ask, "Is my root system expanding—am I learning, repenting, staying curious?" and "Are new shoots sprouting—am I risking again for kingdom?" If either stalls, remedial watering is scheduled: silent retreat, mentorship chat, or serving outside comfort zone. Just as Lebanon's forests grow over decades, believers accept slow ripening; impatience is pruned by Sabbath rhythms. In drought seasons, deep roots keep leaves green (Jer 17:8), reminding saints that feelings fluctuate but covenant sap endures. Ultimately, this horticultural promise guards against relapse by shifting metrics from flash to fruit and by planting expectation of continual, organic, Spirit-given growth.

9.7.2 ▪ Battling Condemnation—Romans 8:1 vs. Accuser's Echoes

The enemy who enticed into backsliding often morphs into prosecutor once repentance begins, flinging "you'll fall again" whispers like fiery darts (Rev 12:10). Believers respond with Romans 8:1 as legal decree—"No condemnation"—not motivational slogan. The Greek *katakrima* denotes final verdict, meaning double jeopardy is impossible because Christ already absorbed sentence (Isa 53:5). Practical warfare starts with thought audits: when a condemning memory surfaces, pause and label it accusation, not conviction; conviction is specific and hopeful, accusation vague and shaming. Speaking truth aloud engages auditory nerves, drowning internal noise—try reading Romans 8:31-39 in first person. Visual anchors help: some keep a stamped "PAID" note on desk; others write 8:1 on bathroom mirror. Community assists—friends trained to answer "I blew it" texts with gospel, not pep talk. Liturgy reinforces verdict: weekly declarations like "In Christ we are forgiven" after corporate confession export theology to the pew. Singing hymns such as "Before the Throne of God Above" weaponizes melody against mental loops. Physical posture—shoulders back, head lifted—refuses shame curvature (Lk 13:11-12). Counselors may guide EMDR or CBT techniques to re-file traumatic memories under forgiven category. If condemnation persists, revisit justification doctrine—books like *Concise Theology*

226

by Packer fortify mind. Remember Zachariah's vision: filthy priest clothed in clean garments while Satan is silenced (Zech 3:1-4). Daily communion with Christ inoculates; accuser cannot breach a heart whose identity rests in blood-bought embrace.

9.7.3 • Perseverance Practices—Micro-Repentance and Quick Return Reflexes

Hebrews exhorts believers to run with endurance, implying marathon mindset, not sprint spurts (Heb 12:1-2). Micro-repentance operates like course-correction nudges: confess sharp word moments after it leaves mouth, rather than letting infection spread (Eph 4:26-27). Set phone alarms labelled "heart check" to pause, breathe, ask, "Any drift since last hour?" Downloading 3-minute examen apps integrates rapid reviews into lunch breaks. Quick return reflex mirrors David's swift "I have sinned" once confronted (2 Sam 12:13); delay fertilizes guilt weeds. Tracking relapse frequency in journal spots patterns; when a spike appears, schedule mentor call. Scripture memory hinged on temptations (e.g., 1 Cor 10:13 for escapism) equips instant counterpunch. Celebrating small victories—seven clean days, one gentle reply—keeps morale buoyant. Exercise and sleep enhance perseverance; fatigue erodes willpower (Mk 6:31). Serving others shifts focus outward, preventing introspection spiral. Periodic fasting resets appetite hierarchy—body learns it can say no, spirit remembers it can obey. Annual spiritual health physical with pastor reviews goals, adjusts Rule of Life. Endurance thrives on hope: visualize finish-line embrace ("Well done," Mt 25:23). Hebrews 12:3 urges reflection on Christ's endurance to prevent weary hearts; meditating on Gethsemane injects resilience serum. Perseverance, then, is not teeth-grit but rhythm-based grace, maintained by dozens of swift pivots back to Father.

9.7.4 • Witness from Scars—Transforming Former Failures into Pastoral Wisdom

Thomas demanded to see nail scars; Jesus did not hide healing marks but used them as authentication (Jn 20:27-28). Likewise, restored believers bear sanctified scars—memories no longer bleeding but still visible, testifying to the Surgeon's skill. Sharing story breaks

227

shame's secrecy, encourages still-struggling peers (Rev 12:11). Testimony guidelines ensure focus on Redeemer, not graphic sin glorification; outline: darkness, turning point, restoration fruit. Celebrate Recovery and Alpha courses recruit scarred leaders precisely because credibility flows from "I've been there." Paul leveraged persecutor past to magnify mercy (1 Tim 1:13-16); modern Pauls mentor younger addicts, giving hope of long-term sobriety. Scars also become discernment sensors—having felt edge of cliff, restored saints smell danger earlier and can warn church. Writing blogs or devotionals translates personal lessons into communal resources. Boundaries persist: share in appropriate settings, with spouse consent, guarding listeners from trigger overload. Yet suppression robs kingdom; God never wastes pain (Gen 50:20). Annual "grace stories" services platform new testimonies, refreshing congregation's faith. Even vocational callings arise: counselors, pastors, social-workers birthed from healed wounds. Thus, scars transition from shame artifacts to royal regalia—evidence that the Great Physician truly heals backsliders and drafts them into His medical corps.

9.8. Eschatological Restoration—Ultimate Healing and Eternal Fidelity

9.8.1 ▪ *"Death, Where Is Your Plague?"—Hosea 13:14 Fulfilled in Resurrection*

Hosea taunts death centuries before the empty tomb: "I will ransom them…and redeem them from death" (Hos 13:14). Paul cites the verse in 1 Corinthians 15:55, declaring Christ's resurrection as down payment on total cure. For backsliders, this eschatological victory means relapse can never reverse ultimate destiny; even final enemy is defanged. The Greek *nikos* (victory) frames Christian perseverance inside cosmic scoreboard already decided. Resurrection also validates embodied hope—our future selves will be incapable of backsliding because glorified bodies will echo obedient spirits (Phil 3:20-21). Meditating on resurrection fuels present holiness: you practice being the person you are destined to become. Funerals for believers serve as prophetic rehearsals; coffins preach "temporary residence." Pain management changes— suffering is pregnant with glory (Rom 8:18). Daily setbacks shrink

228

when contrasted with eternal triumph curve. Believers facing terminal disease cling to Hosea's promise, turning hospice rooms into worship sites. Easter becomes annual booster shot; its afterglow lingers all year for relapse fighters.

9.8.2 ▪ The Marriage Supper of the Lamb—Backslider Became Bride (Revelation 19:7-9)

Hosea's marital metaphor culminates in Revelation's wedding feast where the once-adulterous people don linen bright and clean. Ancient Jewish customs required months of betrothal preparation; similarly, sanctification readies saints for table seating. The menu—fine wine and rich marrow (Isa 25:6)—signals lavish acceptance. Place cards bear new names (Rev 2:17), hinting at finalized identity distances from past labels like "Lo-Ammi." Viewing Christian life as bridal preparation reframes disciplines: purity is no longer rule list but trousseau fitting. Communion anticipates banquet; each sip whispers, "Save room for main course." Evangelism widens guest list; servants sent to highways compel latecomers (Mt 22:9-10). Imagine walking aisle of cosmic cathedral; meditating on that scene stirs fidelity now. When temptation growls, recall fiancé's soon arrival (Jas 5:8). The feast also promises multicultural harmony—every tribe at one table—motiving racial reconciliation today. Feast imagery assures chronic dieters of spiritual famine that satiation is guaranteed; we fast now to feast forever.

9.8.3 ▪ No More Wandering—New-Covenant Hearts Etched with God's Law (Jeremiah 31:33)

Jeremiah prophesies heart surgery: law internalized, rendering external enforcement obsolete. Hebrews 8:10 confirms fulfillment in Christ, announcing that divine handwriting on neural pathways remodels impulse patterns. Backsliding thrives on divided heart; new covenant fuses will and desire. The Spirit acts as built-in GPS, rerouting when veering off course (Gal 5:18). This doesn't negate vigilance but upgrades its power source—like electric fence energized by sun, not battery of self-effort. Daily surrender "keep in step with the Spirit" (Gal 5:25) taps perpetual guidance. Group discernment sessions highlight Spirit nudges that surprisingly converge, proving internal law is corporate as well. Moral formation becomes inside-out artistry: generosity no longer feels heroic but natural, akin to sap producing fruit. Worship lyrics "prone to wander" remain confession of flesh, yet Spirit counters with homing beacon stronger than drift. Eternal state promises zero tug-of-war; vision of God will so satisfy that sin proposal will sound ludicrous (1 Jn 3:2). Until then, believers rehearse future harmony by quick obedience now—prompt forgiveness, instant generosity, reflex prayer.

9.8.4 ▪ Hope Now, Glory Later—Living Today in the Light of Final Wholeness

Christian hope splits into twin beams: *now*—immediate access to throne (Heb 4:16), and *later*—inheritance undefiled (1 Pet 1:4). Holding both prevents despair and presumption. Hope-now empowers risk: entrepreneurs launch kingdom ventures, trusting God to refill accounts; missionaries brave hostile zones, assured of everlasting reward (Mk 10:29-30). Hope-later tempers disappointment: unmet dreams file under "reserve for glory." Practical ritual: before major decision, ask, "Will this choice echo in the new earth?" If yes, proceed boldly; if not, hold loosely. Suffering saint applies two-hand timeline—left hand catalogs present mercies, right hand holds future crown (2 Tim 4:8). Gratitude journals balance pages: one side today's grace, other side promises yet to bloom. Art and creativity flourish as prophetic sketches of coming beauty; painters depict Isaiah 11 peace, composers score Revelation 21 symphonies. Ethical living becomes eschatological signaling—every act of justice previews kingdom constitution. Annual vision retreats include reading final two Revelation chapters aloud on a beach sunrise, imprinting telos on imagination. Even funerals declare hope duality—ashes return to soil (now sorrow) while trumpet awaits (future glory). Thus believers navigate between harbors, sails full of Spirit wind, eyes fixed on horizon where sun never sets, confident that backsliding's scars will dissolve into storybooks read by grandchildren beside the river of life.

Conclusion When Hosea ends with orchards blooming and roots spreading like Lebanon's cedars, he is sketching your future, not sentimental poetry. Restoration is more than damage control; it is placement within a thriving ecosystem of grace where former deserters become sturdy oaks of righteousness. Backsliding loses its narrative power because a greater story now governs your identity—the story of a Shepherd who not only finds lost sheep but teaches them to hear His voice and follow closely. As you leave these pages, remember: relapse is always possible, but immediate return is always available. Keep short accounts with God, nurture practices that keep the soil soft, and let His free love move you from shame to holy confidence. The Great Physician has written "fully restored" across your chart; your role is to live, day by day, in agreement with His diagnosis and His cure.

Chapter 10. Steadfast Mercy— Becoming People of Compassion

Mercy is not a sentimental mood that drifts into the room when life is gentle. In Hosea's pages it is a fierce, covenant-forged force that out-waits betrayal, out-loves rebellion, and out-lasts judgment. God's declaration—"I will betroth you to Me in *ḥesed* and compassion" (Hos 2 :19)—is more than a pledge to Israel; it is a blueprint for every disciple who has tasted unconditional grace. This chapter asks a probing question: What happens to people who live daily under that kind of steadfast kindness? Scripture and history attest that they are gradually re-made into conduits of the very mercy that rescued them—spouses who forgive seventy-seven times, churches where prodigals find open arms, companies that choose fairness over exploitation, and believers who cross cultural fault lines carrying practical compassion. Here we explore how deep reception of God's loyal love heals the inner orphan and ignites an outward revolution of gentleness, justice, and hope.

10.1. The Theology of *Ḥesed*—Mercy Rooted in Covenant Love

10.1.1 ▪ Defining Ḥesed—Loyal Love, Kindness, and Unbreakable Commitment

Ḥesed is one of the most elastic words in the Hebrew Bible, and translators struggle to pin it down with a single English term. It connotes loyal love, covenant faithfulness, deep kindness, and tenacious solidarity all at once. Scholars note that the word carries three simultaneous layers: emotional affection, practical action, and legal obligation. In other words, *ḥesed* feels, moves, and swears. When Ruth clings to Naomi, pledging, "Where you go I will go," she is performing *ḥesed* (Ru 1:16-17). When the Psalmist exults, "Your *ḥesed* is better than life" (Ps 63:3), he is celebrating a love stronger than mortality. Covenant documents of the ancient Near East show kings using cognate terms to guarantee protection for vassals, so *ḥesed* implies shelter under royal wings. Yet unlike human treaties, God's *ḥesed* precedes any merit; He "abounds" in it even to the thousandth generation (Ex 34:6-7). The Septuagint often translates *ḥesed* with *eleos* (mercy) or *charis* (grace), revealing how the New Testament writers inherited the concept. Modern disciples therefore do violence to the word if they reduce it to mere sentimentality; it is more like a legal adoption paper soaked in tears of affection. *Ḥesed* sticks when attraction fades. It picks up prodigals at bus stations at 2 a.m. It keeps vows when memories blur. To receive *ḥesed* is to be folded into a commitment you did not initiate and cannot terminate. To offer *ḥesed* is to treat another person's well-being as your own sacred responsibility. Hosea's entire prophetic burden hangs on that extraordinary definition.

10.1.2 ▪ Hosea's Portrait—From Courtroom Indictment to Marital Restoration

Hosea sketches *ḥesed* on a canvas splashed with betrayal. The opening chapters read like a courtroom, with Yahweh arraigning Israel for breach of covenant: "There is no faithfulness or *ḥesed...* only bloodshed" (Hos 4:1-2). The shocking command that the prophet marry Gomer visualizes the charges; her serial infidelity embodies Israel's spiritual promiscuity. Yet even while pronouncing judgment, God's speeches drip with longing: "How can I give you up, Ephraim?" (Hos 11:8). The same mouth that roars like a lion (Hos 5:14) later whispers marital vows, "I will betroth you in *ḥesed* and compassion" (Hos 2:19). The swing between anger and tenderness reveals that divine wrath is not the opposite of mercy but its servant—clearing debris so *ḥesed* can reach its target. The renaming of the children seals the reversal: "Not-Loved" becomes "Loved," "Not-My-People" becomes "My-People" (Hos 2:23), proving *ḥesed* has the power to rewrite identity records. Hosea thus demonstrates that covenant compassion is not naïve tolerance; it is costly pursuit that absorbs the pain of reconciliation. The book ends with Yahweh himself taking the initiative: "I will heal their backsliding; I will love them freely" (Hos 14:4), a line that functions as the Old-Testament gospel in miniature. Anyone who studies Hosea without sensing a summons to become similarly stubborn in mercy has missed the prophet's beating heart.

10.1.3 ▪ Ḥesed Across Scripture—Ruth, Psalms, Prophets, and the Cross

The golden thread of *ḥesed* weaves through the entire canon. In Genesis 39 Joseph finds favor (*ḥesed*) even in prison—proof that the covenant travels into dungeons. Ruth's midnight threshing-floor proposal is lauded as "greater *ḥesed* than the first" because she seeks legacy for Naomi, not just romance for herself (Ru 3:10). The Psalms hymn the word 127 times; Psalm 136 turns it into a refrain,

"For his *ḥesed* endures forever," after each line of salvation history, inviting worshipers to chant mercy into muscle memory. The prophets fuse justice and mercy: Micah distills religion to "do justice, love *ḥesed*, and walk humbly" (Mi 6:8). In the New Testament, Jesus embodies the attribute—touching lepers (Mk 1:41), weeping over cities (Lk 19:41), and pardoning Peters (Jn 21). Paul's favorite term "grace" (*charis*) echoes *ḥesed*, culminating at the cross where divine loyalty absorbs human disloyalty (Rom 5:8). John frames the incarnation as *plērēs* of "grace and truth" (Jn 1:14), a binary that Hosea had already welded. Revelation ends with the marriage supper of the Lamb—permanent *ḥesed* secured (Rev 19:9). Thus, from Eden's animal-skin covering to Calvary's veil-tearing cry, Scripture drips with the same compassionate DNA. To preach anything less than relentless mercy is to misrepresent the family story.

10.1.4 ▪ Trinitarian Mercy—Father's Heart, Son's Incarnation, Spirit's Indwelling

Mercy is not merely a divine policy but the Trinity's relational atmosphere. The Father "so loved the world" that He gave (Jn 3:16); love initiates rescue. The Son enacts *ḥesed* in skin, dining with traitors and absorbing wrath (Eph 2:4-7). The Spirit applies mercy microscopically—pouring it "into our hearts" (Rom 5:5) and sealing adoption papers (Eph 1:13-14). At Jesus' baptism, the Father's voice of delight and the Spirit's dove kiss the Son's obedience, revealing *ḥesed* as an intra-triune overflow shared with humanity. Trinitarian mercy means believers experience compassion on multiple fronts: cosmic (the Father's plan), historical (the Son's cross), and personal (the Spirit's whispers). It also shapes communal ethics; churches become extensions of that triune hospitality, welcoming prodigals to the family table. Prayer taps the Trinity's compassionate circuitry— addressed to the Father, through the Son, by the Spirit (Eph 2:18). Missional outreach mirrors perichoretic dance: we go because the Father sends, the Son accompanies (Mt 28:20), and the Spirit empowers (Acts 1:8). Understanding mercy trinitarily guards against cheap grace (Father without holiness), moralism (Son without sympathy), or spiritualism (Spirit without flesh). It invites worship that is both awestruck and intimate, kneeling in wonder yet climbing into Abba's lap.

10.2. Receiving Mercy Deeply—Healing the Inner Orphan

10.2.1 • Shame vs. Belovedness—Identity Re-Scripted by Grace (Romans 8:15-17)

Shame is the emotional echo of Eden's fig leaves: it whispers, "You are unworthy of closeness, so hide." Belovedness is the Father's counter-roar: "You are my child; come home." Paul describes conversion as adoption whereby slaves to fear receive the Spirit of sonship and cry "Abba!" (Rom 8:15-17). Yet many Christians still live like spiritual orphans—performing for approval, fearing abandonment, mistrusting celebration. Hosea tackles this orphan spirit directly; God promises, "In you the orphan finds mercy" (Hos 14:3). Practical exercises can move truths from head to heart: lectio on baptism narratives, imagining the Father's voice spoken over you; journaling a letter from older-you in heaven affirming current-you's status; or placing a photo of prodigal's embrace (Lk 15) where you pay bills to remember worth is not wages. Small groups can create "identity circles," where each member declares scriptural names over another—saint, temple, masterpiece. Therapists employ EMDR to untangle traumatic shame neural loops, allowing gospel scripts to rewrite them. It is vital to distinguish conviction (I did wrong) from toxic shame (I am wrong). Daily practice: when failure surfaces, respond, "That was not in line with who I am as beloved," rather than "I'm disgusting." Over time, belovedness becomes emotional reflex; soul runs toward God after sin, not away. Hosea's promise thus migrates from prophecy to physiology—new neural pathways etched by mercy.

10.2.2 • Confession as Mercy Doorway—Falling into, not out of, God's Arms

Confession is often viewed as courtroom plea bargaining, but in Scripture it is more like collapsing into a physician's care. "If we confess our sins, he is faithful and just to forgive" (1 Jn 1:9); the terms "faithful" and "just" infuse confession with covenant

236

confidence, not gamble. Hosea urges Israel to "take words" (Hos 14:2); words function as stretcher carrying wounded honesty into triage. The posture is forward-leaning: confession aims at restoration, not self-flagellation. Practical frameworks include the ACTS acronym—Adoration, Confession, Thanksgiving, Supplication—ensuring confession is sandwiched by grace. Writing sins on dissolvable paper and placing them in water during a retreat dramatizes vanishing guilt (Mic 7:19). Confessing to a trusted friend aligns with James 5:16, adding relational medicine. Regular confession prevents sin layering into callus; think "spiritual flossing." Churches enriched by historic liturgy repeat communal confessions weekly, democratizing the practice—no solo specialists, all in need. The paradox: the quicker you admit failure, the less power failure wields. Thus confession is not an exit from intimacy but the threshold of deeper union.

10.2.3 • Practicing Self-Compassion—Agreeing with Heaven's Verdict

Self-compassion is not self-excuse; it is aligning internal dialogue with God's external declaration of mercy. Jesus told the adulterous woman, "Neither do I condemn you; go and sin no more" (Jn 8:11)— a sentence that balances kindness with call. Research shows that shame floods the limbic system, narrowing cognitive capacity, while compassionate self-talk calms fear centers, enabling change. Daily practice: place hand over heart and speak Romans 8:1 aloud, breathing slowly to embody truth. Replace "I'm stupid" with "I made an error, but I'm learning," mirroring God's growth orientation (Phil 1:6). Sabbath includes treating body kindly— adequate sleep, nourishing food—signaling that redeemed flesh matters (1 Cor 6:19-20). When inner critic pipes up, ask, "Would I say this to a hurting friend?" If not, silence it. Spiritual directors recommend writing a Compassion Charter: a personal pledge to respond to failure as God does. Over time, neurons fire along mercy pathways, making condemnation foreign. Remember, self-hatred does not honor the cross; it implies Christ's sacrifice was insufficient.

237

10.2.4 • *Story Work—Letting Divine Mercy Rewrite Personal Narratives*

God is the Author who edits tragic scripts into redemption arcs (Gen 50:20). Story work invites believers to trace life chapters, naming wounds and noticing *ḥesed* footprints. Joseph said, "God sent me ahead to preserve life" (Gen 45:5), re-narrating betrayal as providence. Tools include timeline mapping—plotting highs, lows, and turning points on paper, then overlaying Scripture promises experienced in each season. Prayerful imagination asks Jesus, "Where were You in this memory?" and often reveals unnoticed presence. Hosea's Israel will one day call former Valley of Trouble a Door of Hope (Hos 2:15); likewise, abuse survivors who experience God's comfort often become compassionate advocates. Sharing rewritten stories in community consolidates healing and multiplies faith. Cognitive-behavioral therapy intersects: reframing distorted beliefs with gospel truth. Sacramental markers—planting a tree on anniversary of sobriety—embody new storyline. Journaling future chapters—"By God's grace, five years from now..."— propels hope. Ultimately story work converts mercy from doctrine to autobiography: you move from studying Hosea to starring in a modern rerun of his redemptive narrative.

10.3. Mercy in the Family—Cultivating Compassionate Households

10.3.1 • *Marital Kindness—Micro-Mercies that Fortify Covenant Vows*

Marriage is the daily theater where *ḥesed* either shines or shrivels. Paul commands spouses to mirror Christ's sacrificial love (Eph 5:25-33), making compassion not optional nicety but marital DNA. Research by John Gottman shows successful couples maintain a 5:1 ratio of positive to negative interactions; micro-mercies—thank-you's, back rubs, coffee mugs ready—accumulate into fortress walls against contempt. Hosea illustrates marital resilience: he buys back Gomer (Hos 3:2), modeling costly reconciliation. Practical tools: "daily debrief" 15-minute listening sessions without devices; weekly Sabbath date where conflict topics are off-limits, focusing on delight. Conflict rules guard tone: "I" statements, time-outs when flooded, prayer pause mid-argument. Forgiveness liturgies—reading Col 3:13 together—reset atmosphere. Households can display covenant symbol (framed vows) in bedroom as visual anchor. Sexual intimacy thrives when undergirded by compassionate attunement; 1 Cor 7:3-5 frames mutual service, not demand. Teaching children to witness parental apologies demonstrates humility culture. Over decades, micro-mercies outlast hormonal surges and career upheavals, proving that compassion, not passion, is the glue.

10.3.2 ▪ Parenting with Grace and Truth—Discipline as Discipleship (Ephesians 6:4)

Paul warns fathers not to provoke but to nurture, blending boundary and warmth. Mercy-based discipline differentiates consequence from rejection; a child may lose screen time yet keep parental delight. Hosea 11 shows God teaching Ephraim to walk, stooping down, then lamenting necessary discipline—a template for parental balance. Practical strategy: use "time-in" (sitting with child to process emotions) before "time-out." Employ natural consequences rather than shame-loaded punishments. Affirm identity before correction: "You're kind; hitting isn't like you." Family devotionals centering on gospel reinforce heart-level motivation. Parents confess own mistakes, modeling need for mercy. Teenagers receive responsibility increments alongside grace safety nets—curfew discussions framed as care, not control. Celebrating repentance— ice-cream after apology—associates confession with joy. Grandparents can reinforce narrative with storytelling of God's faithfulness across generations (Ps 78:4-7). Over time, children internalize compassionate authority, making God's fatherhood plausible.

10.3.3 ▪ Sibling Peace-Making—Training Children in Reconciliation Skills

Cain's failure still echoes in hallway fights; parents must coach siblings to handle conflict redemptively. Teach Matthew 18's steps in kid language: Talk, Listen, Get Help. Implement "peacemaker chairs" where rivals articulate feelings using sentence starters: "I felt ___ when ___." Affirm, then brainstorm solutions. Scripture memory of Eph 4:32 ("Be kind...") reinforces neural scripts. Model apology—parents reconcile disagreements in front of kids. Family meetings review weekly conflicts, celebrate peacemaking wins. Rotate chores to build empathy: when brother washes sister's dishes, resentments soften. Encourage joint projects—puzzles, garden care—requiring cooperation. Storybooks like *The Berenstain Bears Get in a Fight* open discussion. Pray nightly blessing over each child, asking God to knit hearts. Tracking reduction in tattling becomes metric of growth. Eventually, siblings become each other's intercessors, fulfilling Psalm 133's vision of unified brothers.

10.3.4 ▪ Hospitality Habits—Turning Dinner Tables into Mercy Tables

Mercy begins where casseroles land. Biblical hospitality welcomes strangers (Heb 13:2) and frames meals as kingdom previews (Lk 14:12-14). Families schedule "Open-Table Friday," inviting neighbors or church visitors. Kids help cook, set placeholders, and ask guests two get-to-know questions, learning empathy. Prayer before meal thanks God for stories gathered, not just food. Recipes chosen consider dietary restrictions, signaling attentiveness. Conversation guidelines outlaw gossip; practice "high-low-wow" sharing. Table liturgy includes candle signaling Christ's presence and blessing spoken over each guest (Num 6:24-26). Leftovers packaged for take-home extend mercy beyond evening. During holidays, adopt "plus-one rule" so singles, internationals, or widows find family. Hospitality budget line counters scarcity excuses. Follow-up texts express gratitude and sustain relationship. Children observe diversity, dismantling us-them binaries. Thus dinner becomes discipleship lab where steadfast mercy marinates in aroma of roasted chicken and laughter.

10.4. Church as Mercy Community—Structures and Cultures of Compassion

10.4.1 ▪ Preaching the Tender Heart of God—Homiletical Approaches

Mercy culture is fertilized first from the pulpit, because what the preacher magnifies the people imitate. Sermons that merely exhort without unveiling divine tenderness leave hearers inspired for a week but internally underfed for a lifetime. Hosea offers a model: he announces judgment only to pivot to compassion, letting wrath serve mercy rather than eclipse it (Hos 11:8–9). Homiletically that means every rebuke must contain a roadmap back to grace, lest listeners despair. Exegetical preaching can highlight verbs of divine feeling— "My heart recoils within me" (Hos 11:8)—so congregations realize God's holiness includes deep attachment, not aloof perfection. Illustrations should incarnate mercy in everyday scenes: a foster parent's midnight bottle-warming or a boss who keeps an employee on payroll during illness. Preachers can also practice "gospel reversals," showing how Christ absorbs the penalty the text describes, then offers the blessing it promises. Narrative sermons that slow-motion the prodigal's embrace (Lk 15:20) let congregants hear sandals slap and robe rustle, tethering emotions to doctrine. Application sections move beyond "try harder to be nice" toward Spirit-empowered practices—breath prayers of compassion during commutes, or budgeting mercy dollars. Testimonies integrated into preaching—five-minute interviews with congregants who forgave impossible debts—create lived hermeneutics. Finally, tone matters: gentle firmness communicates gravity without caricaturing God as perpetually angry. When pulpits consistently radiate the Father's heart, pews gradually swell with people who feel safe enough to fail and hopeful enough to try again.

10.4.2 ▪ Small-Group Safety—Confession, Accountability, and Gentle Restoration

While sermons plant seeds, small groups are the greenhouse where mercy grows to maturity. Safety begins with covenant agreements— confidentiality, non-judgmental listening, and shared facilitation— so no one voice dominates or shames. Leaders model vulnerability first; if they confess impatience with their kids, others sense permission to unmask deeper wounds. James 5:16 links mutual confession to healing, implying that some ailments linger because secrets thrive. A practical rhythm is the "circle of trust": each person shares a high, a low, and where they sensed God's nearness or absence that week. Groups practice empathetic reflection—"What I hear you saying..."—before advice, honoring Proverbs 18:13's call to listen before answering. Accountability questions stay specific: "Did you show kindness to your spouse when stressed?" rather than nebulous "How was your week?" Gentle restoration follows Galatians 6:1: peers ask, "What small step of obedience feels possible?" and then pray, not lecture. Celebration is equally intentional; when someone reaches thirty days sober, the group erupts in applause and perhaps brings cupcakes. Conflict is inevitable, so groups keep a reconciliation protocol—private clarification, then mediated conversation—preventing unresolved tension from poisoning atmosphere. Regular service projects—foodbank sorting, neighborhood clean-ups—bond members through shared mercy deeds. Over time, newcomers walk into these circles and feel a qualitative difference: air thick with acceptance, conversations tinged with hope, tears welcomed rather than hurried away.

10.4.3 ▪ Diaconal Ministries—Food, Finances, and Friendship for the Vulnerable

Acts 6 introduces deacons to ensure widows are not overlooked; compassion administration is therefore as biblical as preaching. Effective mercy ministries start with listening-surveys: what does the neighborhood actually need—fresh produce, financial coaching, mental-health referrals? Food pantries transition from canned-goods dumping to dignity markets where clients choose items and volunteer alongside staff. Financial ministries blend benevolence grants with six-week budgeting classes, echoing Jesus' pattern of feeding multitudes and then teaching (Mk 6:34-42). Churches establish emergency funds accessible within forty-eight hours, because eviction notices do not wait for committee meetings. Volunteers undergo trauma-informed training, learning to ask, "What happened to you?" not "What's wrong with you?" Friendship is the secret sauce; consistent table fellowship breaks the helper-client divide more effectively than any program. Elderly shut-ins receive weekly phone calls plus quarterly home-communion visits, fulfilling James 1:27's pure religion test. Partnerships with local clinics bring free blood-pressure screenings to church foyers, integrating bodily compassion. Metrics include qualitative stories, not just numbers: a single mom secure in housing, a veteran re-grown in confidence, a refugee laughing freely. When diaconal teams report on Sundays, the congregation sees tithes converted into tangible mercy, and giving rises.

Corporate worship reinscribes compassion every seven days. Lament psalms give sufferers a public voice; reading Psalm 13 responsively teaches that doubt belongs inside, not outside, sanctuary walls. Prayers of the People widen horizons—interceding for prisoners, nurses, and politicians creates empathetic muscle memory. Silent confession allows congregants to unload shame onto Christ before singing triumphal refrains. Passing the peace is not perfunctory; it rehearses reconciliation—members cross aisles to grasp hands with those they avoided. Visual liturgy—banners of refugee journeys, communionware crafted by local artisans—immerses eyes in mercy stories. Benedictions like Numbers 6:24-26 send worshipers as blessing agents; congregants raise hands, both receiving and pledging to give. Special services—Blue Christmas for grief, Healing Eucharists with anointing oil—minister to niche pain pockets. Musical curation matters: songs such as "His Mercy Is More" or "Yet Not I but Through Christ in Me" tilt affections toward grace. Finally, testimonies slot into liturgy—five-minute mercy snapshots after Scripture reading—bridging text and life. When worship is thus saturated, congregants exit with hearts tuned to compassion's key.

10.5. Mercy and Justice—Joining God's Preferential Option for the Weak

10.5.1 ▪ Prophetic Consistency—Hosea, Amos, and Social Ethics Today

Hosea marries mercy with justice, condemning merchants who use dishonest scales (Hos 12:7). Amos intensifies the roar: "Let justice roll down like waters" (Am 5:24). The prophets reveal that compassion cannot be selective—God hates both idolatry and exploitation. Modern churches recapture prophetic balance by preaching sin as both personal rebellion and societal rigging. Bible studies examine housing red-lining alongside ancient land-grab laws in Micah 2:2. Book clubs read *Just Mercy* next to Ruth's gleaning mandate. Pastors issue position papers on payday-lending practices, aligning with Proverbs 22:22. Consistency requires self-critique: if a congregation weeps for trafficked children abroad but ignores local foster-care backlog, cursory compassion has replaced covenant compassion. Discipline includes speaking truth to power; letters to city council cite Isaiah's "Woe to unjust decrees" (Isa 10:1). Prophetic mercy stays hopeful, not shrill, because it trusts God's promise to plant vineyards where violence once reigned (Hos 2:15).

10.5.2 ▪ Holistic Gospel—Reconciling Personal Compassion with Structural Change

Jesus healed individuals and overturned temple-market injustice, embodying holistic mission. A robust theology sees cross and kingdom intertwined: personal salvation births agents of systemic renewal (Col 1:20). Practical outworkings pair crisis relief (food drives) with development initiatives (job-training, micro-loans). Sermons articulate the difference between mercy (alleviating immediate pain) and justice (removing root causes), yet call believers to both. Churches host "poverty simulations" that immerse middle-class members in bureaucratic mazes, converting pity into informed action. Partnerships with civic groups allow policy advocacy without partisan captivity. Holistic gospel also includes spiritual warfare; systemic evil is powered by "powers and principalities" (Eph 6:12), so prayer walks encircle city halls before lobbying appointments. Metrics track rising graduation rates, declining recidivism, and church baptisms simultaneously, proving integration possible.

10.5.3 ▪ Advocacy Pathways—Immigrants, Prisoners, and the Unborn

Scripture commands love for the stranger (Lev 19:34), visitation of prisoners (Heb 13:3), and defense of the voiceless unborn (Ps 139:13-16). Advocacy begins with proximity: ESL volunteers learn immigrant names, pen-pal teams write incarcerated neighbors, and pregnancy-center mentors offer long-term support beyond birth. Policy engagement follows relationship; congregants testify at hearings about driver-license access or sentencing reform. Prayer vigils outside detention centers read Psalm 146, reminding activists that God "executes justice for the oppressed." Churches adopt restorative-justice circles, allowing offenders to make amends to

244

victims, echoing Zacchaeus' quadruple restitution (Lk 19:8). Sanctity-of-Life Sunday moves beyond anti-abortion rhetoric to baby-shower generosity and foster-care recruitment. Advocacy training equips members to draft op-eds, understand legislative cycles, and maintain Christlike tone online. Wins are celebrated—green-card approvals, commuted sentences, healthy newborns—fueling perseverance.

10.5.4 ▪ Creation Care as Mercy—Extending Compassion to All God's Creatures

Romans 8 depicts creation groaning; showing mercy to land and animal honors God's first commission (Gen 2:15). Churches start community gardens on unused lots, donating produce to food pantries—mercy for bodies and soil. Sermons tie Hosea 4:3 (land mourning) to modern species extinction, stirring ecological repentance. Plastic-free fellowship meals and reusable-cup stations demonstrate small-scale obedience. Youth groups host creek clean-ups, memorizing Psalm 24:1 en route. Budget lines fund renewable-energy retrofits; savings go to global missions, linking stewardship and evangelism. Liturgies incorporate a "Season of Creation," praying for farmers and climate refugees. Ethical meat consumption—supporting local humane farms—aligns diet with dominion. Mission trips plant mangrove trees as carbon prayer acts. Creation care is framed not as political fad but as neighbor love, since environmental degradation disproportionately harms the poor. Thus mercy enlarges to cosmic scope, anticipating new-earth harmony.

10.6. Vocational Mercy—Compassion in the Workplace and Marketplace

10.6.1 ▪ Business as Blessing—Ethical Profit, Fair Wages, Generous Policies

Proverbs commends diligent hands but condemns wealth gained by oppression (Prov 22:16). Christian entrepreneurs therefore treat profit as fuel for mercy, not idolatry. They implement living-wage audits, ensuring cleaners earn dignified salaries. Flexible schedules accommodate single parents and Sabbath observance. Percent-of-profits tithes fund community projects, echoing gleaning laws (Lev 19:9-10). Transparent supply chains avoid sweatshops; certifications like Fairtrade signal neighbor love across oceans. Job-training programs hire ex-offenders, mirroring Joseph's rise from prison to palace. Quarterly "Bless Days" donate products to nonprofits. Executives practice open-book management, trusting employees with financial data—compassion through empowerment. When layoffs are unavoidable, severance packages include counseling and reference assistance, reflecting Ruth's gleaning kindness. Investors notice ethical ROI, proving mercy and sustainability coexist.

10.6.2 ▪ Professions of Healing—Medicine, Counseling, and Social Work

Jesus went about "teaching, preaching, and healing" (Matt 4:23), setting template for health vocations. Christian doctors see image-bearers, not case numbers; they pray (with permission) before surgeries. Sliding-scale clinics embody Luke 10's Good Samaritan, pouring oil and wine into wounds. Counselors integrate lament psalms into CBT, giving clients language for pain. Social workers view bureaucratic forms as sacred tools to secure shalom. Ethical dilemmas—end-of-life care, justice-involved teens—are navigated through Micah 6:8 lenses. Burnout prevention is mercy to self: sabbath rhythms, peer supervision, spiritual retreats. Testimonies of holistic healing—body and soul—reinforce vocational calling.

10.6.3 ▪ Education and Mentorship—Forming the Merciful Imagination of Students

Teachers shape worldview scaffolding; compassionate pedagogy sees students as whole persons. Classroom norms include "no joke left behind"—humor never targets vulnerability. Literature choices highlight empathy—reading *Les Misérables* sparks debate on justice and grace. Science labs discuss environmental stewardship ethics. Mentoring programs pair retirees with at-risk youth, meeting weekly for life skills and prayer. Discipline policies shift from zero-tolerance to restorative circles, echoing Matthew 18 reconciliation. School lunches incorporate pay-what-you-can options. College professors host office-hour "mercy moments," listening beyond academics. Over time, graduates enter workforce primed to ask, "How can this vocation bless, not exploit?"

10.6.4 • The Arts and Media—Storytelling that Humanizes the Marginalized

Prophets used poetry; Jesus employed parables. Artists therefore wield mercy through imagination. Filmmakers document refugee journeys, dismantling stereotype walls. Muralists paint local heroes recovering from addiction, transforming graffiti-scarred alleys into galleries of grace. Musicians compose laments for racial injustice, leading audiences into communal sorrow (Ps 137). Journalists adopt solutions-oriented reporting, highlighting grassroots compassion, not only crisis. Christian publishers amplify voices from global church, redressing Western monopoly. Theater troupes perform in prisons, echoing Matthew 25 visitation. Digital illustrators craft comics teaching kids empathy. Funding models like Patreon enable patrons to participate in mercy dissemination. Each art form becomes portable temple where *ḥesed* can be encountered by those who may never enter a sanctuary.

10.7. Cross-Cultural Mercy—Bridging Divides Near and Far

10.7.1 • The Samaritan Principle—Neighbor Defined by Need, Not Similarity

The lawyer in Luke 10 asks, "Who is my neighbor?" expecting ethnic or geographic limits; Jesus answers with a story that obliterates both, centering mercy rather than bloodline. A battered Hebrew lies on the Jericho road, ignored by clergy who share his doctrine and DNA, but rescued by a Samaritan whose theology is suspect and ancestry despised. The parable establishes that compassion is determined by proximity to pain, not proximity to culture or creed. Applying the principle requires first seeing the wounded; cross-cultural mercy begins with slowed pace and open eyes in grocery aisles, border checkpoints, and war headlines. Then comes visceral pity—Luke's verb *splagchnizomai* (10:33) means a gut-level stirring that refuses to stay theoretical. Action follows:

bandaging, transport, financial provision, and promise of return, each step translating empathy into tangible help. Modern Good Samaritans might pay an immigrant's school registration, drive a Muslim neighbor to a medical appointment, or advocate at city hall for refugees' housing rights. Crucially, mercy flows both ways; the Samaritan is donor today but could be recipient tomorrow, teaching mutuality instead of saviorism. The story ends with Jesus' imperative, "Go and do likewise," making compassion the litmus test of genuine discipleship. Churches embody the principle when pot-luck tables feature dishes labeled in Swahili, Spanish, and Khmer, or when English learners read Scripture aloud in their heart language on Sunday. Individual believers can map their "Jericho roads"—the bus routes, chat forums, and sidewalks they travel—and ask which marginalized travelers bleed unnoticed. Prayer journals that list names of people from different ethnicities guard hearts from defaulting to homogenous friendships. The Samaritan principle reminds us that heaven's choir will sing in many tongues (Rev 7:9); practicing that mercy melody now tunes us for the coming concert.

10.7.2 ▪ *Short-Term Teams and Long-Term Partnerships—Best Practices*

Short-term mission trips can either fertilize global compassion or reinforce colonial patterns; intention and preparation decide the outcome. Healthy teams begin with listening: months of virtual meetings where local hosts outline real needs, cultural taboos, and project priorities. Training covers language basics, power dynamics, and the theology of mutual submission (Eph 5:21). Trip itineraries prioritize relational presence—home visits, story exchanges—over selfie-worthy construction sprints. Participants bring seed funds that are stewarded by local leadership after departure, ensuring continuity and protection against "orphaned projects." Debrief sessions each evening invite reflection on cross-cultural observations, Scripture, and emotional highs and lows, integrating head, heart, and hands. Long-term partnerships grow when trips rotate the same site, allowing friendships to mature into sister-church covenants and exchange visits. Mission committees shift language from "help" to "learn and serve," acknowledging the reciprocal nature of the Body (1 Cor 12:21-26). Digital tech sustains connection—WhatsApp prayer circles, shared Bible-reading plans, and joint Zoom worship keep mercy in motion between physical

248

visits. Metrics of success move from buildings erected to testimonies collected—how many local believers felt empowered, how many team members sensed vocational nudges. Every traveler commits to a post-trip action step in their hometown, translating global compassion into local practice. Critiques of short-term work (cost, disruption) are addressed through transparency and post-trip audits of impact. Ultimately, when executed humbly, such exchanges prefigure Revelation's nations bringing their glory into the New Jerusalem (Rev 21:24), each culture gifting distinct treasures to the collective joy of Christ.

10.7.3 ▪ Racial Reconciliation—Listening, Lamenting, and Leveraging Privilege

Paul proclaims Christ has destroyed the dividing wall of hostility, making one new humanity (Eph 2:14-16); racial reconciliation is therefore gospel fruit, not sociological hobby. The journey begins with listening—majority-culture believers suspend defensiveness and attend to minority narratives of historical wounds, policing disparities, and church exclusions. Acts 6 shows early church adjusting structures when Hellenist widows were overlooked, proving that system tweaks are a biblical response to inequity. Lament follows; Psalm 137 and Lamentations teach grief language that names sin without sanitizing it. Corporate services of lament—candles, reading the names of victims, silent kneeling—honor collective sorrow and invite Spirit-led repentance. Education is ongoing: book clubs discuss *The Color of Compromise*, and Sunday-school classes examine the multi-ethnic church of Antioch (Acts 13:1-3). Privilege—unearned advantages in housing, hiring, or policing—is reframed as stewardable talent (Mt 25:14-30); believers leverage it by mentoring under-resourced entrepreneurs, co-signing for loans, or amplifying marginalized voices in decision rooms. Cross-racial friendships deepen over shared meals and joint service, moving conversation from issues to stories. Peacemaking involves truth-telling and forgiveness rituals rooted in Matthew 18; offended parties articulate harm, and listeners confess without deflection. Multicultural worship—different styles, bilingual liturgy—de-centers any one culture, mirroring heaven's throne room. Finally, advocacy emerges: congregations write letters supporting fair-housing ordinances or school equity budgets, interpreting Micah 6:8 as both private kindness and public justice. Progress is slow,

249

setbacks likely, but steadfast mercy perseveres, trusting that the Spirit who joined Jew and Gentile will finish healing today's fractures.

10.7.4 ▪ Digital Mercy—Compassionate Presence in Online Spaces

The internet is today's global Jericho Road—crowded, risky, full of wounded avatars scrolling for connection. Digital mercy starts with tone: Colossians 4:6 commands speech seasoned with salt; believers audit tweets for sarcasm toxins and replace them with grace-truth balance. Social media fasting one day a week curbs outrage addiction, creating space to pray for those who trigger anger. Comment sections can become micro-mission fields—responding to despairing posts with private messages, resource links, and genuine prayer offers. Content curation is compassionate stewardship: sharing verified crisis-relief links during disasters, boosting minority creators, and refusing to repost click-bait rumors. Churches form "digital deacon" teams who monitor livestream chats, welcome newcomers by name, and route pastoral needs to care teams within minutes. Young believers mentor elders on internet empathy, while elders impart discernment about sensationalist headlines—mutual edification across generations. Virtual small groups enable home-bound or geographically isolated Christians to participate in communion services, extending Hosea's *ḥesed* through fiber-optic cables. Cyber-bullying interventions—reporting anonymous abuse, rallying encouragement for victims—mirror Good Samaritan bandaging in pixel form. Data privacy is mercy, too; ministries handle donor info transparently, reflecting Proverbs 11:13's call to guard secrets. Even memes carry mission potential; a well-timed humor post diffuses despondency on a friend's feed. Digital mercy prepares hearts to receive face-to-face gospel conversations, and it amplifies local acts globally, inspiring a ripple of compassion far beyond physical borders.

10.8. Eschatological Mercy—Hope that Fuels Persevering Compassion

10.8.1 ▪ *The Coming Kingdom of Kindness—Isa 11:1-9 and Revelation 21:4*

Isaiah envisions a Day when wolf and lamb coexist, children play over cobra holes, and "the earth is filled with the knowledge of the LORD" (Isa 11:6-9). John parallels the vision with tears wiped away and death undone (Rev 21:4). These texts anchor mercy activists in unshakeable optimism; every act of compassion rehearses conditions already decreed in God's future. Planting community gardens foreshadows Edenic abundance; tutoring sessions hint at the universal knowledge of God. The guaranteed arrival of shalom allows believers to endure short-term setbacks—failed bills, broken truces—without surrendering to cynicism. Eschatological kindness also shapes evaluation metrics: success is measured by faithfulness toward coming reality, not immediate results. Artists paint lions lying with calves as prophetic protest against blood-sport entertainment culture. Parents teach children to treat insects gently, connecting tiny mercies with cosmic peace. Hospice chaplains read Revelation 21 beside hospital beds, reminding families that every goodbye is penultimate. As hope expands, compassion deepens; one can afford to love extravagantly when convinced the future is secure.

10.8.2 ▪ *Final Judgment and Mercy Missions—"Whatever You Did for the Least..." (Matthew 25)*

Jesus' sheep-and-goats discourse links eternal destinies to treatment of the hungry, stranger, naked, sick, and imprisoned (Mt 25:31-46). Paradoxically, mercy—that soft virtue—becomes final exam criteria, underscoring its seriousness. Believers therefore view compassion work as eschatological investment, laying up treasure where rust cannot destroy. Mission committees align budgets with Matthew 25's categories, ensuring outreach portfolios cover food relief, refugee hospitality, clothing drives, medical missions, and prison chaplaincy. Sermons emphasize that works do not earn salvation but evidence authentic faith (Eph 2:10). Personal daily examen includes the question, "Did I meet Christ in the 'least of these' today?" When energy wanes, volunteers picture Jesus saying,

"You visited me," reigniting zeal. Judgment hope also humbles activists; knowing they too rely on mercy prevents self-righteous savior complexes. Conversely, neglect warnings jolt complacent churches to course-correct—closing plush coffee bars to fund free clinics. Final judgment thus functions as both carrot and stick, driving mercy perseverance until the throne confirms every hidden cup of water.

10.8.3 • Suffering, Glory, and the Logic of Compassion—2 Corinthians 1:3-7

Paul calls God "the Father of mercies" who comforts us so we can comfort others, creating a recycling loop of grace (2 Cor 1:3-7). Suffering, therefore, is not compassion's obstacle but its credentialing course. Cancer survivors host support groups; bankruptcy veterans teach budgeting; parents of prodigals lead intercessory nights. This "wounded healer" model mirrors Christ's resurrected scars (Jn 20:27). Glory enters when comfort overflow reaches critical mass, inspiring corporate lament competence and joy resilience. Practically, churches develop testimony banks—video stories of comfort received that become training modules for new caregivers. Pastors normalize grief-share attendance as discipleship, not deficiency. Short-term mission orientation includes sessions on trauma stewardship, recognizing that visitors will witness deep pain abroad. Paul's logic counters prosperity gospel by declaring tribulations transferable currency in God's economy. Consequently, sufferers are honored as frontline ministers, not sidelined liabilities.

10.8.4 • Living Sacraments—How Mercy Today Previews Tomorrow's World

Sacraments are visible words; acts of compassion are likewise eschatological symbols that speak without microphones. When believers forgive debts, they enact the Jubilee economy of the coming age (Lev 25; Lk 4:18-19). When they reconcile enemies, they dramatize swords beaten into plowshares (Isa 2:4). Each adoption showcases household expansion of the New Jerusalem, where no orphan spirit roams. Hospitality to immigrants is a down-payment on Revelation's multi-ethnic city. Environmental clean-ups anticipate the river of life flowing clear as crystal (Rev 22:1-2). Like communion, these acts contain real grace: both giver and receiver are spiritually nourished. Church calendars schedule "Kingdom Preview Days," mobilizing congregants into citywide service, followed by testimonies and Eucharist, merging sacrament and service. Families adopt "Mercy Sabbath" once a month— volunteering in the morning, feasting with new friends at night— practicing eternal rhythms. Kids collect coins for wells, learning that their small sacrifices echo widow's mites immortalized (Mk 12:43-44). Living sacraments rebuke hopeless headlines, providing embodied evidence that a better kingdom already infiltrates broken soil. When skeptics ask for proof of resurrection, believers can point to addiction-free neighbors, debt-forgiven families, riverbanks litter-free, and say, "Taste and see—this is hors d'oeuvres of the age to come."

Conclusion Steadfast mercy is not a program we launch but a river we enter. Its headwaters spring from the pierced side of Christ, its currents are steered by the Spirit, and its destination is a new creation where tears are obsolete. As you step out of these pages and back into kitchens, classrooms, boardrooms, and city streets, remember: the same love that pursued Gomer, that knelt beside lepers, and that prayed, "Father, forgive," now pulses in you. Let it shape your next conversation, your next budget decision, your next response to pain—until small acts of compassion accumulate into a living prophecy of the world to come. For in the end, Hosea's God will have a people whose merciful hearts echo His own, and every healed relationship, every defended vulnerable one, every cup of cold water will have been part of the rehearsal for that eternal day.

Chapter 11. Hope in Judgment— Seeing Discipline through Resurrection Lens

Stand beneath a surgeon's bright lamp and the scalpel no longer feels like an enemy—it is a servant of healing in hands that know exactly where to cut. Hosea invites us to view God's judgment the same way: as precise, purposeful incisions that open a path for life to return. Again and again the prophet links wounding and mending, exile and homecoming, death and unexpected dawn—"He has torn us, that He may heal us ... on the third day He will raise us up" (Hos 6:1-2). Jesus carries that logic all the way to Calvary, where wrath and mercy converge and resurrection proves that divine discipline is never the last word. In this chapter we will trace how the cross reframes every personal setback, every churchwide shaking, and every global crisis—not as random blows but as invitations to deeper repentance and sturdier hope. By learning to look at chastening through a resurrection lens, we discover that even God's "no" is a seedbed for a greater "yes," and that every valley of trouble can become, in His timing, a door of hope.

11.1. Judgment Re-framed—From Retribution to Restorative Surgery

11.1.1 ▪ The Physician's Scalpel—Why Love Must Wound (Hosea 6:1)

Hosea's invitational cry—"Come, let us return to the LORD, for He has torn us that He may heal" (Hos 6:1)—presents divine judgment as a surgeon's incision, not an executioner's stab. A cancer-removing scalpel breaks skin to spare life; similarly, God permits tearing so that infection of idolatry cannot metastasize. Israel's prosperity had numbed spiritual nerves, requiring pain to awaken their senses (Deut 32:15). The metaphor shatters two extremes: the fantasy that a loving God never wounds and the fear that any wound implies abandonment. In biblical logic, the cut and cure are sequential steps of one procedure; to refuse the incision is to forfeit the healing. The prophet even locates hope inside the grammar—*He has torn* (past) *that He may heal* (purpose clause), making restoration the divine intention from the first slice. Modern disciples misinterpret hardship when they separate these halves; they see stitches and forget the coming rehabilitation therapy. Spiritual surgery is often outpatient and incremental: a job loss exposes greed, a relational rupture unmasks control, a physical ailment slows frenetic striving. Hosea assures that the same hand wielding the knife also mixes the balm; orthopedists do not leave bones un-set. Therefore, the faithful posture during discipline is not sullen stoicism but cooperative surrender—holding still so the Physician can complete His work.

11.1.2 ▪ Justice vs. Wrath—Biblical Nuances behind a Loaded Word

"Wrath" in Scripture is not capricious rage but God's settled, active opposition to everything that vandalizes shalom (Rom 1:18). Justice (*mishpat*) describes the right order He loves; wrath is justice in motion against disorder. Hosea alternates these terms to show they are two sides of covenant loyalty: the Lord "will roar like a lion" (judicial wrath, Hos 11:10) precisely because His heart "recoils with compassion" (just love, Hos 11:8). The cross demonstrates that distinction: divine anger toward sin converges with divine love toward sinners, producing substitution rather than annihilation (Rom

255

3:25-26). Misreading wrath as divine temper tantrum leads either to antinomianism ("ignore the Old Testament") or to terror-based legalism. Properly understood, wrath dignifies human pain—it means God refuses to wink at injustice; every abused child, oppressed worker, and betrayed spouse has cosmic Ally. Practically, believers who embrace this nuance repent faster (they know sin matters) and hope deeper (they know mercy triumphs). Preachers should therefore rescue the word "wrath" from caricature by pairing it with covenant vows and showing its ultimate absorption by Christ.

11.1.3 ▪ Discipline as Covenant Faithfulness—Hebrews 12:5-11 and the Father's Heart

Hebrews depicts discipline as signature of legitimacy: "What son is there whom his father does not discipline?" (Heb 12:7). In ancient homes, tutors might punish slaves, but only fathers invested loving correction in heirs; chastening, paradoxically, proves adoption. Hosea echoes this paternal pathos—God "taught Ephraim to walk, taking them by the arms" (Hos 11:3). The Greek term *paideia* in Hebrews includes instruction, guidance, boundaries—not mere punitive strokes. When believers view hardship through this lens, they shift from "Why is God angry?" to "What virtue is God training?"—perhaps endurance (Jas 1:2-4), humility (2 Cor 12:7-9), or empathy (2 Cor 1:3-4). Spiritual disciplines cooperate with divine discipline; fasting, silence, and confession prune self-reliance before crises necessitate harsher cuts. Parents learn from the pattern: discipline that mirrors the Father is purposeful, measured, and hope-oriented, never humiliation for humiliation's sake (Eph 6:4). The goal is "the peaceful fruit of righteousness" (Heb 12:11)—character that can host glory without collapse.

11.1.4 ▪ The Pattern of Down-Then-Up—Death-and-Resurrection Embedded in Scripture

From Eden's exile to Joseph's pit, from exile to return, Scripture beats with a down-then-up rhythm that foreshadows Easter. Jonah descends to watery Sheol before Nineveh hears mercy (Jon 2:6; 3:3). David's songs plummet into lament before soaring into praise (Ps 30). Jesus crystallizes the motif: "Unless a grain of wheat falls into the earth and dies, it remains alone" (Jn 12:24). Hosea captures it in the compressed prophecy, "After two days He will revive us; on the third day He will raise us up" (Hos 6:2), a timetable later mirrored in Christ's burial. Recognizing this narrative arc guards us from premature despair in the "Friday" phases of our stories. It also curtails triumphalism that demands uninterrupted ascent; resurrection hope does not erase cruciform pathways but interprets them. Spiritual formation uses the template: examen names death moments nightly, gratitude anticipates resurrection sprouts. In counseling, sufferers chart personal Good Fridays, Holy Saturdays, and Easter Sundays, tracing God's faithfulness across seasons. Ultimately, the pattern forms a worldview: valleys are tunnels, not cul-de-sacs.

11.2. Hosea's Cycles—Cutting Down to Raise Up

11.2.1 ▪ Valley of Achor to Door of Hope (Hosea 2:14-15)

The Valley of Achor, infamous for Achan's execution (Josh 7:26), becomes in Hosea a launchpad for renewal—"I will make the Valley of Achor a door of hope." The geographical pivot turns a crime scene into a honeymoon suite, revealing God's knack for transforming liabilities into thresholds. Historically, Israel's first defeat in Canaan symbolized covenant breach; prophetically, its memory now spotlights undeserved grace. Personal equivalents might be divorce papers, bankruptcy court, or rehab intake—the places we'd rather forget but God chooses as rendezvous points. The divine strategy is paradoxical: isolate ("I will allure her into the wilderness"), then speak tenderly. Wilderness strips props—Wi-Fi, applause, Baal trinkets—so that whispered promises gain acoustics. Hope (*tiqvah*) literally means "cord"; God threads a lifeline through disaster rubble. Practical application: journal recurring painful memories, ask Spirit to rename each valley; create liturgical milestones— planting a tree on the anniversary of loss—as tangible doors of hope. Hosea's reversal pre-echoes the empty tomb, another disaster site turned gateway.

11.2.2 ▪ Lion's Maul and Shepherd's Call (Hosea 5:14; 11:10-11)

Hosea pictures God first as a lion that "tears and goes away" (Hos 5:14), later as the same lion whose roar gathers children home (Hos

11:10-11). Judgment and salvation share a larynx. The tearing addresses idolatry; Israel trusted Assyria's treaties, so God shreds those illusions. Yet He retreats "until they acknowledge their guilt," leaving space for voluntary return (Hos 5:15). When repentance sprouts, the lion's growl morphs into shepherd's call, and exiles "come trembling like birds from Egypt." The dual image instructs leaders: sometimes love confronts, sometimes it comforts; timing discerns which tone heals. Pastoral care can articulate, "God may feel like He's mauling your career, but He's simultaneously positioning you to hear His call." For intercessors, the passage fuels hope to pray prodigals through both stages—wounding that wakes, voice that guides. Missionally, it warns against demonizing hardship; the lion could be God, not Satan.

11.2.3 ▪ *"You Are Not My People" to "Children of the Living God" (Hosea 1:9-10)*

Lo-Ammi's naming is a shocking covenant annulment—God telling Israel, "You are not my people." Yet in the very next breath Hosea predicts a population boom where ex-iled sons become "children of the living God." Peter applies the reversal to Gentile believers, proving the prophecy's reach (1 Pet 2:10). The oscillation shows that divine identity statements are not frozen; repentance and Christ's mediation can flip destiny. Practical discipleship uses this dynamic: counselors help clients replace self-labels ("failure," "unwanted") with gospel names ("beloved," "chosen"). Baptism services announce, "Now you are God's people," dramatizing Hosea's flip. Ethically, it humbles insiders—today's church could become Lo-Ammi through hypocrisy—while encouraging outsiders that no heritage disqualifies.

11.2.4 ▪ *The Three-Day Motif—Prophetic Echo of Easter (Hosea 6:2)*

Ancient readers noted Yahweh acts decisively on "third days": Isaac's rescue moment (Gen 22:4), Sinai's thunder (Ex 19:16), Jonah's expulsion from fish (Jon 1:17; 2:10). Hosea consolidates the pattern into communal resurrection: "On the third day He will raise us up." Jesus cites Jonah's sign to predict His timeline (Mt 12:40). The motif provides liturgical cadence: Holy Saturday services of silence hold space between tear and repair. It shapes emotional expectation—there is waiting, but it is measured. In crisis counseling, mentors tell sufferers, "You're in day two; day three is coming." Even creation echoes the pattern—seeds germinate in dark soil before green shoots surface. Environmental theologians apply this to ecological grief: forests burned today may sprout new biodiversity later. The three-day hope undercuts nihilism; God schedules revival already on the calendar.

11.3. Christ the Fulcrum—Judgment Meets Mercy at the Cross

11.3.1 ▪ Cup of Wrath Drained—Gethsemane and Golgotha (Matthew 26:39; 27:46)

In Gethsemane, Jesus trembles before the "cup," echoing Old-Testament metaphors of wrath (Isa 51:17). His plea, "If possible, let this cup pass," reveals the cost of substituting for covenant breakers. Golgotha answers the garden: "My God, why have You forsaken me?" (Mt 27:46) signals the cup's final drop consumed. Unlike Israel, who chased Assyrian help, Jesus drinks abandonment to secure eternal presence for His people. This substitution reframes personal guilt: discipline isn't punitive payment—it's rehab for sins already forgiven. Evangelism stands on this ground; we invite skeptics to a Judge who has borne His own verdict. Liturgically, communion cups remind worshipers the wrath-cup is empty; we drink grace instead.

11.3.2 ▪ Divine Justice Satisfied, Divine Love Released (Romans 3:25-26)

Paul calls Christ's cross a "propitiation" displaying God as "just and the justifier." Justice demands sin's wages; love desires sinner's rescue; only the cross satisfies both. Without this nexus, discipline would teeter toward either cruelty (justice without love) or permissiveness (love without justice). For believers, it gives existential security—no accusation can reopen a settled case (Rom 8:33-34). For social ethics, it models restorative justice: punishment aimed at restoration, not mere retribution. In counseling, shame is addressed by pointing to a judgment seat that has become a mercy

259

seat. Worship songs like "In Christ Alone" embed the paradox into congregational memory.

11.3.3 ▪ *Resurrection as God's "Yes" after the "No" of the Cross (Acts 2:24)*

Peter proclaims God "raised Him up, loosing the pangs of death," signaling heaven's endorsement of Jesus' payment. Resurrection is receipt stamped *paid in full*. It also inaugurates new-creation life within believers (1 Pet 1:3). Therefore, any divine discipline now occurs *inside* resurrection life, not on death row. Morning prayers can begin, "Because Jesus lives, today's correction cannot destroy me." Easter calendars influence budgeting decisions—invest in ventures that outlive graves. Apologetics points skeptics to empty tomb as historical pivot—judgment answered, hope unleashed.

11.3.4 ▪ *Living Union—How Believers Experience Both Death and Life (Romans 6:3-5)*

Baptism unites Christians with Christ's death and resurrection, making the down-then-up pattern biographical, not just historical. Temptation resistance relies on this union: "Consider yourselves dead to sin" (Rom 6:11). Suffering shares in His death; joy in ministry tastes resurrection. Paul's thorn keeps him cruciform; visions of paradise keep him hopeful (2 Cor 12:7-10). Spiritual disciplines mirror union: fasting (death), feasting (resurrection); confession (death), absolution (life). Small-group testimonies often feature this oscillation—relapse confronted, new freedom tasted. Eschatologically, union guarantees physical resurrection; current bodily decay is apprenticeship, not apocalypse (2 Cor 4:16). Understanding union transforms discipline from divine distance to shared yoke—He is inside the pain, pulling toward life.

11.4. Personal Discipline—Reading God's Corrections through Gospel Glasses

11.4.1 ▪ *Diagnostic Questions—Pain, Providence, or Consequence?*

Every hardship is not a spanking, yet every hardship can tutor the soul if interpreted wisely. The first diagnostic question sounds like

Psalm 139:24—"Is there any grievous way in me?"; honest self-examination keeps us from blaming Satan for messes we made. If conviction surfaces—an affair, a lie, a neglected Sabbath—then we are probably inside Hebrews 12 discipline, and swift repentance is the doorway to relief. If no clear sin appears, we ask Joseph's question: "Could this be providential preparation?" (Gen 50:20). Training pain—like David's wilderness or Paul's thorn (2 Cor 12:7-9)—forms muscle for future callings. A third category is living in a fallen world: the tower in Siloam fell without tying victims to unique guilt (Luke 13:4). Sorting categories matters because the remedy differs—sin requires confession, training requires endurance, random suffering requires lament and trust. Wise mentors help diagnose; isolation breeds misreading. Scripture is our X-ray: reading Deuteronomy 28 may reveal covenant breach; reading Philippians 1 may reveal gospel advance through chains. Prayerful listening completes the scan—ask, "Spirit, spotlight the lesson." Journaling events and emotions over several weeks often reveals patterns invisible in single-day snapshots. If multiple faithful friends echo the same insight, treat it as divine highlighter. Finally, hold conclusions humbly; Job's friends misdiagnosed, proving even good theology can miss the mark when empathy is thin.

11.4.2 ▪ Repentance, Realignment, and Received Grace

Once sin is identified, biblical repentance is more than regret—it is a mind change (metanoia) that leads to directional change (Acts 3:19). Start by naming the sin with forensic precision: "I harbored racist contempt," not "I made a mistake." Next, look at the cross until the heart softens—Zechariah 12:10 promises mourning when we "look on Him whom we pierced." Realignment follows confession: Zacchaeus returned money fourfold (Luke 19:8), so practical restitution accompanies sorrow. Received grace then replaces penance; we choose to believe Jesus' "It is finished" (John 19:30) louder than our inner debtor's ledger. A helpful practice is proclaiming Romans 8:1 aloud every morning for a week, training neural pathways to expect mercy. Accountability cements new alignment—tell a mentor your plan and ask for check-ins. Replace sin-habits with virtue routines: gossip fast becomes encouragement texts; porn triggers birth Scripture memory cards. Celebrate micro-victories—the Spirit's fruit often appears as first green shoots before full harvest (Gal 5:22-23). When condemnation whispers, distinguish it from conviction: condemnation says "you are your sin," while conviction says "you did that sin—come higher." If relapse occurs, repent faster; quick turnaround erodes shame's foothold. Keep Eucharist central—receiving broken bread regularly reminds the soul that grace is digested, not earned.

11.4.3 • *Spiritual Practices for a Season of Chastening—Silence, Lament, Obedient Steps*

Silence positions the heart under the surgeon's hand; Job stopped arguing before restoration began (Job 40:4-5). Schedule technology-free half-days in a park, letting creation's sermon retune perspective (Ps 19:1-4). Lament is silence's voiced companion—pour out complaint like water (Ps 62:8), using psalms 6, 13, or 88 as scaffolding until words return. Write prayers of complaint and end each with "yet I will trust" (Hab 3:17-18). Fast one meal weekly to embody sorrow and heighten spiritual receptors; each hunger pang becomes a reminder to ask, "Lord, teach me." Pair fasting with simple acts of justice—share saved lunch money with a food bank, echoing Isaiah 58:6-7. Keep obedience incremental: Naaman dipped seven times (2 Ki 5:14); healing emerged mid-routine. Daily examen at night reviews where discipline's lesson surfaced—did a conflict reveal impatience? Did traffic test peace? Place a stone in pocket; every time you feel its weight, whisper, "Form Christ in me" (Gal 4:19). Surround yourself with hopeful music—minor-key hymns moving to major-key resolve mirror the journey from grief to praise. End each week lighting a candle and reading Revelation 21:4 aloud, anchoring discipline inside future glory.

11.4.4 • *Testimony and Transformation—When Scars Become Stories*

Post-discipline, scars shift from shame marks to story ink—like Thomas, people may meet Christ through your wounds (John 20:27-28). Craft a three-minute testimony: pre-discipline drift, God's corrective act, resurrection fruit. Share it first in small group to hone clarity and humility; then, when prompted, in wider settings. Keep Jesus central—if listeners remember your failure more than His faithfulness, edit the story. Document tangible turnarounds: anger index down, generosity index up, peace index steady. Mentor someone facing similar discipline; 2 Corinthians 1:4 calls this comfort recycling. Anniversaries matter—mark one-year sobriety or restored marriage with worship night and guest list of those who prayed you through. Convert discipline lessons into creative output—blogs, poetry, or art exhibit titled "Cut to Heal." Evangelistically, scars authenticate gospel realism: skeptics lean in when grace explains real mess, not sanitized legend. Watch for pride relapse; keep Galatians 6:1 handy in case you grow boastful. Finally, thank the Surgeon often; heaven's choir will include verses that trace every saved soul's chastening-to-glory arc.

11.5. Corporate Purging—When God Judges His Household First

11.5.1 ▪ 1 Peter 4:17 and the Refining of the Church

Peter's sobering assertion—"It is time for judgment to begin at the household of God"—frames scandals and shake-ups within divine pruning, not random bad press. Historically, God cleans house before He renovates neighborhoods; see Ananias and Sapphira's sudden judgment launching awe and evangelistic momentum (Acts 5:1-14). Modern equivalents include exposure of clergy abuse or embezzlement; painful yet necessary amputations to save the Body. Congregations must interpret such moments prophetically—asking "What idols did we harbor?" not "How do we spin PR?" Town-hall lament services foster transparency; leaders read Ezekiel 8, naming defilements that hid behind sanctuary walls. Governance reforms follow: financial audits, external safeguarding reviews, whistleblower hotlines. Preaching series on holiness (1 Th 4:3-8) tenderize hearts, preparing for Spirit conviction. Prayer meetings shift from triumphalism to repentance, echoing Daniel's corporate "we have sinned" (Dan 9:5). Healthy members stay, modeling perseverance rather than exit consumerism. Gifted intercessors stand "in the gap" (Ezek 22:30), pleading for mercy while welcoming fire. Over time, credibility rebuilt attracts seekers who trust a church honest about its mess. Judgment, when stewarded, becomes fertilizer for deeper roots and sweeter fruit.

11.5.2 ▪ *Historic Visitations—Revivals Preceded by Conviction &*
Confession

Every major awakening rode on a wave of brokenness before joy. In
1904 Wales, Evan Roberts emphasized "confess all known sin";
weeping miners lined streets each night. The 1949 Hebrides revival
began with two elderly sisters praying Psalm 24 criteria—"clean
hands, pure heart"—until conviction fell island-wide. At Asbury in
1970 students stood in chapel confessing bitterness and dishonesty
for 144 hours straight; only then did euphoria flood worship.
Patterns repeat: small remnant prays, hidden sin surfaces publicly,
restitution follows (stolen tools returned, debts repaid),
reconciliations ripple, and evangelistic harvest arrives. Teaching
these histories inoculates churches against seeking manifestations
without mortification. Create revival reading groups—Finney's
Lectures on Revival, J. Edwin Orr's works—and close sessions with
guided confession. Annual "Holiness Week" aligns with Lent:
fasting, public testimony slots, and optional all-night prayer watches
petition God for fresh visitation. Expect God to answer by first
exposing compromise—like Malachi's refiner's fire (Mal 3:2-3)—
then igniting renewed mission.

11.5.3 ▪ *Structural Repentance—From Toxic Systems to Transparent*
Cultures

Sin is personal and systemic; dismantling toxic structures is
corporate repentance in action. Start with sociology of power—
James warning against favoritism (Jas 2:1-7) indicts modern
celebrity culture churches. Conduct anonymous staff surveys to
identify fear zones. Restructure leadership plurality—limit single-
leader control, install external advisory boards. Salary transparency
curbs greed; published annual reports mirror 2 Cor 8:21's
"honorable in the sight of men." Address workload injustice—
volunteers exploited under "sacrificial service" rhetoric need
Sabbath safeguards (Ex 23:12). Review preaching archives for
misogynistic or racist ideologies; publicly correct past errors.
Remove abuser monuments—renaming buildings after unsung
servants reflects kingdom upside-down values (Matt 23:11-12).
Offer reparations where harm was financial—scholarships for
survivors, counseling stipends. Create ongoing feedback loops:

suggestion boxes, open-mic forums, third-party conflict mediation. Transparent cultures foster trust, preparing soil for long-term fruitfulness.

11.5.4 ▪ Celebrating Cleansing—Liturgies of Lament and Renewal

After purging, joy must seal the wound; Israel held three-day feasts post-temple dedication (2 Chr 7:9). Design services beginning with lament psalms, silence, and communal confession, transitioning to communion and resurrection hymns like "Christ the Sure and Steady Anchor." Visual symbols help: shred papers listing corporate sins, then compost shreds into flower beds symbolizing new growth. Anoint leadership teams with oil, reciting Isaiah 61:3—"beauty for ashes." Share stories of repentance leading to reconciliation— estranged families restored, stolen equipment returned. Commission congregants to acts of public kindness the following week—paying utility bills, cleaning graffiti—demonstrating inward cleansing outwardly. Conclude with joyful feast—pot-luck titled "Grace Banquet." Annual remembrance of cleansing fosters vigilance against drift, framing judgment episode as God's mercy milestone rather than PR nightmare.

11.6. Cultural Shake-Ups—Prophetic Hope amid National or Global Crisis

11.6.1 ▪ Biblical Precedent: Exile as Seedbed for Renewal (Jeremiah 29; Ezra 1)

Babylonian exile looked like covenant failure, yet Jeremiah's letter reframed seventy years as soil for future hope—"I know the plans I have for you" (Jer 29:11). Exiles built houses, planted gardens, and increased; faith became portable. Cyrus's unexpected decree (Ezra 1:1-4) proves God can leverage pagan policy for redemptive pivots. Modern parallels: Communist crackdowns birthed China's house-church explosion; Rwandan genocide preceded reconciliation ministries now global models. Crises scatter believers into new mission fields—think Ukrainian refugees planting Slavic congregations across Europe. Thus, cultural shake-ups can be greenhouse for gospel multiplication. Interpreting them requires prophetic realism—acknowledging loss like Psalm 137 while expecting seed to sprout like Ezekiel 37. Pastors coach congregations: "Plant gardens where you're displaced." Policy-minded believers heed Jeremiah's charge to seek city welfare—voting, volunteering—in exile contexts.

11.6.2 ▪ *Reading Signs without Speculation—Matthew 24 and Discernment Principles*

Jesus lists wars, quakes, and plagues as "birth pains," warning against date-setting prophets (Mt 24:4-8, 36). Discernment balances watchfulness and work: eyes on horizon, hands on plow (Lk 9:62). Evaluate sign claims by fruit—do they produce fear paralysis or mission urgency? Cross-reference headlines with Scripture within community, avoiding algorithm echo chambers. Practice historical humility—remember past predictions crashed (e.g., 1988's rapture hype). Use crisis news as prayer prompts: earthquake alerts trigger Psalm 46 intercession. Teach eschatology courses emphasizing hope and ethics, not charts alone. Equip believers to discern disinformation—check sources, verify data—obeying Exodus 23:1 warning against spreading false reports.

11.6.3 ▪ *Public Theology of Hope—Witnessing through Service and Advocacy*

In crises, the church's voice should sound less like pundits, more like priests—naming grief and announcing resurrection. Develop rapid-response teams: chainsaw crews after hurricanes, counseling pop-ups after shootings. Advocacy flows from Micah 6:8—churches write op-eds urging humane refugee policies, citing biblical hospitality. Public prayers in city halls model lament and hope. Celebrate artifacts of common grace: vaccine breakthroughs as divine kindness (Jas 1:17). Produce podcasts interviewing believers innovating in crisis—engineers who create water filters, artists painting trauma murals. Hope speech avoids triumphal clichés; instead say, "We don't know why, but we know Who comes alongside" (Isa 43:2). Over time, civic leaders view church not as partisan bloc but as reservoir of resilient mercy.

11.6.4 • Eschatological Assurance—Kingdom Unshakeable (Hebrews 12:26-29)

Hebrews declares God will shake created things so that unshakable kingdom stands. Believers interpret societal tremors—market crashes, culture wars—as reminder of superior citizenship (Phil 3:20). Assurance generates generosity: when stocks plummet, some double giving, confident treasure is secure elsewhere (Mt 6:19-21). Worship in crisis evokes early church under persecution—singing while tremors collapse prison walls (Acts 16:25-26). Teaching on new heavens and earth (Rev 21-22) reframes ecological angst as groan before renewal. Use liturgical responses—leader: "Our hope is in the Lord"; people: "He is making all things new." Children's ministry crafts "kingdom jars"—placing slips of broken-world news inside, praying each Wednesday for Jesus to mend. Personal devotions anchor on Psalm 46—"though the mountains be moved"—memorized to stabilize midnight anxieties. Finally, assurance breeds courage to critique injustice; knowing Rome falls frees prophets to confront Caesar now. The unshakeable kingdom is not escape hatch but ballast enabling fearless engagement.

11.7. Practicing Resurrection Now—Hope Habits in the Midst of Discipline

11.7.1 • Gratitude in the Dark—Finding God's Goodness during Loss

Gratitude is not denial; it is defiant praise that stares at an empty tomb and says, "He is risen—there must still be light." Job, flanked by fresh graves, tore his robe yet blessed the name of the Lord (Job 1:20-21), proving thanksgiving can coexist with tears. Paul instructs sufferers to give thanks "in all circumstances" (1 Th 5:18), a prepositional miracle that turns every setting into a sanctuary. Begin by naming one mercy per day—warm water, a texted verse, the scent of coffee—training the limbic system to detect grace the way soldiers detect movement in night-vision goggles. Keep a lament-and-thanks journal with two columns; honesty about pain on the left, matching evidence of God's nearness on the right (Ps 42:3-5). Speak gratitudes aloud at dinner, echoing Psalm 136's antiphonal rhythm where each anguish-line is answered by "His ḥesed endures forever." Neuroscience confirms what Scripture promised: thankful people sleep better and carry lower cortisol, making them more resilient under discipline. Write gratitude notes to mentors and mail them—blessing rebounds to sender (Prov 11:25). Memorize Philippians 4:6-7, breathing prayer on exhale, "Thank You...," and inhaling, "Guard my heart." On the anniversary of a loss, plant bulbs; each spring blossom preaches resurrection to grieving soil. Use photography: snap daily evidence of beauty and compile a slide show titled "Glimpses of Goodness in My Wilderness." When gratitude feels impossible, borrow language—read Clara Scott's hymn "Open My Eyes" until lines become petitions. Corporate worship should include testimony slots where members recount mid-trial mercies, fertilizing communal hope. Gratitude does not shorten discipline but transforms its acoustic; what once echoed cavernous now resonates with quiet doxology. In darkness we learn gratitude is not the roof of the Christian life but its underground spring, rising precisely when all other wells dry up.

11.7.2 ▪ *Prophetic Imagination—Seeing New Creation Sprouts in Burned Fields*

Prophetic imagination asks, "What could resurrected life look like here?" long before green shoots appear (Isa 43:19). Ezekiel stared at sun-bleached bones and, empowered by the Spirit, pictured living armies (Ezek 37:1-10); disciplined saints do likewise over desolate finances, estranged families, or declining churches. Begin with Scripture-soaked visualization: read Revelation 22 aloud, then close eyes and picture your workplace under that river's healing flow. Artists can turn lament into murals—charcoal depictions of stumps overlaid with watercolor buds, embodying Isaiah 6:13's "holy seed" in the stump. Entrepreneurs practice redemptive design thinking: What product could reverse loneliness? What app could connect widows with gardens? Journal future headlines—"Neighborhood formerly ruled by addiction now hosts mentoring cafés"—then pray them forward. Habakkuk models "though...the fig tree does not blossom, yet I will rejoice" (Hab 3:17-19); declare "yet" sentences over seemingly dead zones. Teach children to imagine lion-and-lamb peace by role-playing conflict reconciliation with stuffed animals. In staff meetings, leave one chair empty to symbolize the needy neighbor your ministry will someday serve, keeping vision tangible. Prophetic imagination resists cynicism's stranglehold by rehearsing God's track record: exile ended, cross became crown, winter always surrenders to spring. Host "Dream Nights" where congregants brainstorm kingdom possibilities without budget constraints, trusting Ephesians 3:20 multiplication. Map neighborhood assets on giant posters, drawing arrows to indicate where resurrection life could flow—unused lots into gardens, vacant stores into literacy hubs. Celebrate even faint sprouts—a recovering addict's first clean week, a city council's pilot reform—as firstfruits (Rom 8:23). Keep prophetic sketches on refrigerator door; daily glances stoke perseverance. By seeing sprouts before they surface, believers partner with the Creator who "calls things that are not as though they were" (Rom 4:17).

11.7.3 ▪ Eucharistic Living—Broken, Blessed, Given for Others

Jesus took bread, blessed, broke, and gave (Luke 22:19); resurrection people adopt the same four-beat rhythm for ordinary lives. We present ourselves for "taking" each morning—Here I am, Lord (Isa 6:8). Blessing follows as God honours us with beloved identity (Matt 3:17). Then comes breaking—discipline phases, inconvenient interruptions, poured-out service. Finally, giving—spending time, talent, and tears for neighbor nourishment. Practically, start days with palms-up prayer, "Take me." At noon speak a blessing over self and coworkers—Numbers 6:24-26—remembering bread declared good before broken. In evening examen ask, "Where was I broken today?" and "How was that brokenness given for someone's hunger?" Hospitality becomes sacramental; a pot of chili ladled at doorsteps proclaims Christ's body for the world. Financial stewardship mirrors loaf-logic: tithe (taken), ask God to multiply (blessed), embrace reduced lifestyle (broken), fund justice projects (given). Parents explain discipline to children through bread analogy—family rules break selfishness so family can feed others with joy. When illness limits mobility, sufferers offer intercessory prayer—hidden crumbs still nourish global harvest. Churches can commission members weekly: leaders lift communion baskets and say, "Go, be bread," turning liturgy to lifestyle. Keep a "broken-for" notebook: jot moments when wounds open doors (2 Cor 4:10-12). Eucharistic living thus flips victim

269

narrative; broken seasons become distribution points for resurrection power.

11.7.4 ▪ Communities of Resurrection—Small Groups as Greenhouses of Hope

Individual hope wilts in isolation, but small groups act like greenhouses retaining gospel warmth (Heb 10:24-25). Structure gatherings around up-in-out rhythm: look up in worship, in toward each member's story, out toward a shared mission. Begin with a resurrection story each week—news of addicts freed, wars abated, or personal breakthroughs—training eyes for good reports (Ps 112:7). Share meals; breaking bread together incarnates Acts 2:46 joy. Practice "hot-seat blessing": one person receives three minutes of affirmations rooted in observed fruit, speaking life over dormant dreams. Rotate leadership to dismantle hierarchy, reminding all they carry resurrection authority (1 Pet 2:9). Create crisis funds; when layoffs strike a member, the group covers rent—embodied Romans 12:13 hospitality. Celebrate sacraments at home—baptize in backyard pools; communion over stew—signaling sacred cannot be quarantined. Group texts circulate praises, turning smartphones into psalm books. Quarterly serve together: clean elder homes, tutor migrants, planting hope beyond walls. Track answered prayers on poster boards; visual evidence fuels persistence. When grief enters—miscarriage, failed visa—circle the sufferer, anoint with oil, and hold silence, embodying Romans 12:15 empathy. Multiply groups every 18 months, sending out "seed teams" to propagate hope elsewhere, echoing tomb-to-world expansion. Conduct exit interviews: Did this group feel like resurrection rehearsal? Adjust accordingly. Over years, such greenhouses cultivate believers resilient enough to thrive under corrective heat yet supple enough to spread fragrant blossoms throughout scorched neighborhoods.

11.8. The Final Word—Death Swallowed by Life (Hos 13:14; 1 Cor 15:54)

11.8.1 • New-Creation Judgment—Everything Wrong Set Right (Revelation 21:5)

"I am making all things new" is no poetic flourish; it is the courtroom decree of the One seated on the throne (Rev 21:5). Judgment in the new creation does not merely punish evil; it reverse-engineers every injustice until righteousness fits each corner like mosaic tiles. Tears wiped (Rev 21:4) signify grievances adjudicated, not ignored. The martyrs' cry for vengeance (Rev 6:10) receives satisfying reply— not vindictive but restorative. Imagine headlines: *War Museums Close; Nations Beat Stockpiles into Tractors* (Isa 2:4). Economic scales recalibrate—workers paid full wages, debts forgiven beyond jubilee. Racial hierarchies dissolve as kings bring diverse glory into the city (Rev 21:24-26). Environmental healing accompanies moral rectitude: desert blooms (Isa 35:1), predators lose hunger for prey. Personal regrets find redemptive edit; what Joseph told brothers ("You meant evil...but God meant good" Gen 50:20) becomes cosmic tagline. Judgment scenes that once terrified now thrill— nothing spoiled will remain unrepaired. Knowing this, believers labour in hope; anti-trafficking offices, reconciliation tables, and recycling centers are prophetic pilot projects. They anticipate adjudication by aligning with it, like musicians rehearsing before maestro arrives. When discipline now feels harsh, recall the destination: a universe whose every atom whispers justice soaked in mercy.

11.8.2 • The Resurrection Body—Personal Discipline Completed in Glory

Our present bodies groan—tendons inflamed by anxiety, brains fogged by depression—but resurrection promises a soma pneumatikon, a Spirit-animated body (1 Cor 15:44). Discipline trains these mortal tents for immortality, like athletes practicing with weighted vests. Paul likens sufferings to childbirth contractions producing glory (Rom 8:22-23). Imagine waking with energy cresting like morning surf, senses tuned to divine frequencies—sight perceiving ultraviolet beauty, taste recognising nuances of

271

Revelation's fruit. Disabilities become trophies; Joni Eareckson Tada envisions standing, leaping, and casting her wheelchair aside. Memory healed: no intrusive shame-reels, only sanctified recollections. Physical resurrection validates bodily ethics—purity, rest, stewardship—because flesh matters. It also nullifies fear of martyrdom; the sword only accelerates upgrade. Spiritual disciplines fit pilgrims for this outfit; fasting reminds stomach glory is coming, exercise honors future continuity between current and glorified frames. Past addictive cravings will metamorphose into uncorrupted desires—nothing to hide, everything to enjoy (Ps 16:11). Resurrection bodies guarantee relational wholeness: hugs without awkwardness, eye contact without shame. This hope fuels perseverance under present chastening; compared to eternal vitality, today's losses are "light and momentary" (2 Cor 4:17). Store this blueprint in mind; let it buoy hospital visits and hospice hymns.

11.8.3 • Cosmic Jubilee—Land, Nations, and Creatures Released from Curse

Leviticus 25's jubilee freed slaves, cancelled debts, and returned land; Isaiah extends the principle to the whole earth (Isa 61:1-4). Paul foresees creation itself liberated from decay (Rom 8:21). Imagine ecosystems exhaling—oceans rid of plastic, coral reefs resurrected like Lazarus. National wounds heal; swords into plowshares symbolizes budget realignment from defense to agriculture (Mic 4:3). Languages remain but unify in worship (Rev 7:9); Babel's fracture mended without erasing diversity. Economic jubilee cancels generational poverty; each family inherits secure dwelling under vines and fig trees (Mic 4:4). Animal kingdom aligns—no factory farms, predators eat hay with cattle (Isa 11:7). The land receives Sabbath rest perpetual; deserts gush springs (Isa 35:6-7). Israel's promised land expands to global scale—a renewed cosmos where Immanuel dwells. Thus, environmental activism and debt-relief advocacy prefigure cosmic jubilee. Churches host "mini-jubilees," forgiving micro-loans every seven years, teaching eschatology through spreadsheets. Worship songs incorporate creaturely choruses—whales and sparrows join choir (Ps 148). Cosmic jubilee reframes current discipline of scarcity; it is God's pruning for abundance.

272

Paul calls afflictions "light" and "momentary" not because they feel lightweight, but because he weighs them on eternity's scale. The Greek hyperbolē of glory ("beyond comparison") suggests exponential payoff. Trials are seed-investments accruing compound interest of joy. Suffering then cannot steal joy; it stocks future reservoirs (Ps 126:5). Daily posture: hold sorrows in one hand, promises in the other—like Simeon cradling infant hope amid Roman occupation (Luke 2:25-32). Practical step: create "Already/Not Yet" lists—left column evidences grace now, right column hopes awaiting fulfillment. Encourage grieving friends with forward-leaning language: "This is chapter-five darkness, but chapter-eight sunrise is scripted." Employ sabbath as weekly rehearsal of final rest; cease striving to taste ultimate peace (Heb 4:9-11). Sing hymns that end with heaven stanzas—"Great Is Thy Faithfulness" transitions from daily mercies to "ten thousand beside." Use art: place an hourglass on desk reminding that pain has an expiry date. Re-narrate setbacks as weight-training; heavier pressures forge stronger faith sinews (Jas 1:2-4). Mentor younger believers by sharing aged scars alongside radiant hope, illustrating sanctified time. Finally, cultivate eschatological imagination through reading Revelation aloud; let city-of-light visions disinfect despair. Living between times means groaning and grinning simultaneously, knowing the Judge of discipline is also the Bridegroom of endless delight.

Conclusion When the Great Physician lays down His scalpel for the final time, scars will remain only as radiant testimonies, not as tender wounds. Hosea's taunt—"O Death, where are your plagues?"—will echo across a renewed cosmos, and discipline will be forever folded into delight. Until that unveiling, we inhabit the holy tension of a people both corrected and commissioned: we accept pruning so that richer fruit can bless neighbors; we interpret shaking as proof that an unshakable kingdom is near. Every time we choose gratitude in loss, practice repentance with expectancy, or offer broken bread in confident joy, we rehearse the pattern of our Savior—crucified, raised, and reigning. May this vision steady your heart: the Judge who wounds is the Redeemer who heals, and His resurrected life is already pulsing beneath every field that looks, for the moment, cut down to stubble. Hope has the final jurisdiction; let it govern your response to every discipline, great or small, until the day our faith becomes sight and all His loving purposes stand complete.

Chapter 12. Bridegroom of Grace—Anticipating Union with Christ

A wedding is the most future-oriented of human ceremonies: two lives stand in the present, yet every vow tilts toward the days still to come. Hosea harnesses that expectancy when the Lord promises, "I will betroth you to Me forever... in steadfast love and mercy" (Hos 2:19). Those ancient words find their full resonance when Jesus steps onto history's stage and quietly calls Himself "the Bridegroom" (Mk 2:19). From that moment the gospel ceases to be merely a rescue plan and is unmasked as a romance in which the Eternal Son woos, wins, and one day weds a once-wayward people. To live as Christians, then, is to live engaged—already spoken for, not yet at the altar—carrying the joy, purity, and restless longing that fill every true fiancée. In this chapter we will trace how Scripture's marriage motif stretches from Hosea's shattered home to John's dazzling vision of the marriage supper of the Lamb, how the Spirit functions as our engagement seal, and how daily disciplines become bridal preparations. Above all, we will explore why seeing Jesus as Bridegroom transforms obedience into desire-driven faithfulness and turns mission into handing out invitations to the greatest celebration the universe will ever host.

12.1. The Betrothal Motif—From Hosea's Vows to Scripture's Grand Romance

12.1.1 ▪ Hosea 2:19-20—Legal Language of Eternal Covenant Love

Ancient Near-Eastern betrothal contracts usually required a bride-price, listed the groom's obligations, and guaranteed the woman food, clothing, and marital rights if the husband later neglected her (cf. Ex 21:10-11). In Hosea 2:19-20 God adopts that legal format yet transforms every clause: the dowry He brings is His own righteousness, justice, *ḥesed*, and compassion—virtues normally demanded of the groom now gifted by Him. The repetition "I will betroth you" three times functions like signing, sealing, and notarizing the covenant. The phrase "forever" (*l ōlām*) overrides the standard conditionality of human marriages, announcing that no later breach will dissolve this union—an astounding claim given Israel's history of serial adultery. The inclusion of "knowledge of God" (v. 20) as one of the bridal promises elevates intimacy to covenant status; in Hebrew idiom *yāda ʿ*can mean marital knowing (Gen 4:1), so God pledges experiential closeness, not mere legal standing. Even the prepositions preach grace: He betroths *to Me*, shifting focus from benefits to belonging. Modern believers reading the verse discover their security does not depend on the mood swings of their devotion but on the granite oath of the divine Groom. The passage also corrects consumer-dating Christianity; covenant precedes compatibility, and love produces beauty rather than waiting to find it. Liturgically, churches can echo Hosea's wording at baptisms—"He has betrothed you"—helping converts feel less like club members and more like engaged lovers. Finally, the text foreshadows Trinitarian involvement: righteousness (Son), steadfast love (Father), and knowledge (Spirit who reveals, 1 Cor 2:10) all converge, hinting that the whole Godhead signs the wedding license.

12.1.2 • Old-Testament Espousals—Sinai, Song of Songs, and Prophetic Poetry

At Sinai God descends in cloud and fire, issues vows ("You shall be My treasured possession," Ex 19:5-6), and the people respond, "All that the LORD has spoken we will do," mimicking a collective "I do." Ezekiel later retells that scene with bridal imagery: the Lord covers Israel with His garment, a cultural act of engagement, and adorns her with jewels (Ezek 16:8-13). The Song of Songs celebrates this covenant romance from the standpoint of desire—"My beloved is mine and I am his" (Song 2:16)—showing that legal commitment fuels, rather than quenches, passion. Jeremiah grieves when Israel "forgot their bridal love" of wilderness days (Jer 2:2), implying that early covenant years were a honeymoon of trust. Isaiah 54:5 explicitly names God as Husband and promises widowed Zion a singing future. Ruth's story adds Gentile inclusion: a Moabite widow enters the Davidic line via a redeemer-groom, prefiguring global bridehood. Together these texts sketch a progressive revelation: covenant starts formal, grows poetic, broadens ethnic boundaries, and deepens emotional range. Reading them sequentially is like watching a courtship montage where each scene adds nuance—security, longing, fidelity, and redemption. For discipleship, these passages help couples frame marriage as theater of the gospel and help singles anchor identity in being eternally spoken for.

12.1.3 • Bride Images in the Psalms and Wisdom Literature (Psalm 45; Proverbs 31)

Psalm 45 is simultaneously a royal wedding ode and a messianic prophecy; the groom's throne is "for ever and ever" (v. 6), pushed beyond any earthly king toward the ultimate Son. The bride, clothed in gold of Ophir, is told to forget her people and father's house (v. 10), echoing the Genesis leave-and-cleave command and foreshadowing Christian allegiance that surpasses biological ties (Lk 14:26). Her companions follow with "joy and gladness," prefiguring the multi-ethnic church entering the king's palace (v. 15). Proverbs 31, often reduced to chores, actually celebrates a covenant partner who embodies wisdom—the poem's acrostic structure from aleph to tav suggests completeness, making the excellent wife a living

277

alphabet of grace. If read ecclesiologically, she mirrors the active, marketplace-present Bride of Christ who feeds, clothes, and blesses the poor (Prov 31:20). These wisdom portraits teach that bridal identity is not passive; beauty includes righteous deeds that Revelation will later call "fine linen" (Rev 19:8). Singing Psalm 45 in worship marries doxology to eschatology, letting congregants rehearse their own entry procession. Studying Proverbs 31 in mixed-gender settings prevents typecasting and highlights missional entrepreneurship as bridal virtue.

12.1.4 ▪ Continuity and Development—How NT Writers Extend the Motif

New-Testament authors do not invent but intensify the spousal theme. Jesus' first miracle at Cana (Jn 2:1-11) occurs at a wedding, subtly signaling that He will supply covenant wine when human jars run dry. Paul in 2 Corinthians 11:2 claims pastoral jealousy "to present you as a pure virgin to Christ," showing apostolic ministry as bridal preparation. Ephesians 5:25-32 lifts marriage from mere metaphor to sacrament of union; earthly husbands embody Christ's cleansing love "with water and the word," echoing Ezekiel 16's bathing imagery. John's Apocalypse then unveils the telos: "the bride has made herself ready" (Rev 19:7). Development also appears linguistically—*mystērion* in Eph 5:32 wraps the motif in sacred depth; union is more than symbol, it is ontological participation. Still, continuity remains: righteousness, steadfast love, and knowledge promised in Hosea reappear as Christ's righteousness imputed, love poured into hearts (Rom 5:5), and knowledge of God through the Spirit. The trajectory moves from promise to presence to consummation, teaching believers to live in "already-not-yet" engagement tension. Pastors can craft sermon series tracing this continuum, helping congregations locate themselves between betrothal and banquet.

12.2. Christ the Bridegroom—Incarnation, Cross, and Empty Tomb

12.2.1 • John the Baptist's Friend-of-the-Bridegroom Role (John 3:29-30)

John likens himself to the best man whose joy peaks when he hears the Bridegroom's voice, not when he gets a spotlight. His declaration, "He must increase, but I must decrease," supplies a template for every gospel herald: success equals transferring affection from messenger to Messiah. Jewish wedding customs placed the friend in charge of guarding the bride, arranging logistics, and announcing the groom's arrival with a shout at midnight (cf. Mt 25:6). John fulfills that duty by preaching repentance, cleansing Israelites in water as bridal mikveh, and identifying Jesus as Lamb-Groom. His joy "now complete" rebukes ministry envy; true servants celebrate when people leave their platform for Christ's embrace. Preachers today stand in that lineage; altar calls are not brand recruitment but betrothal ceremonies. John's wilderness location also signals that genuine covenant renewal often starts outside institutional walls, challenging comfortable religion. The best-man analogy yields homiletical checkpoints: Are our sermons voice-amplifiers for the Groom? Are we handling the Bride with purity? Do we step aside when He enters?

12.2.2 • Wedding Parables—Invitations, Garments, and Wise Readiness (Matthew 22; 25)

Jesus tells of a king who prepares a banquet yet receives snubs from the invited elite (Mt 22:1-14), turning the streets into invitation routes for the marginalised—tax theology for evangelism: if some refuse grace, widen the guest list. The shocking twist is a guest expelled for lacking wedding clothes, teaching that acceptance requires transformation, not mere RSVP. In Matthew 25:1-13 ten virgins await the groom; five pack extra oil, embodying sustained devotion, while five let lamps die, exposing borrowed spirituality. Both parables highlight urgency—doors eventually shut—and warn against presumption. Scholars note that oil often symbolizes the Spirit; vigilance is Spirit-dependence, not adrenaline. Pastoral application: discipleship trains believers to carry private reserves of prayer and Scripture, so public crises don't darken their witness. Small groups can host "lamp-check nights" assessing spiritual disciplines. Evangelistically, the parables compel invitational lifestyles—street corners are workplaces, chats, digital spaces—handing out wedding flyers indiscriminately yet urging proper attire, i.e., Christ's righteousness (Gal 3:27).

12.2.3 ▪ Purchasing the Dowry—Blood, Water, and the Side Opened for a Bride (Ephesians 5:25-27)

First-century grooms paid *mōhar* to secure a bride; Christ pays with "himself," a dowry surpassing silver (1 Pet 1:18-19). The piercing of His side releases blood and water (Jn 19:34), echoing Eve drawn from Adam's side—bride birthed from sleeping groom. Early fathers saw baptism (water) and Eucharist (blood) flowing as twin sacraments of nuptial formation. Paul says Christ cleanses the Church "by the washing of water with the word" so she stands without spot—a direct allusion to bridal bath rituals. The verb "present" (*paristēmi*) evokes formal giving of the bride; Jesus is both groom and father-figure escorting the Church down the aisle. This dowry changes ethics: if the price tag of my neighbour is divine blood, how dare I demean them? It also stabilises assurance; what Christ bought He will surely claim (Phil 1:6). During communion, ministers can mention dowry imagery, letting the cup remind saints of their infinite value.

12.2.4 ▪ Resurrection as Public Betrothal Announcement—He Is Risen to Wed

In Jewish culture, engagements became public when contracts were displayed or wine shared; resurrection is God's banner "This Jesus...you crucified, God raised" (Acts 2:32-36). The angel's words, "Come, see the place where He lay, then go quickly and tell," parallel bridesmaids spreading good news (Mt 28:6-7). Paul calls resurrection "firstfruits" (1 Cor 15:20), hinting that wedding harvest has begun. Empty tomb appearances function as rehearsal dinners—Emmaus meal, Galilee breakfast—previewing marital fellowship. Christ greets Mary with her name (Jn 20:16), intimate as groom's whisper under veil. Ascension then parallels the groom returning to prepare the home (Jn 14:2-3); Pentecost deposits the Spirit as

280

engagement ring, proving He will return. Thus, Eastertide spirituality cultivates hopeful longing; singing "Christ the Lord is Risen Today" doubles as bridal chorus. Believers scan world events like brides glancing at calendars, counting days until promised return.

12.3. The Spirit as Engagement Guarantee—Presence, Power, and Preparation

12.3.1 ▪ *Arrabōn: The Spirit as Down-Payment of Glory (2 Corinthians 1:22; Ephesians 1:14)*

Paul twice calls the Spirit an *arrabōn*—a commercial term for earnest money ensuring full payment. In first-century commerce failure to complete purchase forfeited the deposit, so God binds His reputation to the Spirit's indwelling. The metaphor shifts assurance from feelings to divine escrow; even on dull days the guarantee remains. The Spirit's presence is experiential: inner testimonium (Rom 8:16), unexplained peace (Phil 4:7), and awakened hunger for holiness. These foretastes differ in degree, not kind, from coming glory—the same Spirit who now sparks prayer will one day flood resurrected senses. Practical discipleship: during worship pause to acknowledge the earnest—"Thank You, Spirit, for being preview." In counseling, remind doubting hearts that longing for God is itself evidence of deposit. Eschatologically, the Spirit's permanence contradicts ancient near-eastern divorces; this engagement will not collapse due to bride price failure.

12.3.2 ▪ *Bridal Gifts—Spiritual Charisms as Wedding Shower from Heaven (1 Corinthians 12)*

First-century brides received gifts to equip new household; similarly, charisms—prophecy, generosity, administration—are bridal shower items empowering the Church's witness. Paul frames them as manifestations "for the common good" (1 Cor 12:7), discouraging comparison envy at the party. Variety mirrors cultures bringing treasures to the wedding feast (Rev 21:26). Practically, churches should run discovery courses titled "Unwrapping Your Bridal Gifts," connecting talents to nuptial narrative. Using gifts becomes dress rehearsal—healing prayer previews future

281

wholeness, words of wisdom foreshadow face-to-face knowing (1 Cor 13:12). Abusing gifts is akin to spoiling wedding china; Paul's rebuke in 1 Cor 14 aims to protect marital ambiance. When blessings flow, credit the Groom, fostering gratitude rather than self-exaltation.

12.3.3 ▪ Inner Beauty Regimen—Fruit of the Spirit as Bridal Adornment (Galatians 5:22-23)

Ancient brides spent months in perfume (Est 2:12); the Spirit's fruit polishes inner character: love as primary fragrance, joy as radiant smile, peace as poised posture. Patience and kindness form relational etiquette, goodness and faithfulness craft trustworthy reputation, gentleness accents speech, and self-control preserves purity. Unlike gifts, fruit cannot be microwaved; it ripens through abiding (Jn 15:4). Trials act as heat lamps accelerating sweetness (Jas 1:2-4). Accountability friendships serve as mirrors, politely noting spinach between teeth: envy, irritability, pride. Spiritual disciplines—silence, service, scripture—supply nutrients. Fruit display draws seekers; suitors of false religions notice the Bride's aroma and inquire. Teaching series can frame each trait as section of wedding dress—stain one, entire gown compromised. Yet grace runs the laundry; confession applies Christ's bleach, whiteness restored (Isa 1:18).

12.3.4 ▪ Groaning and Interceding—Spirit and Bride Say "Come" (Romans 8:23; Revelation 22:17)

Engaged couples count days; the Spirit intensifies that ache by groaning within believers for full adoption, redemption of bodies (Rom 8:23). His sighs are wordless prayers, deeper than language (Rom 8:26), harmonising with creation's groans and the Bride's whispered "Come!" The convergence surfaces in Revelation 22:17 where Spirit and Bride speak a single imperative—the only time Scripture records them in unison. Corporate worship that intercedes for Christ's return aligns with this duet; songs like "Even So, Come" tune congregations to bridal pitch. Personal practice: conclude daily devotions with Maranatha, inviting Groom into traffic jams and boardrooms. Missional urgency flows; every evangelistic conversation is sending more voices to echo "Come." Lament likewise joins the groan—tears for injustice become betrothal angst. Fasting embodies longing; emptiness of stomach rehearses not-yet embrace. The Spirit also answers the groan in down-payments: revival outpourings, healings, racial reconciliations—mini-honeymoon visits assuring final wedding. Studying eschatology without Spirit's ache risks speculation; with Him, it fuels affection. In counseling grief, remind mourners that sighs have translator in heaven. As anticipation crescendos, holiness follows—no bride dallies with old flames on eve of wedding. Thus, Spirit-induced yearning is both promise keeper and purity purifier.

12.4. Personal Union—Identity, Intimacy, and Imitation

12.4.1 ▪ *"Bone of My Bones"—Mystical Union Explained (1 Cor 6:17; John 15)*

Union with Christ is not a poetic flourish; Paul says, "Whoever is joined to the Lord becomes one spirit with Him" (1 Cor 6:17). That little phrase *one spirit* reaches back to Adam's exclamation over Eve—"bone of my bones" (Gen 2:23)—and forward to Jesus' vine-and-branches discourse where life-sap flows continuously from root to fruit (Jn 15:4-5). Mystical union means the believer's truest address is *in Christ* (2 Cor 5:17) even while their mailing address remains earthly. Identity therefore shifts from biography to Christography: successes no longer inflate worth and failures no longer collapse it (Phil 3:8-9). Every spiritual blessing—adoption, redemption, inheritance—is delivered to that union address (Eph 1:3-14). The doctrine guards against moralism; fruit grows because branch abides, not because branch strains. It also guards against passivity; sap that truly courses inevitably pushes out buds of obedience (Jn 15:8). Union undergirds assurance: if Christ's life is ours, our salvation is as durable as His resurrection (Rom 6:5-9). It reframes temptation: sexual sin is not a private lapse but a violation of marital oneness with the Lord (1 Cor 6:15-16). Daily meditation can rehearse union by breathing in "Christ in me" and exhaling "and I in Christ" (Col 1:27). In suffering, believers remind themselves that nothing—"tribulation, or distress, or sword"—can sever the marital bond (Rom 8:35-39). At communion the bread inside the body dramatizes Christ inside the believer. Baptism pictures the wedding ceremony—plunged into His death, raised into His life (Rom 6:3-4).

283

Thus, mystical union is the fountainhead from which intimacy flows and imitation follows.

12.4.2 ▪ Daily Communion—Prayer as Pillow-Talk and Scripture as Love Letter

If union is fact, communion is experience. Jesus invites secret-place intimacy: "Go into your room and shut the door" (Mt 6:6). There the Bridegroom shares whispers too delicate for public homily (Song 2:14). Prayer becomes pillow-talk when we address God not only as Sovereign but as "My beloved and my friend" (Song 5:16). Conversational rhythms can mirror marriage check-ins: adore, listen, request, and rest in silence. Scripture then functions as love letter; the Spirit highlights lines that feel handwritten—Jeremiah's "I have loved you with an everlasting love" (Jer 31:3) or Zephaniah's serenade (Zeph 3:17). Lectio divina slows reading to savor tone and nuance much like reading a cherished note repeatedly. Keeping a "God's terms of endearment" journal trains the mind to anticipate kindness instead of condemnation. Worship music adds melody to prose; singing truth engages affections that prose alone cannot reach (Eph 5:19). For busy seasons, breath prayers—"Jesus, my joy"— tuck intimacy into commutes and queues. Couples' devotion can become triple fellowship: spouse, spouse, and Christ the Bridegroom (Ecc 4:12). Retreat days operate like anniversary get-aways, re-centering identity on belovedness. Communion of course climaxes at the Table, where bread and wine become tactile "I love yous" (1 Cor 11:24-26). Cultivated daily, these practices keep engagement rings glinting even in mundane chores.

12.4.3 ▪ Holiness of the Bridal Chamber—Fleeing Spiritual and Sexual Adultery (1 Th 4:3-5)

Paul roots sexual purity in betrothal imagery: "This is the will of God, your sanctification…that each of you know how to control his own body in holiness and honor" (1 Th 4:3-4). To violate the marriage bed—physically with pornography or spiritually with idols—is to defile the bridal chamber reserved for Christ (Jas 4:4). Holiness therefore feels less like taboo policing and more like guarding honeymoon sheets. Practically, believers install filters, craft media plans, and pursue accountability not to earn love but to

284

protect intimacy already pledged. Fasting trains appetites to submit, reminding bodies they belong to Another (1 Cor 6:19-20). Inner idols—greed, status, political absolutism—also seduce; examine bank statements and screen time to locate rival lovers. Corporate worship includes confession liturgies, laundering garments weekly (1 Jn 1:9). Counseling wounded sexuality points sufferers to Jesus who "cleanses with water and the word" (Eph 5:26); shame becomes hem healed by His touch (Mk 5:34). Parents disciple teens with positive vision—marriage as garden, not gate, sexuality as covenant gift, not forbidden fruit. Singles steward desire through creative service and close friendships, demonstrating that romantic delay need not stifle relational richness. Holiness culture celebrates restorative testimonies, showing stained gowns turned radiant (Isa 1:18). Ultimately purity is relational vigilance—eyes fixed on the Groom so counterfeits fade.

12.4.4 ▪ *Suffering with the Groom—Sharing Cross to Share Crown (Rom 8:17)*

Paul links heirs with co-suffering: "If we suffer with Him, we may also be glorified with Him" (Rom 8:17). Engagement to the Crucified means splinters inevitably reach our shoulders (Lk 9:23). Yet shared pain forges intimacy; couples who navigate trial together exit bonded. When believers endure ridicule, they participate in Jesus' rejection by His hometown (Jn 1:11). Physical illness can echo Gethsemane's cup, whispered "yet not my will" shaping trust (Lk 22:42). Persecuted saints experience the Bridegroom's solidarity—Stephen saw Him standing to honour his martyrdom (Acts 7:55-56). Suffering also prunes distractions, focusing eyes on wedding day hope (2 Cor 4:17-18). Lament psalms give bridal voice to anguish, preventing stoic silence. Community bears burdens as bridesmaids lifting train over muddy ground (Gal 6:2). Communion in affliction anticipates communion in reign—"If we endure, we will also reign with Him" (2 Tim 2:12). Practice framing setbacks aloud: "This is lighter than the joy set before me." Keep resurrection stories—job provision, healed relationships—as reminders that Friday always points to Sunday. Scarred places then become unique contact points for others' comfort (2 Cor 1:4). Thus, cross-sharing is courtship's final proof of unwavering love.

12.5. Corporate Bride—Cultivating a Bridal Culture in the Church

12.5.1 • Worship as Bridal Processional—Adoration before Action

Sunday gatherings rehearse the approach to the aisle; call to worship is the musical cue for the congregation-bride to rise. Songs that spotlight God's beauty—"One thing have I asked" (Ps 27:4)—train eyes on the Groom before petitions rush in. Liturgical flow mimics covenant progression: adoration, confession, assurance, and communion mirror pledge, cleansing, gifting, and feast. Visual aesthetics matter: banners of lilies and vineyards recall Song themes; fragrance diffusers with frankincense subtly evoke temple-wedding continuity. Processionals may include scripture carried high, symbolizing Groom entering. Moments of silence cultivate awe— bride catching first sight. When worship teams choose keys to accommodate congregational singing, they act like tailors ensuring gown fits. Testimony slots function like toasts, declaring qualities of the Groom and fidelity of the Bride. Generosity offering ranks as gift-exchange; bride returns love tokens to fiancé's mission (Phil 4:18). Closing benediction sends people out like betrothed showing ring to world. Regular evaluation asks: Did adoration outweigh announcements? Did awe linger in parking lot? A bridal worship culture inoculates against consumer spectatorship.

12.5.2 • Table Fellowship—Eucharist as Foretaste of Marriage Feast (1 Cor 11:26)

Paul says the church "proclaims the Lord's death until He comes" whenever it breaks bread, bridging cross and consummation. The loaf signals one body (1 Cor 10:17), a unified bride tasting future banquet (Rev 19:9). Set-up teams treat table linens like altar cloths; care communicates value. Words of institution highlight nuptial frame—"This cup is the new covenant," wedding language from Ex 24:8. Many traditions include intinction, symbolizing inseparable body-blood union. After distribution, congregants stand to sing doxology—practice for "Hallelujah!" thunder in heaven (Rev 19:6). Leftover elements are consumed, not trashed, honouring sacred meal. Home groups replicate table fellowship with pot-luck "agape feasts," knitting weekday lives into bridal fabric (Acts 2:46).

Teaching children to tear bread and dip trains next generation in expectancy. Fasting before communion heightens longing; feast then tastes sweeter. Global flavors—injera, naan, tortilla—remind church of multi-ethnic bride. Thus weekly Eucharist is both photo and appetizer of the coming Supper.

12.5.3 ▪ Discipline and Spotless Garments—Ephesians 5:26-27 Applied to Congregations

Christ washes His bride with water and word; likewise, local churches practice formative discipline. Preaching that confronts gossip or greed functions as washing cycle. When sin persists, Matthew 18 steps operate like stain-removal, aiming not ejection but garment purity. Members' covenants set expectations: fidelity to Scripture, financial integrity, peacemaking. Restoration stories are celebrated—dirty robes bleached to dazzling (Rev 7:14). Leadership modeling transparency, confessing from pulpit, prevents culture of hidden mold. Annual vision nights review fruit of discipline—reconciled marriages, debt freedom—connecting purity to flourishing. Small groups conduct "garment checks" by asking, "Where is Christ inviting fresh washing?" This culture counters legalism with gospel detergent: repentance plus promise of radiant future. Visitors sense authenticity and crave identical cleansing.

12.5.4 ▪ Diversity of Bridesmaids—Ethnic Unity and Shared Adornments (Rev 7:9)

John sees every nation before the throne wearing white, indicating equal invitation and equal cleansing. Local churches mirror this by platforming multicultural voices—Scripture read in Spanish, Swahili, Korean. Worship sets weave global melodies, letting each culture bring dowry treasures (Ps 96:3). Shared adornments include baptism identity, Spirit gifts, and mission calling; ethnicity enriches but does not divide. Anti-racism work becomes bridal harmony, not political side gig (Eph 2:14). Pot-luck fellowships celebrate cuisines, dismantling food-police suspicions. Hiring practices pursue representation; bridal party without diversity misrepresents Groom's guest list. Conflicts are inevitable; peacemaking teams facilitate Matthew 18 dialogue across cultural misunderstandings. Joint service projects—refugee tutoring, neighborhood beautification—

bond bridesmaids through sweat and laughter. Story nights allow testimonies of how Jesus found people in various nations, enlarging collective wonder. Ultimately diversity showcases the Groom's attractiveness—only divine love can gather such disparate friends and make them family.

12.6. Bridal Mission—Inviting the Nations to the Wedding

12.6.1 • *"Go to the Highways"—Evangelism as Sending Wedding Invites (Matthew 22:9-10)*

The king in Jesus' parable orders servants to invite "both bad and good," demolishing merit criteria. Evangelism thus resembles heralds distributing embossed invitations marked "admit freely, attire provided." Gospel presentations highlight gift righteousness garments (Isa 61:10). Street evangelists can literally hand invitation cards to church Alpha dinners. Social media posts function as digital couriers; testimonies captioned "You're invited." Hospitality evangelism—barbecue in front yard—models banquet open-door. Apologetics answers RSVP objections—*Is the banquet real? Will the king accept me?* Prayer walking neighborhoods is postal route preparation, softening soil for invitations. Rejected invites don't discourage; servants move to next cul-de-sac. Metrics shift from conversions to invitations faithfully delivered. Regular testimony Sundays recount those who said yes, inspiring more heralds.

12.6.2 • *Mercy and Justice Witness—Displaying Groom's Character to the Poor*

The Bridegroom defended the vulnerable (Lk 4:18); His fiancée mirrors that posture. Food pantries, legal-aid clinics, and anti-trafficking teams serve as hors d'oeuvres of kingdom generosity. Isaiah 58 links true fasting to shared bread; mission committees allocate budgets accordingly. Mercy deeds authenticate invitation—hungry guests trust a feast promised by givers who feed now. Justice advocacy—writing lawmakers for fair housing—proves wedding hall has room for the marginalized (Mic 6:8). Short-term mission trips repair roofs and preach hope, embodying word-and-deed courtship. Serve-teams wear T-shirts "Loved & Sent," clarifying

288

motive. Outcome: recipients often ask reason for hope (1 Pet 3:15), opening gospel door.

12.6.3 ▪ Apologetics of Beauty—Holiness and Art that Stir Longing for the Groom

Beauty bypasses intellectual defenses, awakening ache for transcendence. Church art galleries display paintings on Hosea, leading viewers from betrayal to bridal joy. Choral concerts of *Messiah* end with "Worthy is the Lamb," echoing wedding anthem (Rev 5:12). Christian architects design hospitable spaces flooded with light, symbolizing invitation to glory. Believers curate Instagram feeds of creation splendors tagged "Handiwork of my Groom," evangelizing through wonder. Holiness itself is beautiful: integrity in business, fidelity in marriage, gentleness online. Such ethical aesthetics cause observers to "glorify God" (Mt 5:16). Apologists quote Tolkien's eucatastrophe to illustrate gospel's happy ending. Poets craft spoken-word on divine romance for open-mic nights. When skeptics ask for rational proofs, believers add experiential evidence: "Taste and see" (Ps 34:8).

12.6.4 ▪ Martyrdom and Perseverance—Love Stronger than Death (Song 8:6)

"Many waters cannot quench love," and history proves it. Early martyrs sang wedding hymns en route to arenas, viewing execution as bridal entrance. Revelation pictures conquerors who "loved not their lives even unto death" (Rev 12:11). Modern persecuted believers embrace prison as pre-banquet waiting room. Their testimonies kindle Western courage: if they keep lamps burning under threat, surely comfort-wrapped saints can stay awake. Mission training includes martyrdom theology—students read *The Insanity of God*. Perseverance also applies to long obedience: caregivers for Alzheimer relatives, pastors in small villages, missionaries in slow-fruit fields. Each daily faithfulness says, "I still choose You," echoing Ruth's vow. Anniversary celebrations of conversion re-pledge allegiance. Hope of a Groom returning with reward sustains grit (Heb 10:35-37). Thus, unquenchable love, proven in pressure, becomes highest apologetic—death itself confesses the Bride's unwavering yes.

289

12.7. Preparing the Dress—Practices of Expectant Purity and Joy

12.7.1 • Oil in the Lamps—Watchfulness, Fasting, and Sabbath Anticipation

Jesus' parable of the ten virgins (Mt 25:1-13) teaches that readiness is not a mood but a stockpile. Oil represents sustained devotion—inner reserves of the Spirit that cannot be borrowed at midnight. Watchfulness begins by training the body's rhythms: setting phone alarms for Daniel-style prayer breaks (Dn 6:10), lighting a candle at dusk to whisper "Come, Lord Jesus" (Rev 22:20), and extinguishing it at dawn to thank Him for delay that allowed another day of mission. Weekly fasting loosens fleshly impatience and converts hunger pangs into bride-like longing; each skipped meal is a reminder that the Groom, not groceries, ultimately satisfies (Mk 2:19-20). Sabbath serves as 24-hour rehearsal dinner—ceasing productivity to taste coming rest (Heb 4:9-11). Believers prepare by curating what fills their metaphorical lamps: podcasts that lift eyes to heaven rather than stoke outrage, playlists saturated with hope, and Scripture memory that drips oil into thought patterns (Ps 119:11). When cultural crises ignite fear, lamp-keepers refuse panic buying; they examine wick length through self-assessment questions: Am I harboring secret sin? Am I nursing grievance? (1 Th 5:6-8). Communities hold "oil-checks" each quarter, inviting members to describe practices sustaining flame, then celebrating creativity—one paints prophetic art, another tenders silence walks. Parents model watchfulness by turning off cartoons on Saturday nights, gathering children to brief candlelit compline, shaping generational expectation. Corporate worship may open with doorkeeper prayer: "Blessed are those who stand at Your gates" (Ps 84:10). The goal is not survivalism but radiant welcome; trimmed wicks emit brightest light, attracting latecomers to the procession. Thus, oil discipline weds urgency and delight: urgency because doors will close, delight because Groom is worth the wait.

12.7.2 • Praise and Lament as Seamstress Needles—Stitching Hope through Pain

Every bridal gown requires thread and needle; in kingdom tailoring, praise and lament alternate stitches. The Psalms juxtapose "Why, O Lord?" (Ps 22:1) with "Yet You are enthroned" (Ps 22:3), teaching hearts to pull sorrow and adoration through the same fabric. Lament prevents cynicism; it acknowledges rips in the dress—abuse, injustice, unanswered prayer—refusing plastic smiles. Praise prevents despair; it embroiders gold promises over torn places, declaring future beauty (Isa 61:3). Practically, believers draft two-column prayers: grievances left, God's attributes right, then pray them aloud, crossing lines with "yet." Small groups host "sand-prayers," releasing pain onto sand trays, then tracing thank-You words across grains to symbolize redemptive overlay. Annual Good Friday services create communal lament spaces; Easter sunrise answers with jubilation, teaching cyclical stitching. Music ministries curate set lists that move from minor-key ache to major-key triumph, mirroring Revelation's arc from martyrs' cry (Rev 6:10) to wedding chorus (Rev 19:6). Personal journals include monthly lament psalms rewritten in one's own vocabulary followed by spontaneous hymns. Counselors guide trauma survivors to narrate hurt inside larger covenant story, sewing dignity back into torn identity (Joel 2:25). When churches only praise, fabric frays under hidden tension; when only lament, it unravels into gray threads. Balanced stitching produces tensile strength able to handle wedding-day dancing. Ultimately, Jesus models duet: He weeps at Lazarus' tomb (Jn 11:35) then thanks Father for hearing Him (Jn 11:41), hemming sorrow and gratitude into seamless robe of trust.

12.7.3 • Spiritual Friendships—Bridal Party Accountability and Encouragement

In ancient Jewish weddings, bridesmaids guarded the bride, assisted with adornment, and accompanied her to meet the groom; spiritual friendships fulfill similar roles today. Jonathan's covenant with David—"You will be king, and I will be next to you" (1 Sam 23:17)—illustrates friend as destiny-protector. Bridal party discipleship means meeting regularly for heart-examination: What voices competed for your affection this week? How did you respond? (Heb 3:13). Friends text Scripture screenshots at 3 p.m., an hour many slump, reminding each other of chosen status (Jn 15:16). They celebrate small obediences—deleting an unclean app, reconciling with a sibling—like bridesmaids cheering each fitted seam. When one staggers, others lift; Ecclesiastes' "threefold cord" (Ecc 4:9-12) becomes lifeline. Practically, triads use apps like Marco Polo to send video prayers, maintaining presence across time zones. Annual retreats offer space for confession bonfires—burning index cards of idols, then exchanging prophetic encouragements sealed in envelopes to open later. Older saints mentor younger, passing down legacy jewels of wisdom (Titus 2:3-5). Cross-cultural friendships enrich gown diversity, adding African kitenge patterns or Korean silks to collective attire (Rev 7:9). Friendships guard against dateless loneliness narratives; singles realize they already have a bridal party beyond romance. Healthy boundaries keep support mutual; no friend replaces Bridegroom. When betrayal wounds, community applies Matthew 18 restoration, mending torn lace. Together they rehearse Revelation rehearsal dinners—potluck feasts where each dish symbolizes a God attribute—and toast, "To the Lamb and His Bride!"

12.7.4 ▪ Prophetic Imagination—Seeing the Coming Wedding in Ordinary Days

Prophetic imagination animates mundane tasks with eschatological meaning. Folding laundry becomes practicing garment stewardship for white linens of Revelation 19:8. Sweeping floors envisions future streets of gold where no dust settles (Rev 21:21). Gardeners see each seed buried as type of resurrection, whispering, "Soon the Bride will bloom." Educators view lesson plans as dowry investment into children's future roles in palace administration (2 Tim 2:2). Commuters interpret brake lights as waiting liturgy—pause before glory arrival. Artists doodle wedding rings in meeting margins, embedding hope within corporate culture. Parents rename bedtime story "princess and king" endings as gospel foreshadowings. Prophetic imagination also reframes news: reports of ceasefires spark meditation on everlasting peace treaty; disaster coverage ignites prayer, "Come renew the earth." It fuels creativity: bakers craft wedding-cake cupcakes for neighbors, sharing that one day joy will overflow like frosting. Vision boards on refrigerators showcase verses, bridal imagery, and justice goals, aligning aspiration with

292

telos. When cynicism whispers "same old world," imagination counters with Hebrews 11 substance evidence. Churches host "Hope galleries," displaying members' sketches of future kingdom scenes. Even suffering becomes canvas: hospital IV poles imagined as lampstands awaiting oil. Prophetic sight is cultivated through Scripture immersion—Isaiah's wolf-lamb tableau, John's crystal river—then prayed into senses. Ultimately, such gaze keeps hearts upright; no slouching fiancé forgets the date when every sunrise rehearses wedding march.

12.8. The Marriage Supper of the Lamb—Eschatological Consummation and Eternal Delight

12.8.1 ▪ Revelation 19:6-9—The Liturgical Liturgy of Heaven's Feast

John hears a roar "like many waters," echoing Niagara's volume, announcing not war but wedding. The imperative "Let us rejoice and exult" is heaven's loudest call-to-worship, and the reason given— "the marriage of the Lamb has come"—elevates nuptial joy above every prior celebration. "Fine linen, bright and clean," equates righteous deeds with bridal couture, proving sanctification threads will endure flames (1 Cor 3:13-14). The angel's command to write, "Blessed are those invited," certifies RSVP list—scripture's only beatitude delivered by an angel. Liturgically, present Eucharists echo future liturgy: sursum corda ("lift up your hearts") anticipates lifted goblets at cosmic toast. Hallelujah appears here for first time in New Testament, fourfold, indicating crescendo moment. This scene answers Psalm 23's table in enemy presence; foes are now removed, cup overflow eternal. Homiletically, preachers portray the menu: Isaiah's aged wine (Isa 25:6), fruit from life-tree (Rev 22:2), manna's flavor revisited. Feast imagery validates bodily resurrection—taste buds resurrect for divine cuisine, denying Gnostic squeamishness. Communal singing of Handel's "Hallelujah" rehearses this thunder; each soprano line foreshadows seraphic accompaniment. Hope for this supper relativizes current dietary restrictions—celiac, diabetes—knowing healed bodies will indulge freely. Missionally, feeding programs are appetizers served in King's name. Finally, the "Lamb" title preserves cruciform

293

identity: Groom bears scars at his own banquet, so ex-Gomers can attend unashamed (Rev 5:6).

12.8.2 ▪ New-Creation Honeymoon—Garden-City, River, and Throne (Rev 22:1-5)

Honeymoons combine intimacy and exploration; Revelation's garden-city offers both. A crystal river flows from throne—the couple's shared dwelling—symbolizing unbroken communion. Either side grows the tree of life, twelve fruits monthly—no seasonal infertility; delight is continuous. Leaves heal nations, suggesting honeymoon ministry: the newly wed Bride participates in ongoing restoration of cultures, a redeeming tour instead of idle seclusion. Night is banished; lamp of Lamb illuminates streets—a perpetual candlelit dinner. Names on foreheads signify covenant tattoos— identity unsnatchable. Unlike original Eden, this garden boasts urban architecture, marrying wilderness beauty and civilization creativity; redeemed technology and art become love gifts exchanged. Honeymoon length? "They will reign forever," endless. Meditating on this scene fuels environmental care now—no littering the future honeymoon suite. Couples celebrate anniversaries by planting trees or cleaning rivers, prophesying landscape to come. Pain of childlessness eases knowing fruitfulness awaits in cosmic orchard. Artists draw river murals in baptisteries, linking initial union rite to final habitat. Lecture series titled "City of Intimacy" help urban planners integrate kingdom aesthetics. Thus, the promised honeymoon dignifies ordinary place-making endeavours and soothes pilgrimage fatigue.

12.8.3 ▪ Beatific Vision—Face-to-Face Knowing and Unending Intimacy (1 Jn 3:2)

John assures that "when He appears, we shall be like Him, for we shall see Him as He is." This beatific vision marks climax of betrothal—veil lifted, eyes locked, transformation instant. Moses glimpsed backside glory and face shone (Ex 34:29); how much more when Bride beholds Groom's unveiled splendour. Augustine called vision "the end for which we are created"; Thomas Aquinas placed it above every miracle. Psychologically, deepest human longing is to be fully known yet fully loved—here realized. All partial mediations—Scripture, sacraments, conscience—converge into direct perception. No prayer distance, no interpretive darkness, only flooded awareness: "Now I know in part...then face to face" (1 Cor 13:12). Identity completes: insecurities evaporate, self-loathing impossible before blazing affection. Ethically, hope of seeing Him purifies "just as He is pure" (1 Jn 3:3); vision anticipation motivates holiness better than fear of hell. In worship today, lifting eyes during doxology prefigures that gaze. Contemplative prayer trains spiritual sight, quieting noise so eyes of heart sharpen (Eph 1:18). Mystics describe moments of infused love; these foretastes sustain through deserts. Ultimately, the everlasting honeymoon is not endless activities but endless beholding and reflecting—glory circulating like blood in resurrected veins.

12.8.4 ▪ Living in the In-Between—How Blessed Hope Fuels Present Faithfulness (Titus 2:11-14)

Paul ties grace past, discipline present, and glory future in one sentence: grace "has appeared," trains us to live godly, while we "wait for the blessed hope." Hope is therefore pedagogical—teaching to say "no" to ungodliness and "yes" to zeal. When inbox overwhelms, recall RSVP to celestial banquet; tasks align with kingdom agenda. Budgeting becomes eschatological exercise—investing in treasures moth cannot steal. Conflict resolution speeds up; who wants wedding prep sullied by grudges? (Eph 4:32). Mission urgency rises; Groom desires full banquet hall (2 Pet 3:9). Endurance in chronic illness borrows future vitality, echoing Paul's "weight of glory" calculus (2 Cor 4:17). Sabbath celebrates partial arrival—week-long work rests point to eternal rest (Heb 4:9). Fasting stores appetite for feast; it is protest against fast-food of sin. Ethical stances—sexual fidelity, honest dealings—become bridal loyalty displays. Catechesis memorizes Apostle's Creed clause "He will come again," embedding anticipation in children's earliest theology. Art of waiting includes joy hobbies—gardening, music—activities that will continue post-renewal, blending rehearsal and refreshment. Communal benedictions send congregants into week with wedding-march chord: "May the God of peace sanctify you...at the coming of our Lord Jesus" (1 Th 5:23). Hope keeps lamps aflame when culture's storms blow; no trial can cancel invitation sealed by Spirit. Thus, living in-between is not limbo but lively engagement—eyes on horizon, hands on plow, heart on the Groom.

295

Conclusion History will end with music, linen bright and clean, and a cry that rings through galaxies: "Blessed are those invited to the wedding feast of the Lamb!" (Rev 19:9). Between this moment and that banquet, the Church walks the aisle of time dressed in unfinished garments, yet every stitch is being woven by grace. When we remember that the One who disciplines us is also the Lover who cannot wait for the unveiling, holiness stops feeling like tight shoes and starts feeling like a tailor's final fitting. Each act of mercy is a rehearsal dinner, each Eucharist a taste of the coming toast, each prayer of "Come, Lord Jesus" the heartbeat of a bride leaning toward the doors. May the vision of Christ as your Bridegroom steady trembling hearts, awaken fresh affection, and send you back into the world shining with the quiet confidence of someone already chosen, already cherished, and soon to be forever embraced.

www.ingramcontent.com/pod-product-compliance
Lightning Source LLC
Chambersburg PA
CBHW061817040426
42447CB00012B/2698